Regulation and Deregulation of the Motor Carrier Industry

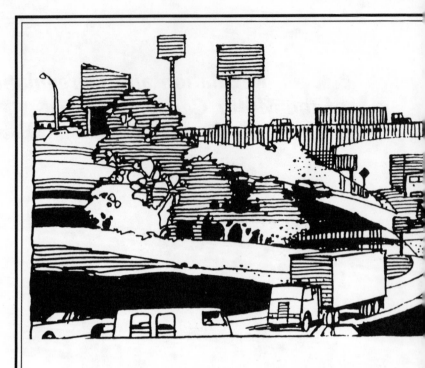

Edited by
JOHN RICHARD FELTON
and
DALE G. ANDERSON

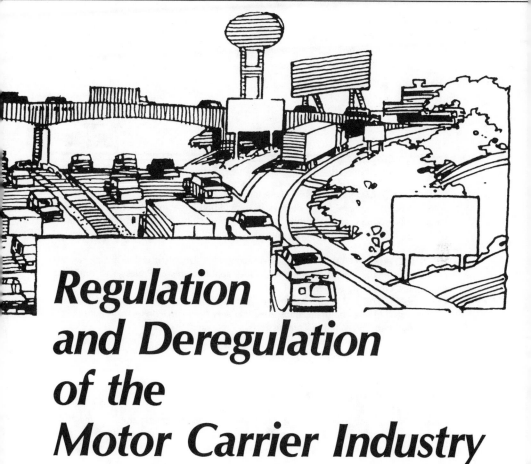

Regulation and Deregulation of the Motor Carrier Industry

IOWA STATE UNIVERSITY PRESS, AMES

DALE G. ANDERSON is Professor of Agricultural Economics, University of Nebraska-Lincoln. He holds M.S. and Ph.D. degrees in Agricultural Economics from the University of Nebraska-Lincoln. He has published numerous monographs and articles on the economics of rail and motor carrier transportation and agricultural products and inputs.

JOHN RICHARD FELTON is Professor of Economics, Emeritus, University of Nebraska-Lincoln and has also held a series of summer appointments as Professor of Agricultural Economics, University of Nebraska-Lincoln. He is the author of *The Economics of Freight Car Supply* (1978) and numerous articles, monographs, and contributions to books and proceedings. He was Chairman, Transportation Panel, Task Force on Increasing Productivity in the Food Industry, National Commission on Productivity (1972).

© 1989 Iowa State University Press, Ames, Iowa 50010

Manufactured in the United States of America

First edition, 1989

Library of Congress Cataloging-in-Publication Data

Regulation and deregulation of the motor carrier industry / edited by John Richard Felton and Dale G. Anderson.—1st ed.
    p. cm.
    Bibliography: p.
    Includes index.
    ISBN 0–8138–0071–4
    1. Trucking—Government policy—United States. 2. Trucking—United States—Deregulation. 3. Trucking—Law and legislation—Economic aspects—United States.   I. Felton, John Richard, 1917–.   II. Anderson, Dale G.
HE5623.R428   1989
388.3'24'0973—dc19   88–9366
                                  CIP

Contents

Preface

The year 1985 marked a half-century since the federal government undertook the comprehensive regulation of the trucking industry and five years since there was substantial statutory relaxation of such control. Despite inherent structural characteristics that militated against monopoly, the industry was the object of regulation of entry, rates, and service that was so extensive in nature as to rival that applicable to the nation's public utilities. The railroads, threatened with the competition of a dynamic new industry, and trucking firms, confronted by large numbers of actual and potential entrants, together with a depression of unparalleled severity, provided a milieu in which trucking regulation could be enacted, notwithstanding the absence of public interest in the venture.

Once regulation was firmly established, the beneficiaries—both the regulators and the regulated—resisted fiercely any relaxation of the constraints providing power and position to the former and protection and profits to the latter. Somewhat ironically, the almost ideally competitive characteristics of the trucking industry generated strong incentives for its members to contend that it should be regulated as a monopoly. Had the industry exhibited characteristics that might have facilitated high concentration, extensive product differentiation, and interfirm collusion, opposition to deregulation might not have been so unremitting.

At any rate, economic regulation of trucking continued virtually unchanged for more than forty years despite a rising tide of criticism by members of the economics profession over the last three decades. Theoretical and empirical studies raised doubts as to the significance of scale economies in the industry, questioned whether destructive competition was the alternative to regulation, and endeavored to assess the social cost of entry and rate regulation.

Ultimately the intellectual impact of economic analysis and the economic impact of skyrocketing petroleum prices created an environment more conducive to fostering increased efficiency through a relaxation of those controls that reduced average truckloads, mandated circuitous routing, necessitated interlining, and validated cartelized ratemaking. Regulatory reform began in the late 1970s with a series of appointments to the Interstate Commerce Commission of persons who were committed to an interpretation of the Motor Carrier Act of 1935 that reconciled the public interest with efficiency and competition rather than with the preservation of the traffic and revenues of existing trucking companies.

The movement for regulatory reform culminated in the passage of the Motor Carrier Act of 1980, which released the genie from the bottle or opened Pandora's box, depending upon one's perspective. Both metaphors, however, suggest that the structural, behavioral, and performance changes that followed from regulatory relaxation will be difficult to reverse. Many new firms have entered the industry, existing firms have acquired more extensive commodity and geographic authorities, and old habits of collective ratemaking are giving way to more aggressive marketing and pricing behavior. While the process of transformation from cartelization to independence is not complete, it gives every evidence of being irreversible.

The chapters comprising this volume were authored by faculty members and former graduate students of the University of Nebraska-Lincoln. Most chapters were written initially as independent essays, and about half were published as journal articles. Together they comprise a coherent body of literature on the evolution of trucking regulation and on the evaluation of its economic consequences. Since about one-half of the chapters appeared previously, if at all, only in working-paper form, this volume has the merit of assembling these interrelated studies into a single monograph.

This book summarizes partial results of research under University of Nebraska, Nebraska Agricultural Research Division Project 10-71 and North Central Regional Research Project No. 137, "Effect of Changes in Transportation on Performance of the U.S. Agricultural Transportation System."

Lincoln, Nebraska
May 1986

Regulation and Deregulation of the Motor Carrier Industry

CHAPTER 1

Background of the Motor Carrier Act of 1935

Just as state regulation of railroads antedated federal regulation, so did state regulation of commercial trucking precede federal control over entry, rates, and the service rendered by motor carriers. Also, as with the railroads, the states endeavored to regulate interstate as well as intrastate highway transportation until the Supreme Court held, in *Buck* v. *Kuykendall,*[1] that in so doing, the states were infringing upon an enumerated power of the federal government, that is, the authority of Congress to regulate commerce "among the several states."

Presumably, the historic *Wabash* case should have warned the states that they were invading federal prerogatives when they attempted to regulate the entry or rates of interstate carriers. In *Wabash, St. Louis and Pacific Railway Co.* v. *Illinois,* the Supreme Court nullified the attempt of Illinois to apply its prohibition against long- and short-haul discrimination to an interstate rail shipment.[2] Despite this precedent, however, state legislators may well have believed that highway carriage was sufficiently different from railroad transport to justify regulation of the interstate aspects of highway transportation pursuant to the state's power to protect the health, safety, and welfare of its citizens. After all, in *Cooley* v. *the Board of Wardens of the Port of Philadelphia*[3] the court had held that, in the absence of federal preemption of the field, the

By John Richard Felton.

states might legislate in matters affecting interstate commerce, provided that it was an issue of local concern, characterized by considerable diversity from one locale to another, and that the effect on interstate commerce was merely indirect or incidental.[4] When, however, the state of Washington attempted to prevent a bus company from operating between Washington and Oregon by requiring it to obtain a certificate of convenience and necessity, there could be little doubt that the effect upon interstate commerce was both direct and substantial.

The day after the *Buck* decision, Representative Cable introduced a bill to impose federal regulation upon interstate highway carrier operations. It was to be followed by some thirty-three more bills on the subject prior to the passage of the Motor Carrier Act of 1935 a decade later.[5]

Pre-Depression Views

Initial support for federal regulation came primarily from the National Association of Railroad and Utility Commissioners (NARUC), representing the state commissions whose regulatory effectiveness had been jeopardized, and the railroads whose surface transportation monopoly and "value of service," that is, discriminatory, rate structure were being eroded by the advent of highway carrier competition. With the exception of some large common carrier trucking firms, which favored some form of federal entry restrictions, trucking operators and shipper groups during the latter part of the 1920s were for the most part opposed to federal regulation. Even the Interstate Commerce Commission in 1928 declared: "There is not at present the need in the public interest for the regulation of motor-truck lines. . . . "[6]

Growing Support for Truck Regulation

As the Great Depression deepened during the early 1930s, however, there was a growing number of converts to the cause of federal regulation of interstate motor transport. On the basis of a survey of shippers and carriers of agricultural products, Edwards and Park noted that many agricultural carriers "expressed a desire to have legal regulation of the trucking business as to rates, liability, service, and franchise, in order to free the business [from rate cutting and easy entry]."[7]

By 1932 the Interstate Commerce Commission had also changed its views as to the need, in the public interest, for highway carrier regulation. While conceding that there was "little present demand by shippers for such regulation"[8] and that there had been a "marked improvement [in] the financial responsibility of truck operators,"[9] the commission, nonetheless, concluded that the newness of the industry, ease of entry, absence of regulation, and insufficient operator awareness of costs condemned the industry to chronic instability and excessive competition.[10] The commission summarized its appraisal of the injurious consequences of unrestrained competition of motor vehicles with the railroads and with each other, as follows:

1. An instability in charges for transportation affected by the competition, resulting in widespread and unjust discrimination between shippers and uncertainty as to the basis upon which business may be done.
2. The loss of much capital invested in both the railroads and the motor vehicles.
3. Radical changes in the railroad rate structure which, in the final analysis, may result in loading the traffic which is not affected by the competition with the utmost charges it is able to bear.
4. A tendency to break down wages and conditions of employment in the transportation industry.
5. Increase in the hazard of use of the highways.[11]

Two years later Joseph B. Eastman, federal coordinator of transportation, expressed even greater alarm over the "disorganized" and "economically unsound" position of intercity trucking operations.[12] While recognizing that the depression had exacerbated the problems of the industry, he identified the small scale of operations; easy entry; and the existence of different types of carriers, that is, private, common, and contract, as the crux of the industry's difficulties. Despite the fact that trucks accounted for only about 5 percent of all intercity ton-miles, the coordinator declared that truck competition, "much of it destructive," was responsible for undermining railroad value-of-service ratemaking, "since it made the traffic vulnerable on which the relatively higher rates are charged."[13] The ultimate consequence of such "free and uncontrolled [rate] competition," in the view of the coordinator, was that "cost of service would inevitably be the controlling factor, and rates would tend to seek that level."[14]

Thus the coordinator clearly understood the impact of truck competition upon a railroad rate structure wedded to the value-of-service principle, in which commodities high in value in relation to their bulk were systematically charged higher rates than those of lower value. Commodity value-weight ratios were a convenient index of elasticity of demand for transport and provided an obvious opportunity for price discrimination by a railroad industry long possessed of monopoly power. So long as the overall earnings of the railroads were subject to regulatory constraint, such discriminatory rate structures could logically be demonstrated to confer benefits not only upon the shipper who was charged the lower rates, but even the shipper against whom discrimination was practiced. Whether or not the conditions posited by the "added-traffic" theory were realized with sufficient frequency to produce the mutually beneficial consequences predicted by the theory, it was the stock-in-trade of transportation economists as well as regulatory commissioners.[15]

Under any circumstances, it must be regarded as somewhat anomalous for the coordinator to have charged the trucking industry with eroding a discriminatory railroad rate structure, at the same time that he assailed it for being "a breeder of discriminations."[16] No less contradictory, perhaps, was his criticism of the large capital losses suffered by the trucking industry together with the contention that "no responsibility is felt by the motor-transport industry today to maintain unprofitable service."[17]

The federal coordinator also reported the results of a survey that revealed overwhelming support among various individuals and organizations for the imposition of federal regulation (nature and scope unspecified) upon interstate highway transport (see Table 1.1). Conspicuous by

Table 1.1. Views of Various Individuals and Groups on Federal Regulation of Highway Transport, Circa 1934

Group	View on Federal Regulation of Interstate Busses and/or Trucks	
	Favor	Oppose
Shippers (mostly corporations)	156	15
Individuals, including lawyers, professors, engineers, etc.	54	1
Chambers of commerce	65	3
Railroads and associations of railway executives	7	0
State regulatory commissions	4	1
Trade associations	25	3
Truck and bus operators and motor associations	25	6
Taxpayers' associations and railroad employees	6	0
Traffic organizations and rate bureaus	15	1
Unclassified	10	4
Total	367	34

Source: *Regulation of Transport Agencies, A Report of the Federal Coordinator of Transportation,* Sen. Doc. No. 152, 73d Cong., 2d sess. (Washington: GPO, 1934), 227.

their absence from the list of respondents are automobile manufacturers and farm organizations, both of which remained adamantly opposed to regulation of the trucking industry.

Economics Profession on Regulation

Presumably included among the "professors" in the coordinator's list of respondents were members of the economics profession. While there was apparently no poll inquiring about the views of professional economists on the desirability of economic regulation of highway carriers, most seemed to support it to some greater or lesser extent. At a 1928 session of the American Economic Association devoted to commercial motor transportation, William M. Duffus declared: "Most students of transportation will agree, I think . . . that there must be some sort of central planning looking toward the coordination of our various transportation agencies on a sound economic and financial basis."[18] At the same meeting Henry R. Trumbower contended that transportation, "both rail and highway, should be regarded as a regulated monopoly" and that cost minimization in transportation could best be achieved by giving railroads "the first opportunity to enter the field of highway service and coordinate it with rail service."[19] The final participant in this session, M. H. Hunter, maintained: "All common carriers should be required to secure certificates of convenience and necessity," but, since competition among contract carriers should insure maintenance of reasonable rates, "the interest of the public can be adequately served by evidence of good intent and financial responsibility."[20]

Johnson, Huebner, and Wilson of the University of Pennsylvania, while conceding that there were some differences of opinion on the matter, declared that the "best informed" believed that intermodal coordination was of "special importance" and that its achievement "can best be brought about by having all agencies of transportation . . . subject to regulation that is intended to promote the balanced development of an integrated system of transportation."[21] Shan Szto, who studied under Johnson, Huebner, and Wilson at the University of Pennsylvania, must be counted as one of the more ardent supporters of regulation. He condemned excessive, unwise, and undue competition as of "no benefit to anybody."[22] The intensity of competition tended to "make the field unattractive to responsible business people" and contributed to "the probable interruptions and irregularity of a type of service which acquires its value to the community largely by reason of its stability and continuity."[23]

Finally, he dismissed the argument that regulation would raise truck rates as "a subtle appeal and . . . a strong factor in creating opposition on the part of the public."[24]

Harold G. Moulton and his associates at the Brookings Institution in their monumental study, *The American Transportation Problem,* condemned the instability and competitive waste that characterized the trucking industry and recommended the formation of intermodal transportation companies as a means of insuring cost minimization in intercity transport:

> . . . one of the surest means of promoting real integration, of getting traffic routed in the most economical way, is by developing transportation companies as distinguished from railroad, or highway, or waterway, or airline companies. In principle, there can be no objection to boat or truck companies engaging in railroad business or vice versa—as long as public control is adequate to prevent abuse.
>
> If transportation is to develop in a comprehensive way along national lines, regulation by the federal government must be extended to all agencies operating interstate: carriers by water, carriers by air, and carriers on the highway, as well as rail carriers and pipe lines.[25]

Sidney L. Miller, whose *Inland Transportation* appeared the same year as the Brookings' study, addressed not just the "problems" of an unregulated highway carrier industry but the unalloyed "evils" arising from the absence of federal control. These evils included discrimination, that "canker of business"; "disturbance of markets"; waste of resources; highway congestion; financial irresponsibility; and diversion of traffic from railroads.[26]

D. Philip Locklin, whose first edition of *Economics of Transportation* appeared in 1935, continued through the six subsequent revisions of what was for many years the leading text in the field of transportation economics to be a staunch supporter of highway carrier regulation. As he appraised the inherent characteristics of motor transport: "The ruinous type of competition does develop; discrimination in rates does appear; the condition of overcapacity does not correct itself automatically; and the struggle for survival in the face of inadequate revenues leads to deterioration of safety standards, evasion of safety regulations, financial irresponsibility, and generally unsatisfactory service."[27]

On the other hand, relatively few professional economists appear to have been opposed to, or even skeptical with respect to the merits of, regulation. G. Shorey Peterson, while not necessarily aligned against regulation of motor carriers, did express a number of reservations. The industry "is almost wholly devoid of those features which have made a large degree of monopoly inevitable"[28] and while the "benefits of a wise restriction of competition seems clear enough . . . the case for regulation — except as it applies to safety and responsibility — is not especially impressive."[29] Moreover, he declared himself against internal subsidization, and he maintained that "regulation which seriously burdens part of a group of competing carriers is *prima facie* bad."[30]

The most forthright opponent of motor carrier regulation among professional economists, however, appears to have been W. T. Jackman. In his view such regulation was likely to be both unnecessary and ineffective:

> It is said that the regulation [by franchise] of such vehicles [common carrier trucks] in the public interest would prevent destructive rate cutting and enable railways to work alongside of them in rendering essential public service. It is doubtful if this kind of regulation is desirable. Motor trucks which are used as plant facilities and those which are employed by private carriers . . . could not be brought under regulation as to their facilities and charges. This would leave a very narrow field for the common carrier by motor truck. Moreover, the latter, if subject to regulation as to its rates and services, would be likely to lose a large share of its business to the private carrier, through rate reductions below those fixed for the common carrier. The nature of the motor truck carriage resembles more closely the tramp vessel service on the ocean, the rates of which are regulated effectively by competition; and until we have more complete information it would seem desirable not to hedge the motor trucks about by hampering restrictions as to rates and service.[31]

Opposition

In marked contrast to the generally favorable stance of transportation economists on the issue of federal motor carrier regulation, agricultural groups were unanimous in their opposition. The National Grange, whose antirailroad sentiment was so unremitting that the campaign during the 1870s and 1880s to regulate the railroads came to be known as the "Granger Movement," was unequivocally against subjecting highway carriers to economic regulation. In hearings before a House subcommittee in the spring of 1935, a representative of the National Grange distinguished between public-utility-type rate regulation designed to protect the public from monopolistic exploitation and regulation aimed at "stabilizing," that is, raising, rates to protect the industry:

> Hitherto the prime purpose in regulating utilities in this country has been to protect the public against excessive rates and charges . . . to speak of imposing minimum rates can mean only one thing, that present rates are not high enough and that we intend to make provision by law for raising rates to a higher level. To us, such a proposal seems utterly preposterous. If any change is necessary in existing law to bring about equal competitive opportunities, we favor the elimination of some of the restrictions on the railroads which were necessary when they had a monopoly of land transportation.[32]

At the same hearing, other agricultural spokesmen gave voice to similar sentiments. A representative of apple growers interpreted the proposed legislation as a device by which large trucking companies could "eliminate the small independent truck owner," and he referred to the latter as "the salvation of the rural section, so far as transportation costs are concerned."[33] The traffic manager of the American Livestock Association likewise declared his organization to be "unalterably opposed" to motor truck regulation, maintaining that the purpose of the railroads in requesting it was "to hamstring their competition and keep away from the basic or primary principle upon which rates should be constructed, namely, the cost of performing the service."[34] The president of the Farmers' Educational and Cooperative Union of America said that it seemed to him that the bill was "designed to consolidate in one vast system all the transportation facilities of the country and would amount to the same as creating one great transportation monopoly and eliminate all competition, in the matter of transportation between our highway carriers and our railroads."[35] Finally, a representative of the National Cooperative Milk Producers Federation testified that there was "no demand among dairy farmers nor from our contract haulers for regulations of the type contemplated by the proposed bill nor do we believe that there is any general public demand for such regulation."[36]

The opposition to highway carrier regulation on the part of agricultural groups, newspaper publishers,[37] and the powerful automobile manufacturers, coupled with widespread public apathy, might have prevented or at least delayed passage of federal legislation had it not been for the *Schechter* decision[38] in which the Supreme Court held the National Industrial Recovery Act (NIRA) to constitute an unconstitutional delegation of congressional legislative authority. As long as the trucking industry could establish and maintain legally binding codes of fair conduct to cartelize the industry, its primary representative, the American Trucking Associations, Incorporated (ATA), persisted in its opposition to the bill that was ultimately to become the Motor Carrier Act of 1935.[39] The collapse of self-regulation under the National Recovery Administration (NRA) codes, however, induced the ATA to shift from the ranks of the opponents of economic regulation to those of the supporters.[40]

While agricultural organizations were unable to prevent the passage of the Motor Carrier Act,[41] they did obtain an important concession. Section 293(b) provided for the exemption from regulation of "motor vehicles used exclusively in carrying livestock, fish (including shell fish), or agricultural commodities (not including manufactured products thereof)."[42] It did not exempt the trucking of farm supplies, unless carried on the farmer's own vehicle, but it excluded from entry and rate regulation the much greater volume of unprocessed agricultural products.

Insofar as the remainder of the for-hire trucking industry, congressional policy as expressed in Section 202 was to preserve inherent advantages, foster sound economic conditions, promote adequate and economical service at reasonable charges without unjust discrimination or destructive competition, improve intermodal coordination, meet the needs of commerce and national defense, and cooperate with states and motor carrier organizations in the administration of the act. If one were to judge by the subsequent course of commission implementation of the policy, it was prevention of "destructive competition" and cooperation with motor carrier organizations that the commission pursued with the greatest fervor.

Writing shortly after the passage of the Motor Carrier Act, James C. Nelson, who lacked the advantage of forty-five years of hindsight, nonetheless expressed a number of reservations with respect to the probable consequences of regulation.[43] He noted the phenomenal growth of the industry prior to the adoption of federal regulation and the reduced rates achieved through competition, and he pondered whether regulation might blunt the initiative of trucking companies as it had the railroads. Furthermore, he expected some as yet indeterminate but inevitable effect on rates from the curtailment of supply, even though private trucking would impose some upper limit on the magnitude of such increases. He also contended that isolated and rural communities, lacking the volume of traffic to justify regular service, would suffer from territorial and commodity restrictions placed on anywhere-for-hire truck operators. He also predicted higher rates of return and increased industry concentration, coupled with higher wages and reduced employment of labor. Finally, he maintained that while the railroads might "gain some competitive advantages . . . from controlled competition and stabilized rates . . . it is too much to expect that they will find in federal regulation of motor carriers the answer to their difficulties."[44]

Conclusions

While opinions differ as to the role of the railroads in the adoption of federal railroad regulation in 1887, there is no doubt that they were ardent advocates of federal highway carrier regulation in the latter half of the 1920s and first half of the 1930s. Railroads saw trucking companies enjoying the geographic flexibility inherent in highway transport and the route and rate flexibility arising from the absence of federal regulation, and they sought to subject trucks and busses to the same rigidities as beset them.

More detached observers, such as the federal coordinator of transportation, who were imbued with the "public service" conception of transport and the obligation of common carriers to serve all who request service, foresaw that an unregulated trucking industry would ultimately transform the traditional value-of-service railroad rate structure into one based far more closely on cost of service. The internal subsidization of low-value by high-value commodities would be lost in the process, and the burden of fixed costs, in this view, would fall even more heavily on low-value, long-distance railroad traffic.

The Great Depression no doubt added to the ranks of the proponents of federal highway carrier regulation. Competition as a method of organizing economic activity was under concerted attack, and trucking was the personification of a competitive industry. Easy entry and exit; "unstable," that is, flexible rates; ad hoc routes and schedules; and a generally casual modus operandi were repellent to those familiar with the operational and regulatory rigidities characteristic of the railroads. Published rates, established schedules, and financial responsibility for loss and damage that the railroads exhibited seemed to them more important than any tendency toward lower rates that might flow from competition in highway transport.

Finally, the trucking industry itself, after being denied the opportunity for continued self-regulation under the NRA codes, expressed a clear preference for government-enforced cartelization. Whatever may have been the industry's reservations with respect to the bureaucratic delays, inefficiencies, and inflexibilities possibly accompanying federal regulation of entry, rates, and service, it was apparently prepared to embrace them as an alternative to the vagaries of the market.

CHAPTER 2

Trucking Regulation, 1935–1980

The Motor Carrier Act of 1935[1] was for the most part a product of the Great Depression. Across the heartland of America the economic distress of the depression was compounded by drought that had brought crop failure, dust storms, and further economic hardship. Passage of the law should thus be viewed in the context of the desperate economic conditions then confronting the nation. The willingness of government to seek drastic cures for economic malaise of such major proportions is not surprising. What is perhaps more surprising is the persistence with which the regulatory solution has been applied. Indeed, forty-five years were to pass before substantive changes were made in the original legislation. It is instructive to review the regulatory changes that did occur over that period and the events that led eventually to major changes in the form of the Motor Carrier Act of 1980.[2]

The close of the 1970s marks the end of an era in regulation of transportation activities generally. Relaxation of the regulatory environment in the motor carrier industry was part of a larger movement that fundamentally reformed long-standing institutional arrangements in rail and air transport as well. The era began with dogged attempts by the Interstate Commerce Commission to consolidate and extend its regulatory authority over the trucking industry. It closed with that same com-

By Dale G. Anderson and Ray C. Huttsell, Jr.

Ray C. Huttsell, Jr. is Transportation Economist, Missouri Public Service Commission. He received his Ph.D. in Economics from the University of Nebraska-Lincoln in 1979.

mission at the forefront of regulatory reform, effectively deregulating entry into for-hire motor carriage in the late 1970s through administrative fiat.

The new regulatory era is clearly a product of a new economic environment and of a revised political order. It is also a product of the regulatory experience itself. It is in a major sense the outgrowth of legislative, judicial and administrative experience that has accumulated since passage of the original act in 1935. It is this experience the present chapter explores.

Transportation Policy

One rationale for extending regulation to the motor carrier industry in the first place was to bring some measure of evenhandedness to the regulation of freight transportation generally. It was hoped that regulation of motor carriage might provide a measure of protection to the already regulated railroads. But while the physical and economic interconnectedness of the several modes had not gone unrecognized, no official statement of national transportation policy was forthcoming until the passage of the Transportation Act of 1940.[3]

The policy statement contained in the preamble to the act of 1940 recognized that effective regulation must consider the problem of intermodal competition, or the division of traffic among competing modes, in addition to the special problems confronting each of the separate transportation modes. Thus Congress established a policy calling for impartial regulation of all modes of transportation, preservation of the inherent advantages of each, promotion of efficiency, furtherance of sound economic conditions, and condemnation of unfair or destructive competitive practices. Congress attempted to clarify its intent in the Transportation Act of 1958 by declaring that "Rates of a carrier shall not be held up to a particular level to protect the traffic of any other mode. . . ."[4] The new language was aimed largely at preventing the commission from disallowing railroad rate reductions designed to meet intermodal competition.

Although the resulting statement of policy was widely viewed as being vague and subject to varying administrative interpretation, no serious efforts at revision were made until the establishment of the U.S. Department of Transportation (DOT) in 1967. The law creating the new agency called for the DOT to develop a statement of national transportation policy. The resulting statement, completed in 1975, called for sharply reduced regulatory oversight of rates and entry and a reduction of barriers to intermodal cooperation. The statement acquired no legal status as it was not adopted by Congress.

A National Transportation Policy Study Commission was created as a provision in the Federal Highway Aid Authorization Act of 1976. The commission recommended establishment of a uniform policy for all modes of transportation and called for less economic regulation and more freedom of competition among carriers. Adoption by Congress of a new policy statement was delayed, however, until passage of regulatory reform laws in 1980.

Entry and Exit

Of the major provisions of the Motor Carrier Act of 1935, those affecting entry have been of singular importance in shaping the structure and performance of the industry. Indeed, control of entry was the central purpose of the act.

COMMON CARRIAGE. Historically, the burden of proof has been on applicants to show their proposals are "required by the present or future public convenience and necessity."[5] The ICC, until late in the 1970s when major administrative changes began to occur, has interpreted this statutory requirement to mean the applicant must prove:

> . . . Whether the new operation or service will serve a useful public purpose, responsive to a public demand or need; whether this purpose can and will be served as well by existing lines or carriers; and whether it can be served by applicant with the new operation or service proposed without endangering or impairing the operations of existing carriers contrary to the public interest.[6]

Demonstrating that a proposal satisfied the foregoing criteria often proved extremely difficult, even where performance of existing carriers was deficient.

One of the primary objectives of commission policy has been to "preserve competition" by protecting established competitors. Consequently, the ICC has held from the outset that established carriers are usually entitled to capture all the traffic within their respective territories.

> We think that, in order to foster sound economic conditions in the motor-carrier industry, existing motor carriers should normally be accorded the right to transport all traffic which they can handle adequately, efficiently, and economically in the territories served by them, as against any person now seeking to enter the field of motor-carrier transportation in circumstances such as are here disclosed.[7]

Given this position, persuasive evidence that existing service was inadequate or unsatisfactory has been required by the commission to support a showing of public convenience and necessity.[8]

A U.S. District Court ruled in 1964 that this interpretation of the former statutory requirements was too stringent. In the opinion of the court, existing service did not have to be inadequate before a grant of authority was warranted.[9] However, potential entrants who did not rely upon deficiencies in the performance of established carriers to gain entry were expected to present substantial evidence indicating a future need for their services.[10]

Even where existing service was shown to be inadequate, the commission frequently gave established carriers an opportunity to remedy deficiencies before issuing new licenses. This occurred so often that a U.S. District Court concluded in 1967:

> The invariable rule of the Commission is and has been for a long time that no certificate affecting the area of another carrier will be issued until that other carrier has been furnished an opportunity either to improve or correct his service to such route or decide whether he wishes to or can furnish the added service sought by the applicant carrier.[11]

The court found the commission's practice in this regard so "constant and consistent" that it could be compared to a "rule of property."[12]

The Supreme Court reversed the foregoing ruling in the same year in *United States* v. *Dixie Highway Express, Inc.*[13] Referring to two of its own earlier decisions, the court declared that the "invariable rule" did not constitute a vested property right.[14] Nevertheless, the evidence is clear that the commission accorded greater importance to the standard of public convenience and necessity and the protection of established carriers from competition than to fulfillment of the public's need for service.

The commission has also interpreted very strictly the legislative mandate in the act of 1935 to consider the fitness and ability of applicants to provide service. Professor Thomas Gale Moore examined all of the published ICC entry cases covering a span of twenty months and determined that the commission's definition of applicants' ability turned largely on whether or not they were already in the trucking business. Not one of the cases involved a strictly new entrant. Moore concluded:

> The fact that there were no cases of pure *de novo* entry is not surprising. It takes months, in some cases years, for a case to be determined under commission procedures, and to show that an applicant is able, the would-be carrier must have access to a sufficient number of trucks and to a sufficient number of experienced drivers with some shippers ready to utilize the proposed service. All of this would be very expensive and difficult for a truly new entrant to show.[15]

Because of the burdensome expenses, fewer than 10 percent of all the new grants of authority in fiscal 1976 went to persons outside the industry.[16]

CONTRACT CARRIAGE. Contract carriage may be defined as for-hire transportation under specific contracts or agreements that do not fall within the legal boundaries of common carriage. Contract carriers are not required to offer their services to the public at large without discrimination. They are free to select the shippers they wish to serve and to negotiate contracts with them while refusing to haul for others.

Legal conflicts arising over the problem of distinguishing between common and contract carriage were inevitable. Congress drew upon the experience of the states when it formulated the original act of 1935. Early attempts by the states to regulate contract carriers were overturned by the U.S. Supreme Court. On three separate occasions the Court declared unconstitutional state laws that brought contract carriage under the umbrella of regulation.

In the first case a Michigan statute required all motor carriers operating for hire to obtain a license as a common carrier. The Court declared that compelling a firm to undertake the obligations of a common carrier was tantamount to taking private property for public use without just compensation.[17] Similar rulings were handed down in two subsequent cases.[18]

Finally, in 1932 the Court upheld a Texas law governing contract carriers.[19] The essential difference in the Texas statute was that it imposed a modified set of controls over contract carriers. Contract carriers were expected to acquire "permits" rather than "certificates of convenience and necessity." They were not obliged to provide services they did not undertake voluntarily, and the powers of the state commission were limited to the control of minimum rates. Maximum charges were not subject to regulation. The Court probably favored the Texas statute largely because it has the appearance of regulating contract carriers only to the extent necessary to facilitate the control of common carriers.

The contract-carriage provisions of the Motor Carrier Act of 1935 were patterned after the system of controls adopted in Texas and sanctioned by the Supreme Court. First, contract carriers were required to obtain only a permit rather than a certificate of convenience and necessity. After a finding that the applicant is fit, willing, and able, a permit was to be issued if the commission determines that an applicant's proposals are consistent with the public interest. The phrase "consistent with the public interest" has been held to imply that the commission must consider the adequacy of existing facilities and the convenience of shippers but that neither test is conclusive.[20] Second, the ICC was authorized to prescribe minimum rates for contract carriers but not maximum rates. Although the act of 1935 required only that contract carriers publish their minimum charges, a 1957 amendment[21] made it mandatory for contract carriers to publish and adhere to their actual rates.

The commission's protectionist posture toward competition from contract carriers is apparent from the persistent controversy over the degree to which the scope of contract carrier applications should be limited. In a leading case in 1939 the commission decided an appropriate policy was to restrict contract-carrier service to the transportation of certain types of commodities tendered by a particular class of shippers. A common form of the restriction limited a contract carrier's operations to such merchandise as was dealt in by wholesale, retail, and chain grocery and food businesses.[22] Thus a carrier could transport canned goods for a grocery store but not for a canner. The rationale for restrictions of this sort was that contract carriers should be limited to specialized services that cannot be provided by common carriers.[23]

Specialization thus became a secondary test of contract carriage. A second leading commission decision in 1941 held that specialization was an essential characteristic of contract carriage. Evidence of specialization was held to include rendering a service with physical characteristics designed to meet the peculiar needs of a shipper, or a very limited number of shippers, a circumstance making the carrier virtually a part of the shipper's organization.[24]

The question of whether the commission had the power to restrict contract carriers to a limited number of shippers was subsequently taken before the U.S. Supreme Court. Owing to an aggressive solicitation program, a contract carrier had been able to increase the number of its contracts from thirteen to sixty-nine. The ICC ruled in 1954 that the firm had converted its operations to common carriage without proper authorization.[25] The Court in its 1956 decision disagreed with the commission's ruling, saying that "a contract carrier is free to aggressively search for new business within the limits of his license."[26]

Congress responded by amending the act in 1957. The amended version of the definition of contract carriage specified that a contract carrier must operate:

> . . . under continuing agreements with a person or limited number of persons — (a) by assigning motor vehicles for a continuing period of time for the exclusive use of each such person; or (b) designed to meet the distinct needs of each such person.[27]

In addition, the amendment required the commission to specify in the terms of a permit "each person or number of class of persons for which the carrier may provide transportation."[28]

The commission interpreted the foregoing directives to mean that the number of shippers a contract carrier was allowed to serve depended upon the degree of specialization. Where the service was highly specialized to meet the peculiar demands of a narrow class of shippers, the commission held in a 1962 decision, "that a large number of shippers belonging to a limited class satisfied the requirement that service must be restricted to a limited number of persons."[29] Later in the same year the commission ruled that carriers performing less highly specialized service were subject to having their activities limited to six or eight separate shippers, an interpretation which came to be known as the "Rule of Eight."[30] The commission ordered contract carriers to comply with the restriction or apply for authority to operate as a common carrier.[31]

In a more recent (1976) decision the commission determined that a carrier was not serving a limited number of persons if it was providing service for diverse industrial entities over a wide geographical area.[32] Moreover, contract carriers were required to devote each vehicle to the exclusive use of a single shipper or perform specialized services designed to meet the peculiar needs of each shipper. Specialization was thus a key test of contract carriage. By 1978, however, the tide had turned; in one of a series of reformist rulings, the commission eliminated the "Rule of Eight" in an effort to relax entry barriers to contract carriage.[33] The deletion was later formalized in the Motor Carrier Act of 1980.

A feature of the 1957 amendment illustrates the commission's earlier protectionist philosophy. A "grandfather" provision in the amendment allowed contract carriers affected by the altered language to convert their permits to certificates without showing public convenience and necessity.[34] In a case involving ten conversion applications under the amendment redefining contract carriage, the commission ruled that the terms of the form permitting restricting service to commodities handled by a particular class of shippers should be retained in the reissued certificates.[35] One student of commission policy reports that in at least sixty-five authorized conversions similar restrictions were continued.[36]

The 1935 act prohibited firms from holding authority to operate as both a common and contract carrier except where the commission found there was "good cause." The ostensible purpose of this prohibition was to prevent charging some shippers common carrier rates while reducing rates to other shippers under specific contracts when both groups received substantially similar services.[37] The commission resisted awarding dual authority except where the two services were so dissimilar as to be nonsubstitutable or where they were between different points and places.[38] In a sharp reversal of earlier interpretations the ICC in 1978 allowed dual operation of contract and common carriage by a single licensee except where there was "realistic opportunity" for rate or service discrimination.[39] Elimination of the rule was sustained in 1980 by the District of Columbia Circuit Court.[40] The Motor Carrier Act of 1980 formalized the new provision and extended it to allow contract and common carrier goods to be carried in the same vehicle at the same time.

PRIVATE CARRIAGE. The commission has always held that transportation of commodities the carrier owns is not sufficient to convert a for-hire carrier into a private one. The distinction between private and for-hire operations is found in the so-called primary business test[41] and in the requirement that users must fully control drivers and vehicles and bear all risks.[42] Agreements among two or more private carriers to exchange traffic are therefore forbidden. If the primary business of a firm is the manufacture or sale of goods, transportation services performed incidental to such activities are private and not for hire. This principle was clearly enunciated in the 1949 *Lenior Chair Case*:

> If the facts establish that the primary business of an operator is the supplying of transportation for compensation then the carrier's status is established though the operator may be the owner, at the time, of the goods transported and may be transporting them for the purpose of sale. . . . If, on the other hand, the

primary business of an operator is found to be manufacturing or some other noncarrier commercial enterprise, then it must be determined whether the motor operations are in bona fide furtherance of the primary business or whether they are conducted as a related or secondary enterprise with the purpose of profiting from the transportation performed.[43]

The foregoing policy was upheld in the courts in 1950 and 1951 cases[44] and written into law by a 1958 amendment to the act.[45]

The ICC has generally excluded carriers from performance of both for-hire and private services except where it could be shown that no adverse effects for regulated truckers would result.[46] Private carriers have as a result been all but foreclosed from carriage of regulated backhaul traffic. In 1978, however, a reform-minded commission agreed to accept applications from private carriers for contract and common carrier operating authority in a ruling [47] subsequently upheld by a U.S. Court of Appeals.[48]

It has long been understood that commonly owned corporations, as separate and distinct legal entities, may not transport for one another for compensation under the claim of private carriage when the transportation performed does not satisfy the "primary business test" as applied to the transporting corporation.[49] The commission determined in 1943 that transportation activities on behalf of subsidiaries is not an integral part of the business in which the parent corporation primarily engaged.[50] The ICC had under consideration in the late 1970s a rule permitting intercorporate hauling where the parent corporation owned 80 or more percent of the subsidiaries involved;[51] action was forestalled by passage of the act of 1980 that allows such hauling but only in cases of 100 percent interest.

Operating Restrictions

As a result of narrow commodity authorizations and territorial grants, the operating rights of regulated carriers often became extremely complicated. Some carriers accumulated 200 or more certificates covering assorted commodities and overlapping territories. One large carrier was discovered to have 244 separate operating grants requiring a volume of 124 pages to describe. The ICC regularly received, as a consequence, more than 30,000 inquiries annually as to whether a particular carrier may handle a particular shipment.[52]

Commodity restrictions have been the most important limitation upon operating authority. After examining several decisions of the commission involving interpretations of carriers' commodity authorizations, one student of the problem concluded:

> Operating rights of some of these carriers are so narrow that survival is dependent upon the continued movement of particular products in commerce and upon the whims of a few shippers, not necessarily on the willingness to serve or on carrier operating efficiency. The carriers do not possess operating mobility, so loss of traffic requires them to seek additional operating authority, to engage in "gray area" activities, to sell their franchises, or to drop out of business.[53]

A sample survey of intercity common and contract carriers conducted in 1941 confirms that regulated carriers are frequently limited to narrow commodity authorities. Professor James C. Nelson has summarized the results of that survey.[54] Of the sampled certificates and permits, 62 percent were found to be restricted to special commodities. Of the carriers which did not employ specialized equipment, 40 percent were limited to one commodity or commodity class and 83 percent to six or fewer.

Rigorous route and territorial restrictions also have been imposed upon intercity regulated carriers. The Nelson survey revealed the extent to which truckers are constrained by geographical limitations:

> Seventy percent of the regular-route common carriers possessed less than full authority to serve intermediate points; more than one-tenth had no such authority. More than 90 percent of the irregular-route carriers were limited to radial service; that is their traffic had to be accepted at, or delivered to, one or more specified points within their territories. Most such carriers had no choice but to operate through points which they could not lawfully serve, "leap frogging" between noncontiguous points or areas, or between noncontiguous points and an area.[55]

The sample also disclosed that approximately one-third of the carriers had return-haul limitations, and nearly 10 percent lacked the authority to carry traffic on return hauls.[56]

An extreme example indicates how far the ICC was prepared to go in order to suppress competition among motor carriers. In 1970 the state of California asked the ICC to promulgate a rule which would allow "for-hire motor carriers of hazardous materials to utilize the nearest, direct route . . . in lieu of circuitous routes . . . "[57] The petition was supported by the U.S. Departments of Transportation and Defense, but the commission found the rule to be unjustified. A primary reason for the denial was stated as follows:

> Existing competitive relationships might be seriously undermined by the adoption of the proposed rule or its alternatives which, in effect, might allow certain carriers to alter their routes and provide a new service without the necessity of proving a need for such service.[58]

In other words, the prevention of competition was more important than protection of the public from hazardous materials.

There have been exceptions to the generally pervasive mantle of regulation, exceptions that exempted certain classes of traffic from regulation. Shipments of newspapers and unprocessed agricultural commodities were exempted from regulation in the original act. Motor carriers under control of railroads, water carriers, or freight forwarders, operations of which are regulated as part of the service of the carrier whose services are being supported, were exempted from regulation under the original act of 1935. A 1938 amendment likewise exempted the transportation of property (and persons) incidental to transport by aircraft since the latter traffic was under the jurisdiction of the Civil Aeronautics Board. Purely local transport operations such as those entirely within a "commercial zone" surrounding certain municipalities were also exempt. Section 204(a)(4a) provides for issuance of "certificates of exemption" to carriers engaged solely in operations within a single state to allow transportation in interstate or foreign commerce in cases where it is of a character or volume such as to be of little consequence to the National Transportation Policy. Hawaiian motor carriers, for example, were exempted as a group under this provision. A 1962 amendment, Section 206(a)(6), permitted motor carriers that operate wholly within a single state to carry interstate as well as intrastate goods under the surveillance of the state commission alone.

In other instances exempt carriers have subsequently been brought under regulation. Freight forwarders were subjected to regulation in 1942 when Part IV of the Interstate Commerce Act became law. Forwarders were not permitted to own or control regulated carriers, but other carriers were allowed to own and control them. Forwarders were required to utilize common carriers for their line hauls. A 1950 amendment declared freight forwarders themselves to be common carriers. The exempt status of agricultural products and of agricultural cooperative enterprises has varied somewhat over time; these exemptions are of particular significance and are discussed in more detail.

The Agricultural Exemptions

The motor carriage of agricultural commodities for compensation was exempted from regulation under the act of 1935. A 1952 amendment to the law exempted horticultural products as well.[59] In what became known as the "poisoned vehicle" doctrine, the commission ruled any truck that had at any time been used to carry regulated commodities was forever after barred from operating under benefit of the agricultural exemption. Congress, however, amended Section 203(b) of the law in 1938 in a somewhat ambiguous effort to make the commodity rather than the vehicle the key to the exemption. The courts clarified legislative intent, ruling in two separate cases in 1951 that a vehicle can be used in the transport of both regulated and unregulated commodities as long as both are not carried at the same time.[60]

Because the preponderance of exempt freight moves in one direction, carriers without authority to haul regulated commodities on return trips were confronted with substantial excess capacity. To alleviate spatial imbalances and utilize capacity more efficiently, some exempt haulers have attempted to obtain return loads by offering reduced rates. In an effort to suppress resulting competition between regulated and unregulated haulers, the ICC endeavored to limit the exemptions to commodities traveling from producing areas to markets.

The statutory language framing the exemptions specifically excluded "manufactured" products of agriculture. Initially, this language was employed by the commission to deny exempt status to farm products that had undergone even the slightest degree of processing.[61] The U.S. Supreme Court frustrated this policy in 1956 by declaring a "substantial identity test" in the following terms:

> At some point processing and manufacturing will merge. But where the commodity retains a continuing substantial identity through the processing stage we cannot say that it has been "manufactured." . . . [62]

An immediate outcome of the case was the inclusion of fresh and frozen poultry in the list of exemptions.

Subsequently, the commission requested Congress to limit the exemption to farm-to-market movements. Congress responded in 1958 by restricting exempt commodities to those already recognized while returning some items, such as frozen fruits and berries, frozen vegetables, cocoa beans, coffee beans, tea, bananas, and certain wool products, to the regulated category.[63]

By the late 1970s the commission's view had become far more permissive. In response to long-standing pleas for equalizing exemptions treatment across modes the ICC exempted railroad shipments of fresh fruits and vegetables in 1979.[64]

Agricultural Cooperatives

The motor transportation activities of agricultural cooperatives were exempted from the original provisions of the Motor Carrier Act of 1935, but unlike the exemptions granted to agricultural commodities there was not corresponding language in the act limiting the backhaul uses of vehicles owned by cooperatives. Where locational imbalances generated excess capacity, cooperatives began to haul farm supplies as well as merchandise unrelated to farming for account of nonmembers. To restrain competition between cooperatives and common carriers for freight moving to producing regions, the commission sought to limit shipments by cooperatives through an interpretation of the Agricultural Marketing Act of 1929.

The Agricultural Marketing Act provided that cooperatives may not deal in farm products, farm supplies, and farm business services for nonmembers in an amount greater than the value of such business transacted for members.[65] The commission contended that this was an absolute prohibition against cooperatives transporting nonfarm-related products. However, a U.S. Circuit Court of Appeals ruled in 1965, in *Northwest Agricultural Cooperative Association, Inc.* v. *Interstate Commerce Commission,*[66] that this was an unduly strict interpretation. The court formulated an "incidental and necessary" test:

> . . . Northwest's transportation of nonfarm products and supplies was incidental and necessary to its farm-related transportation both in character and in amount — incidental because limited to other empty trucks returning from hauling member farm

products to market, and producing a small return in proportion to Northwest's income from trucking farm products and farm supplies; necessary because it is not economically feasible to operate the trucks empty on return trips, and because the additional income obtained is no more than that required to render performance of the cooperative's primary farm transportation service financially practicable.[67]

Having been frustrated by the court, the commission sought redress from the Congress.

Congress responded with a compromise. An amendment to the Motor Carrier Act was passed in 1968 providing that cooperatives could transport commodities unrelated to farming for nonmembers only to an extent incidental to their primary transportation operation and necessary for its effective performance. Such transportation could not exceed 15 percent of the total tonnage handled annually.[68] The commission interpreted the "incidental and necessary" test to mean that services performed for hire for nonmembers must:

> . . . as a minimum, be rendered so as to equalize or prevent an economic loss which would have resulted from an otherwise empty movement of a vehicle employed on the prior or subsequent trip in member transportation.[69]

This position was supported by a U.S. Court of Appeals ruling in 1969 that the amendment does not permit for-hire transportation for persons generally simply because the association's activities might otherwise be unprofitable.[70] The act of 1980 increased the upper limit on tonnage to 20 percent.

Rate Regulation

RATE LEVELS. Prior to passage of the Motor Carrier Act of 1980, Congress had never given the commission explicit criteria for determining the reasonableness of the general level of motor carrier rates. In the absence of specific instructions, standards of revenue entitlement have been altered or refined periodically in response to pressure applied by the rate bureaus, shipper organizations, the courts, and other government agencies. The development of public policies toward establishing the general level of rates evolved gradually.

Between 1935 and 1943 the commission used its powers to set minimum rates to forestall competitive rate reductions.[71] One scholar, who
examined the early minimum-rate-level proceedings, concluded that two
criteria were predominant.[72] The commission looked, first, for evidence
of declines in the overall level of motor carrier rates. Declining rates
were regarded as clear evidence of depressed earnings. Second, the commission endeavored to maintain motor carrier rates equal to or above
rail rates. An equitable division of traffic between rail and truck carriers
was thought to require close correspondence between rates for the two
modes.[73] Congress required the commission in its 1940 amendment to
Section 15a (rule of rate making) to give due consideration to the "effect
of rates on the movement of traffic by the carriers for which the rates are
prescribed." The act, which put the burden of proof on carriers in rate
reduction hearings, was an outcome of a view that intermodal competition rather than monopoly power had become the major regulatory issue.[74]

The commission relied almost exclusively between 1935 and 1965
upon the operating ratio as a test of reasonableness in both maximum
and minimum rate-level cases. An operating ratio of 93 before interest
and taxes was found to be reasonable in several cases.[75] Alternative
measures of revenue need such as fair return on fair value and return on
investment, used in the control of railroad earnings, were summarily
rejected.[76] Although the commission came under frequent pressure from
shipping conferences and from various agencies of the federal government, especially the U.S. Department of Agriculture, to include indica-
tors other than financial performance in its oversight of rates, it consist-
ently refused to give such evidence serious consideration.[77] Not until
1962 did the ICC begin to warn against an unconditional application of
an operating-ratio standard.[78]

Notwithstanding its adoption of the operating ratio as the sole test
of revenue requirement, the ICC continued to seek intermodal rate par-
ity. Over a period of some twenty years, requests for or approval of
increases in rail rates were invariably followed by similar requests from
motor carriers.[79] Rates for small shipments increased much faster than
those for larger shipments for which railroads competed more effectively.[80]

A new era was set in motion by a 1965 decision by the U.S. Court of
Appeals for the District of Columbia Circuit.[81] In this case, the court
reversed a decision of the Washington Metropolitan Area Transit Commission. The transit authority had employed the operating ratio as the
sole test of reasonableness. The court held that the operating ratio was

not a sufficient standard when used without reference to other factors pertaining to the ability of the firm to attract capital and maintain its financial integrity.[82]

The commission's initial decisions were affected little if at all by the latter ruling. It was not until four years later that the commission began to broaden its criteria; in the meantime, it rejected numerous requests for rate increases based on the contention that cost and revenue data supplied by the rate bureaus were not statistically sound. Rate of return was given virtually no consideration.[83] The operating ratio still provided the primary means of determining revenue need, but the commission did demand more reliable estimates of revenue and expenses employed in calculating operating ratios.

The final period extends from 1969 to passage of the act of 1980. While since 1969 the commission strengthened its requirements for the collection of financial data, it failed to formulate clear decision rules for judging the adequacy of revenues. The clearest statement coming from the ICC regarding earnings control standards concerned the appropriate use of the operating ratio:

> . . . It is a clear misuse of the operating ratio to take the path pursued by respondents, i.e., to calculate such ratios, either present or projected, and conclude from the bare ratios either that present revenues are insufficient or that proposed revenues are justified. The true course is to determine what are the legitimate expenses and capital requirements for providing the required service; the amounts determined can then be translated into operating ratios, both to compare the rate level with the revenue need and to test the rate structure by comparing profit margins on various weight brackets and other categories of traffic.[84]

Thus the commission finally rejected the operating ratio as the sole indicator of revenue entitlement.

Beyond this conclusion, interpreting the published orders of the commission in motor carrier rate cases is hazardous at best. In five rate-level cases decided in 1969, the commission failed to provide a consistent rationale for granting rate relief. Relief was awarded in one instance because the 10 percent rate of return on equity for a sample group of carriers was regarded as too low.[85] In another case relief was denied on the grounds that the proposed rates would have generated a rate of return on net investment before taxes of 26.7 percent and a rate of return on equity of 22.6 percent after taxes. Such returns were considered too high.[86] Both decisions failed to indicate what an adequate rate of return would have been.

The commission attempted to answer the question of what constitutes an adequate return in two other 1969 cases. Increased revenues for carriers in New England were found to be warranted where it was shown that these carriers had earned lower rates of return on equity and net investment than the corresponding national averages for regulated carriers.[87] This approach involves circular reasoning; it presumes that the realized earnings of the other carriers are within the range of a fair rate of return. In another instance the commission compared the carriers' rates of return on equity to those of seven regulated and unregulated industries and awarded a rate advance upon a finding that the other industries had a higher average return.[88] This method avoids circular reasoning, but it fails to provide a rational for using nontransport industries as an earnings standard.

More recently, the commission has employed a modified operating-ratio test as the primary determinant of revenue needs.[89] In a 1969 case an amount intended to reflect capital requirements was added to reported expenses and the estimated revenue need fell below actual revenues in the recent past.[90] Hence the requested rate increase was approved; the basis for selecting the range of returns employed was not identified, however. Return on stockholder's equity finally replaced the operating ratio in 1978 and a "threshold guideline" of 14 percent was established by the commission.[91]

Historically the ICC has sought to suppress rate reductions fostered by either intermodal or intramodal competition. Of the 173,248 rail, motor, and water tariffs filed with the ICC in 1962, the Board of Suspension and Investigation considered only 5,710 and allowed the others to take effect without formal review. Approximately 95 percent of the suspensions involved requests for rate decreases.[92]

One study examined 350 requests for rate reductions resolved by the ICC between March 14, 1960, and May 25, 1962.[93] More than 90 percent of the cases involved either intramodal truck competition or intermodal competition with motor carrier proponents and rail protestants or the reverse. Seventy percent of the cases were denied. In cases where formal cost evidence was introduced, 80 percent were denied because the proposed rates were judged to be too low or the evidence was deemed insufficient to support an approval.[94]

COLLECTIVE RATEMAKING/ANTITRUST IMMUNITY. The functions of the territorial motor carrier rate conferences were patterned after the comprehensive procedures developed by their predecessors, the railroad rate bureaus. Determination of rates and rules governing various tariffs is undertaken on behalf of the member carriers. Committees composed of member carriers consider rate proposals submitted to them after shippers and other interested parties are given a chance to be heard. Shippers and the general public are, however, excluded from sessions where specific proposals are discussed and voted upon by the membership.

The early rate agreements fashioned by the railroad traffic associations were declared illegal under the Sherman Act of 1890. Shortly afterward Congress strengthened the authority of the ICC by giving it the power to prescribe maximum rail rates upon complaint and after hearing.[95] The price-fixing activities of the rail rate bureaus remained unchallenged for many years. Finally, however, in 1945 the Supreme Court ruled Congress had not given the ICC the authority "to remove rate-fixing combinations from the prohibitions contained in the antitrust laws."[96] Congress responded to the ruling in 1948 by enacting the Reed-Bulwinkle Act, which exempted rail and motor carrier rate bureaus from the provisions of the antitrust laws.[97] President Truman's veto of the legislation was overridden by the Eightieth Congress.[98]

Under the protection afforded by antitrust immunity, rate bureaus have inhibited independent pricing decisions by member carriers. A student of rate bureau policies has described the effect:

> A carrier's incentive to engage in rate cutting is dampened if it expects everyone to learn about and to follow that cut promptly. The publication requirements of regulation permit rate bureaus to learn about proposed rate reductions in advance of their effective date, and to notify members so that they can follow those reductions immediately. By reducing the expected returns from rate reductions, publication requirements aid rate bureaus in maintaining rates above the competitive level.[99]

Where the threat of immediate price matching does not deter rate reductions, the rate cutter can expect vigorous protests from rate bureau members. Indeed, the number of protested rate reductions climbed from 227 in 1946 to 4,712 in 1962. The latter protests represented more than 90 percent of the rate filings suspended and investigated during 1962.[100]

Further evidence of the competition-inhibiting effect of rate bureaus is exemplified in a 1975 ICC decision forbidding protests of independent rate proposals by the bureaus themselves.[101] Within six months the commission acknowledged that there had been "a substantial increase in the publication of independent action proposals and a decrease in the number of protests filed."[102]

JOINT RATES AND THROUGH ROUTES. Before the passage of the Motor Carrier Act of 1980, motor common carriers of property could not be required to establish through routes and joint rates with other such carriers or with rail and water lines but could do so voluntarily if the division of joint revenue provided reasonable compensation to all participating carriers. A through route is an arrangement between connecting carriers for the continuous carriage of commodities on a single billing from an originating point on the line of one carrier to a destination on the line of another. The rate charged for the continuous service is known as a through rate. Through rates may be either combination rates or joint rates. A combination rate is the sum of the separate rates determined by participating carriers. A joint rate is a single charge from origin to destination that is typically less than the sum of the local rates fixed by the connecting carriers.

RELEASED VALUE RATES. Before the enactment of the 1980 legislation, common carriers under the jurisdiction of the ICC were responsible for the full value of articles lost, stolen, or damaged in transit.[103] A carrier could not restrict its liability unless it first obtained permission from the commission to establish released rates.[104] Such rates put a ceiling on the loss and damage responsibility of the carrier in return for reduced transportation charges. In the past the commission has required that the items subject to released rates must possess two characteristics concurrently before it would give its approval. First, the articles must have an unusual susceptibility to loss, theft, or damage. Second, the value of the commodity must be highly variable. Only the joint occurrence of a high risk of loss and an uncertain value has been viewed as justifying limited liability.[105] This stand is consistent with the commission's ruling in 1962 that Congress intended the power to permit released rates to be used infrequently.[106]

The requirement that ICC approval be gained for released rates tended to discourage innovative motor carrier pricing by favoring uniform rates. Encouraging uniform rates irrespective of the risk and consequences of unlimited liability generates a cross subsidy between types of traffic. Commodities with a low expected value of loss subsidize traffic with high expected losses.[107] Greater freedom for shippers and carriers to negotiate the extent of the carriers' liability might be expected to lessen any extra burden imposed upon low-risk traffic while promoting broader price and service options.

Trailer-on-Flatcar Service

The use of truck trailers on railroad flatcars (TOFC) has confronted the commission with persistent issues involving intermodal competition and coordination. Coordinated rail-truck movement combines the more flexible collection with delivery capabilities of trucking with the lower line-haul costs of railroads. Moreover, the small capacity of truck trailers reduces the optimum size of a shipment and lowers storage and handling costs.[108] The railroads, however, have retarded the adoption of such joint services by resisting cooperation with motor carriers and by failing to establish joint rates that pass on the cost savings to shippers.[109]

Although legislation has not given the ICC the authority to compel coordinated rail-truck service, the commission had ordered the railroads to offer TOFC service to motor carriers on the same terms as offered to private shippers and freight forwarders. Motor carriers also have been granted the privilege of utilizing TOFC service as a substitute for any part of a service they are authorized to perform.[110] However, motor carriers have been forbidden to transfer freight to or from railcars except at points they are authorized to serve, even though they may possess the authority to serve both the origin and destination of a shipment.[111]

Merger/Concentration

The total number of Class I, II, and III regulated carriers declined sharply between the time when the last grandfather authorizations were awarded in the early 1940s and the late 1970s when new commission policies began to reverse the trend. Of the 26,000 such carriers in operation in 1940, only about 15,000 remained by 1972.[112] Trends in the volume of business were sharply in the other direction; traffic increased from 19.6 billion ton-miles in 1939 to 101.4 billion in 1961 and freight revenues grew from $792.2 million to nearly $7.5 billion.[113]

The tempo of consolidation activity accelerated markedly during the 1950s, resulting in the emergence of a number of large carrier systems, some of transcontinental scope.[114] By the early 1960s many light-density routes were served by only three or fewer carriers. Single-line service over relatively dense routes was generally provided by as few as two to as many as ten firms. Only a dozen carriers were authorized to provide general commodity service on regular transcontinental routes.[115]

In 1963, the number of Class I motor common carriers authorized to transport general commodities in single-line service be-

tween Seattle or Portland and Chicago was two over direct routes
and four over direct and circuitous routes; between San Fran-
cisco and Chicago, five over direct routes and seven over direct
and circuitous routes; between Los Angeles and Chicago, six
over direct routes and nine over direct and circuitous routes;
between Seattle or Portland and Minneapolis-St. Paul, three over
direct routes and three over direct and circuitous routes. . . .
Thus, a small number of large-size carriers characterizes transcontinental market structures, with even fewer carriers authorized to render specialized service in liquid or dry bulk
commodities.[116]

These significant increases in concentration are clearly inconsistent
with scale relationships in the industry. Theoretical and empirical evidence for constant returns to scale is overwhelming (see Chapter 3). The
growth in concentration is explained not by scale imperatives but by the
quest of trucking firms for rationalization of fragmented operating
authorities awarded at the onset of regulation. Indeed, the passage of
time has brought new patterns of demand, new and improved public
roads, improvements in carrier technology, and other changes to which
carriers must adapt if major inefficiencies are to be avoided. These
changes have often magnified deficiencies inherent in the original certificates.

The ICC has authority to restrict mergers of existing trucking firms
as well as the entry of new carriers. The act of 1935 required commission
approval of consolidations involving more than twenty vehicles. The
provision was changed in 1965 to exempt mergers involving carriers having combined annual gross revenues of less than $300,000.[117]

While the commission has long acknowledged the need for rational-
ized operating authorities, it held fast until the late 1970s to the view that
restraint of competition was a higher priority. Restricted entry was, after
all, the purpose of regulation. But the dilemma had a solution. The
obvious need for more flexible authorities, authorities which might
smooth seasonal fluctuations in traffic, improve backhaul opportunities,
reduce circuity of travel, limit service to unprofitable intermediate
points, and overcome interlining problems, could be accommodated by
mergers. Thus the commission actively encouraged mergers at the same
time that it actively discouraged new entry and expanded authority for
existing carriers.

Even the issuance of grandfather rights following the passage of the
act of 1935 was a slow and laborious process. The burden of proof was

on applicants to show that their prior service was of sufficient intensity and duration to warrant their certification. Many applications had not been acted upon by 1941 and many were eventually denied in part or in whole.[118]

Most of the decline in the number of regulated carriers over the forty-year period subsequent to 1935 resulted from unification proceedings.[119] "Improved service" was mentioned in "well over 75 percent of all cases surveyed" as the ICC's reason for approving mergers, according to James Johnson who made an exhaustive analysis of merger trends and of the commission's policies toward mergers.[120] Expected improvements included faster service from elimination of interchange, improved load factors from authority to carry new products and to serve new points, better balance of traffic patterns to meet changing market conditions, service to new points (often near existing route structures), less circuitous routes, reduced pickup and delivery costs, and reduced loss and damage claims.[121]

The ICC invariably ignored railroad protests of adverse effects of mergers on intermodal competition until 1950 when it denied the unification of the Pacific Intermountain Express (P.I.E.) and Keeshin systems on this basis. The commission concluded that railroads were the low-cost mode for most commodities moving long distances and that protection of this comparative advantage required denial of the proposed merger.[122] The case failed to be a turning point, however, as the commission subsequently reverted to its earlier policy of discounting the adverse effects of mergers on the railroads.

Nor was major weight given to the implications of proposed consolidations for competing motor carriers. The ICC did require that benefits to shippers from "new service" mergers outweigh damage to protestants. The commission has generally approved mergers that were seen as beneficial, even though competing truckers might suffer loss of traffic and revenue, as long as damages were not expected to be "substantial."[123] The commission ruled in 1942 that large size alone was not sufficient cause for denial of merger applications when the joining of eight firms to form the nation's then largest single trucking firm was approved.[124] The Supreme Court upheld the commission's action in a 1944 case.[125]

The extent of premerger interlining between firms seeking consolidation has been a major ICC consideration. Less disruption of the needs of customers and the business of competitors was expected where interlining was substantial. Thus the commission was most favorably disposed toward end-to-end mergers.[126] Dormancy of operating rights was also a key factor in commission decisions, the transfer of dormant rights seldom being allowed in consolidation proceedings. The reason for dormancy was generally not a consideration.[127]

Finally, it appears that larger trucking firms have been more successful than smaller ones in rationalizing their operating rights.

> Large truckers have been able to round out their operations with additional grants of commodity, route, or other authority, or by purchase of rights; but highly restrictive carriers, typically small firms, have not. Thus, the patterns of restrictions resulting from granting "grandfather" rights have not been basically altered.[128]

Trends in the structure of regulated motor carrier markets are at sharp variance with those of markets served by less regulated or unregulated carriers, both in the United States and elsewhere. While data are not at hand to support a detailed assessment of the structure of unregulated, for-hire trucking, all available evidence points to the presence of atomistic and highly competitive markets. Evidence comes from many sources, including the ICC itself,[129] the "Doyle Report" of 1961,[130] and studies undertaken by the USDA.[131] A study by Walter Adams and James Hendry showed that by 1955 the largest 100 Class I motor common carriers had 45 percent of the revenues of Class I carriers of general freight and 26 percent of the revenues of all Class I, II, and III regulated truckers.[132] James C. Nelson summarized the picture as follows:

> Whatever estimate is closest to the true situation, there are a large number of exempt for-hire truckers; they operate on a small scale, averaging 2.2 tractors and 2.5 semi-trailers per firm; their operating and service areas are not restricted except that they can only lawfully haul exempt commodities; their rates are determined by competitive rather than administered or regulated pricing; and they are highly mobile and operate under constant cost conditions.[133]

Motor carriers are far less restrictively regulated in a number of other industrialized countries than in the United States. The experience of these countries confirms that trucking, in the absence of controls on entry, service, and rates, is an inherently competitive industry. Thomas Gale Moore, in a study of trucking regulation in five European countries — Great Britain, West Germany, Belgium, the Netherlands, and Sweden — concluded that in this otherwise diverse group of nations a relaxed regulatory environment has led in each case to enhancement of competition.[134]

Nelson draws similar conclusions from a study of regulatory environments in Great Britain, Australia, and Canada. In Britain for-hire carriers gained substantial additional traffic from own-account truckers following deregulation. While there was some growth of larger firms, the entry of many smaller ones has led to a "workably competitive" outcome. In Australia many small firms and an even larger number of small owner-operators have persisted in the denser routes in a deregulated environment. While only four multimodal freight forwarders compete for long-haul, small-shipment/LTL traffic, the potential entry of a very large number of smaller carriers into these and other truck and rail markets has led to workable competition here as well. Canada has never had interprovincial regulation. Such intraprovincial regulation as remains after a series of deregulatory moves is much less restrictive than that found in the United States prior to 1980. Canadian trucking has been a rapid-growth industry and the number of long-distance truckers has easily been sufficient to provide competitive rates.[135]

Regulatory Reform

Nearly four decades and several cycles of economic ups and downs were to pass before the regulatory environment woven from the economic distress of the Great Depression of the 1930s was to show signs of unraveling. While there were both advances and reverses in court interpretations and on occasion in administration of the act of 1935, the trend was clearly toward institutionalization of regulatory oversight and expansion of its scope. The commission sought to solidify its regulatory control over motor carriers and their rail and water competitors. Congress was generally supportive in this endeavor.

Dissatisfaction with the gradually tightening regulatory fabric began to be apparent, however, evolving slowly at first, growing significantly in intensity during the 1960s as an expanding volume of research findings highlighted its deficiencies, and culminating in the late 1970s in major reforms undertaken by the commission itself. Finally, in the face of rapidly growing sentiment for less stringent regulatory controls and in recognition of the substantial reforms already accomplished by the commission, Congress enacted the compromise act of 1980 gaining reluctant support from both the trucking industry and those who sought its total deregulation.

Meanwhile, the fledgling motor carrier industry had been growing rapidly and by the close of World War II had become far larger and more financially secure than it was in 1935. Funding of the interstate highway system in 1956 gave major impetus to growth of intercity motor carriage and contributed to trucking's growing share of a growing transportation market.

Calls for reform grew louder in the late 1950s and early 1960s, along with mounting research evidence of regulatory shortcomings. Research results increasingly supported reduced regulation and greater reliance on market forces.[136]

President Kennedy's special transportation message to Congress in 1962 called for a lower regulatory profile. President Johnson focused attention on greater intermodal cooperation and in a special message to Congress in 1966 called for the creation of a federal department of transportation.

Congress complied and the U.S. Department of Transportation (DOT) became a reality in October 1966. By the 1970s both the new DOT and the President's Council of Economic Advisers were pressing for regulatory reform. The DOT began submitting each year legislation to Congress calling for major reform of motor carriage and other modes of transportation.[137]

The tempo of research findings critical of regulation grew during the 1970s with the publication of a number of government-sponsored reports.[138] Ralph Nader's Study Group published a report in 1970 calling for restructuring of the ICC, liberalized entry to transportation markets, abolition of rate bureaus, and application of antitrust laws to transportation firms.[139]

The turning point came at the middle of the decade with the emergence of the OPEC oil crisis of 1974 and the northeastern railroad problems of 1975. Congress began to face the need for reform legislation and the ICC came under increasing pressure to change its operating procedures. Passage of the Railroad Revitalization and Reform Act in 1976 brought major regulatory changes to the railroad industry and signaled for the first time a willingness of Congress to consider regulatory reform. The National Transportation Policy Study Commission established by Congress in 1976 advocated easier entry and exit into motor carriage, establishment of a "zone of reasonableness" in ratemaking, and recommended bringing ratemaking under the mantle of antitrust laws.[140]

These events gradually began to be reflected in commission decisions in favor of more relaxed oversight of entry and operating rights. In a 1974 ruling involving Sunkist Growers, for example, the ICC declared

that cooperative "member transportation" included FOB origin shipments of packinghouse sales to nonfarmer consignees such as whole-
salers, jobbers, and chain stores.[141] Cooperatives were thereby afforded
greater leeway in serving nonmember customers. In another rule-making
proceeding in the same year the ICC enlarged the "operational circuity
reduction" from 15 to 20 percent. The ruling allowed carriers to deviate
from their regular, prescribed routes as long as the mileage savings did
not exceed 20 percent of the total miles traveled.[142]

More significant administrative reforms began in 1977 following
changes in commission membership in that and the previous year and the
appointment by President Jimmy Carter of Daniel O'Neal as chairman.
Motor carrier operating authority applications began to increase sharply
in late 1976 when it became apparent that ICC entry policies had become
less restrictive. The annual number of authority cases closed by the commission nearly quadrupled between 1975 and 1980.[143] By 1979 more than
98 percent of the applications were being approved.[144]

The commission took a number of administrative actions between
1977 and 1980 substantially easing entry into the trucking industry. Rule-
making procedures opened in 1977 resulted by 1978 in relaxed rules
concerning transfer of dormant operating rights; transfers were to be
allowed even where protesting carriers were thereby harmed, as long as
public benefit from approval outweighed harm to protestants.[145] The
U.S. Court of Appeals for the First Circuit upheld the commission's
authority to depart from traditional standards of convenience and necessity, in appropriate cases, in granting operating rights.[146] The District of
Columbia Circuit in the same year ruled that harm to existing carriers is
a relevant factor in granting operating authority only when there is also
injury to the public.[147]

The commission announced a policy in 1978 aimed at facilitating
the elimination of gateways in connection with consolidation applications.[148] In another action the commission adopted rules allowing carriers to hold both common and contract carrier authority where such is
not inconsistent with public interest or national policy.[149] Section 210a of
the act of 1935 permits such "dual operations" of a firm only when they
are in the "public interest." The restriction historically had been interpreted so as to prevent such operations. The commission departed from
this position in 1978 in its declaration that "public interest" is met as long
as "no special evidence indicates that rate or service preference is likely
for any one shipper by holding both kinds of operating rights."[150] The
U.S. Court of Appeals for the District of Columbia Circuit sustained the
commission's interpretation in a 1979 case.[151] Finally, in 1978 the com-

mission curtailed the rights of rate bureaus to change or cancel rates established by independent action; rate bureaus were required thereafter to obtain the written permission of participants in the traffic prior to publication of tariffs.[152]

The trend continued in 1979 as additional commission directives made entry still less restrictive. The commission pursued its thrust of the previous year in favoring public rule makings having general applicability over a case-by-case approach; adjudication of operating authority cases was speeded up markedly.[153]

A liberalized policy was formulated for granting operating authority to applicants intending to use it primarily as an incident to the transportation of their own goods and their own nontransportation business.[154] Prospective rates became an entry consideration for the first time when the commission ruled that the ability of an applicant to offer cost-based lower rates was a valid consideration in entry proceedings.[155] In another proceeding the burden of proof was relaxed for awards of single-line authority as substitutes for previous joint-line service with a connecting carrier. As a result, applicants need only show that prior joint-line operations are no longer suited to shippers' needs.[156]

The commission agreed for the first time in 1979 to allow private shippers to operate in the dual capacity of private and for-hire carriers. The policy was aimed at saving energy by facilitating backhauls.[157] In another important policy change, intervention in operating rights proceedings was limited generally to protestants who are already authorized to perform the service in question, have the equipment to perform the service, and who have actually performed such service.[158] The U.S. Court of Appeals for the District of Columbia upheld the new rules in a 1980 decision.[159]

In another significant policy change, the "burden of proof" was shifted to protestants in application proceedings once the applicant has shown need for service exists. Protestants under the revised policy were required to prove that the new service would impair their own ability to serve.[160] Final rules were issued relaxing application procedures and burden of proof requirements for applications for pickup and delivery service in support of water traffic within commercial zones of port cities.[161]

A final series of actions taken during 1979, although of relatively limited scope, fit the pattern of the closing years of the era and served to relax further the regulatory environment. First, the commission allowed carriers to substitute water service between any Alaskan and other western U.S. ports whether or not carriers were authorized to serve the port of interchange.[162] Second, the size of the area surrounding air terminals within which transport incidental to shipment by aircraft was exempt was expanded from 25 to 35 miles from airport boundaries.[163] Additionally, rule-making proceedings were initiated that would allow freight forwarders and railroads to establish contract rates with each other.[164] The commission further ruled that a regulated freight forwarder could provide exempt service by establishing an affiliate company for the carriage of exempt agricultural products.[165] Finally, trucking companies were permitted to issue tariffs under which services of one company could be substituted for those of another. The resulting traffic sharing was expected to improve load factors.[166]

The commission had initiated several additional rule-making proceedings during 1980 that were preempted by passage of the act of 1980. One would have permitted owner-operators and small truckers carrying exempt agricultural commodities to obtain authority to carry regulated products on their return hauls.[167] A second action would have allowed regulated truckers to carry exempt agricultural commodities in mixed loads.[168] The same proceeding would have simplified procedures for carriers with one-way authority to obtain authority for return-haul traffic. A third rule-making was begun that would have allowed regular-route carriers to serve all intermediate points on their routes.[169] Finally, the commission proposed to allow regular-route carriers the option of traveling between terminal points on their routes by the most direct routes.[170]

CHAPTER 3

Inherent Structure, Behavior, and Performance

The structural, behavioral, and performance characteristics of an industry are strongly influenced by technological considerations. The marginal technical rates of factor substitution, the complexity of and rate of progress in the underlying engineering art, factor indivisibility, and so on all affect the organization of an industry. When an industry is subject to extensive regulation, however, it is not always easy to ascertain the extent to which industry performance has been modified by the structural and behavioral changes induced by the regulatory process itself. Thus in the telephone and electric light and power industries, for example, it may not always be clear to what extent monopoly markets are the result of technological imperatives or of the exclusivity of the franchises or certificates of convenience and necessity under which they operate.

While the technological attributes of the telephone and electric light and power industries might lead an investigator to conclude that, absent regulation, significant monopoly elements would remain, the highway transportation of freight is a substantially different situation. Here, a priori reasoning as well as much of the empirical evidence would suggest

Reprinted with permission from John Richard Felton, "The Inherent Structure, Behavior and Performance of the Motor Freight Industry," *International Journal of Transport Economics* 5, no. 1 (Apr. 1978):23–35.

that whatever monopolistic elements are present in the industry are rather exclusively the product of that regulation.

Technology of Motor Freight Transport

Perhaps the technological characteristic of motor freight transport that serves most to account for its inherent market structure is the suitability of its right-of-way for multifirm operation. This, in turn, encourages the separate ownership of vehicles and way, with the flexibility and geographic mobility inherent in such a division of ownership.

A second technological characteristic is the relatively small load and vehicle units. For the most part the load and vehicle units are identical, but in some cases the vehicle unit may consist of several load units, that is, a tractor and one or more trailers. At any rate, the motor freight vehicle unit tends to be dwarfed by the rail and water vehicle units (the train, the vessel, and the flotilla).

A third characteristic is the relatively simple technology of the industry. Loading, unloading, dispatching, and driving of trucks are relatively uncomplicated and unchanging operations. Furthermore, whatever technological changes occur in the principal input industries, road construction and motor vehicle production, they are unlikely to exert any marked effects on the technology of motor freight haulage.

Market Structure: Concentration

The number and size distribution of firms in an industry are the result of a number of forces including: (1) economies of scale; (2) advantages of size, whether they arise from the limiting of competition through merger or from the realizing of the pecuniary gains associated with large-scale promotional activities; and (3) barriers to entry.[1] The technological characteristics of the motor freight industry would appear to militate against high concentration.

In some industries alternative technologies are available for plants of different size or the differential multiplication of inputs makes it possible to achieve a better balance of processes. In the road haulage industry, however, technology and input ratios are largely unaffected by plant size. Larger size involves merely the addition of vehicle units of similar characteristics and of drivers in direct proportion to the additional vehicles. If there are any indivisibilities that could yield even modest economies of scale, they would appear to be associated with terminal operations.

In the absence of diseconomies of scale, the mere lack of economies of scale would not preclude mergers to restrict competition. The existence of a large number of firms and very low barriers to entry would seem to militate against such an outcome. The mergers that did occur would presumably be motivated by some objective unrelated to the realization of monopoly profits.

Promotional activity is not ordinarily an important feature of industries in the producers' goods sector. With the exception of household-goods transportation, virtually all motor freight haulage is an input in the production process. Since the buyers of such transport services are not generally influenced by promotional activities, the ability to advertise on a national basis is not a factor promoting the growth of the firm.

As noted earlier, merger for monopoly presupposes sufficient barriers to entry to render the effort worthwhile. Bain has identified the factors that may give existing firms advantages over potential newcomers as strategic patents on products or processes, substantial monopoly control of a crucial raw material or other input, and substantial differentiation of products.[2] It is obvious that existing trucking firms are not likely to be the beneficiary of important patents, of the control of vital inputs, or of any significant consumer attachments.

While all of the foregoing considerations would suggest that road haulage is inherently an industry of low concentration, the number and size distribution of firms are also dependent upon the size of the market. All transport markets tend to be extensively segmented by commodity and by pairs of origins and destinations. It is not easy, however, to identify the sellers in the market for the transportation of a particular commodity from a particular origin to a particular destination. To count only those firms actually engaged in transporting a particular commodity between two points during any short time span may convey an erroneous impression of market concentration. The reason is that the nonspecialized nature of many trucks, together with the geographic mobility they exhibit, makes intermarket transference a relatively simple phenomenon even in the short run. In sum, the technological characteristics of motor freight transport make entry into the industry extremely easy, and even though transport markets are extensively segmented, entry into industry submarkets is even easier because of the flexibility and mobility of the industry's major asset, the truck.

Market Structure: Condition of Entry

The "condition of entry" is usually defined as the percentage by which established firms can raise prices above a competitive level without attracting entry into the industry. In the absence of barriers to entry, established firms have no advantage over potential entrants, and this percentage is zero.[3] At the other extreme, the barriers to entry may be so high that established firms can exact a monopoly price without the risk of new firm entry. When the "entry forestalling" price, as Bain calls it, exceeds the monopoly price, entry is blocked.[4]

Economies of scale introduce two distinctly different and largely unrelated kinds of barriers to entry. If minimal efficient scale of plant operation would constitute a significant percentage of the output in the market in which the plant will operate, the potential entrant must choose between a suboptimal plant size or a reduction in the price of the product induced by its own augmentation of industry output. A second barrier to entry imposed by scale economies is absolute capital requirements. The larger the dollar investment necessary to a minimal efficient scale, the more difficult it will be to accumulate the resources essential for successful entry.

Neither the percentage effect nor the absolute capital requirements of the trucking industry would appear to raise appreciable barriers to entry into the trucking industry. According to the 1972 Census of Transportation, there were some 600,000 trucks capable of general commodity transportation in the United States.[5] Even if a trucking firm required sixty vehicles to achieve minimal efficient size, this would constitute only $\frac{1}{100}$ of 1 percent of national capacity.

As for absolute capital requirements, Bain's study of twenty manufacturing industries found absolute capital requirements for a minimally efficient plant varying from $500,000 to $2,000,000 in shoe manufacturing to $500,000,000 or more in automobile and steel manufacturing.[6] The contemporaneous study of motor carrier size and efficiency by Merrill J. Roberts revealed that the median asset size of some 114 Class I carriers of general freight operating over regular routes in north central United States was less than $350,000.[7] If absolute capital requirements impose no substantial barrier to entry into shoe manufacturing, certainly they impose none into motor freight transport.

Market Structure: Product Differentiation

Not only is product differentiation a potential barrier to the entry of new firms, but also it affects the competitive relationship among established firms. Presumably product differentiation provides each seller with some insulation from the pricing policies of its rivals and enables those sellers whose consumer attachments are the strongest to achieve larger market shares or higher prices or both. At any rate, product differentiation is inconsistent with a purely competitive market, creating the presumption that industry performance will fall short of the ideal. In sum, product differentiation will probably induce excess capacity, prevent prices from approaching average costs over the long run, and include expenditures that are merely persuasive rather than informational.

The factors giving rise to product differentiation include variations in product quality or design, buyer ignorance, and seller promotional activity. Owing to the sophistication of the consumers of highway carriage of freight, neither ignorance nor promotional activity should be a significant element in motor carrier product differentiation. Variation in the quality of service might be expected, however, to be present even in a completely unregulated environment. Such variations in service might include the quality of the equipment and the frequency, speed, safety, and reliability of service.

All in all, product differentiation would not appear to be an important characteristic of highway freight transportation.[8] Such differentiation as is present may merely involve a more precise meeting of consumers' preferences without providing any protection for successful innovators from imitation by existing or potential truck operators.

Business Behavior

Business behavior, or conduct, is typically held to include pricing policies, product policies, and predatory tactics with respect to rival sellers. The market structure of highway freight transport should render prediction of seller behavior relatively easy.

Truck rates in an unregulated setting might be determined in various ways.[9] Some truck operators might establish rate schedules they would observe with greater or lesser degrees of fidelity and either for brief or more extended periods of time. Others might operate after the fashion of a tramp steamer, with the rate for each shipment the subject of negotiation between the carrier and shipper. Rates might also be established by long-term contract between shipper and carrier. Finally, the rate might be set by the shipper or by the receiver of the shipment.

Whatever the nominal method of rate setting, low seller concentration, the very easy condition of entry, and meager product differentiation would appear to preclude significant departures from a purely competitive price. Collusion would seem fruitless since the possibility of intermarket transference would render infeasible even short-run, price-raising activities.

Inasmuch as the production of transportation service must take place at the same time as its consumption, seasonality in the demand for truck service should be reflected in seasonal variations in rates. Seasonal variations in the demand for the transportation of particular commodities would be insufficient to generate equivalent seasonality in the demand for truck services, however, if the truck were capable of transporting different commodities and the peak demands for different commodities occurred at different times.

Product policies would presumably be responsive to the peculiarities and special requirements of individual shippers. They would constitute a mode of competing and consist primarily in adapting to the preferences expressed by consumers in an imperfect buyers' market. Obviously, not all truck operators would possess the appropriate equipment or would be able to fulfill the time and locational expectations of all shippers, but the market structure of trucking would appear to render even extensive variations in buyer preferences consistent with a competitive outcome.

Market structure would also appear to rule out predatory or exclusionary practices by existing trucking firms. Whether the structure would promote destructive, ruinous, or cutthroat competition has been the subject of far more extensive debate. This issue will be considered as an aspect of the inherent economic performance of the highway freight carrier industry.

Economic Performance

The most relevant criteria of the inherent economic performance of the motor freight industry would probably be: (1) the extent to which actual firm size corresponds to the optimum size; (2) the extent to which capacity is utilized, that is, neither excess nor deficient capacity is prolonged; (3) the extent to which price in the long run tends to approximate average costs; (4) the extent to which product quality is as good as underlying technology and consumer preferences will permit; and (5) the extent to which the industry is progressive, that is, inventive or innovative. Each of these criteria will be explored in turn.

If economies of scale are exhausted rather quickly in highway freight transportation, it does not follow that smaller or larger firms are incurring significantly higher cost than those of optimum size. The scale curve for plants of suboptimum size may increase very gradually and enterprises of larger than minimum efficient scale may not incur appreciable diseconomies of scale. While it is difficult to deduce an optimum size for motor freight transport on strictly a priori grounds, whatever the size, it is unlikely that even extensive departures from the optimum (as measured by capacity) would result in substantial increases in cost over that incurred by a trucking firm of optimum size.

Excess capacity in highway freight transport might arise from seasonal fluctuations in the demand for transportation, from interlocational variations in demand, or from irrational entry. Of these only interlocational variations in the demand for transport would appear plausible.

Seasonal fluctuations in the demand for a service that must be produced at the same time it is consumed automatically generate peak-load pricing in a competitive industry. Such a pricing system tends to impose all, or the bulk, of investment cost upon peak users in proportion to their contribution to the peak and upon off-peak users, generally, only to the extent of the short-run marginal costs of performing the service. The utilization of capacity at prices that would fail to cover the short-run marginal cost of such service would detract from, rather than enhance, economic performance.

Excess capacity might also arise from imbalances in traffic as among different shipment origins. Forward and backhaul traffic movements create a peak-off-peak pricing problem analogous to seasonal fluctuations in the demand for transportation.

In a competitive market interlocational imbalances in demand should cause the rates on backhauls to fall to the level of the additional costs associated with picking up, transporting, and delivering such commodities. Various factors can, of course, account for such imbalances. A community such as Washington, D.C., which is engaged primarily in the production of services, would tend to exhibit a limited demand for freight transport. An area specializing in commodities high in value in relation to their weight would also tend to manifest a lesser (though probably more inelastic) demand for transportation than an area specializing in low-value commodities. Imbalances may also arise because the exports from different areas require specialized equipment unsuited to general commodity transport. At any rate, all such causes of excess capacity are consistent with satisfactory economic performance.

Finally, excess capacity might be endemic to the industry because of the exceptionally low entry barriers and the "excessive" or "destructive" competition fostered thereby. As D. Philip Locklin has observed:

> Although there has been a tendency to discount the overcapacity or "excessive-competition" contentions as merely the rationalization of the desire of the railroads and the existing motor carriers to obtain protection from additional competition, the matter cannot be dismissed so easily. The phenomenon of overcapacity does occur in the industry. . . . the special conditions existing in the motor-carrier industry have resulted in a tendency for overcapacity to develop and to persist, and . . . under these conditions competition does not function as the theorist assumes. The ruinous type of competition does develop; discrimination in rates does appear, the condition of overcapacity does not correct itself automatically; and the struggle for survival in the face of inadequate revenues leads to deterioration of safety standards, financial irresponsibility, and generally unsatisfactory service.[10]

If "excessive competition" is to be other than a pejorative term, it must be given some operational content. For competition to be excessive, presumably the first requirement is that total industry revenues fall short of total industry costs. Such deficiencies in revenues must be more than merely transitory, however, for temporary deficiencies can occur in any industry as a result of general recession, technological innovations, population shifts, factor price increases, and changes in consumer tastes. To be termed "excessive," it would appear necessary for revenue deficiencies to be prolonged.

The conditions conducive to a persistent tendency for total revenues to be less than total costs would include not merely an atomistic structure and ease of entry, but also a demand declining relatively if not absolutely, a relatively inelastic demand, rising factor productivity induced by technological change, and low mobility of industry resources. While this description might fit large segments of agriculture, it has little relevance to highway freight transportation.

As an indicator of absolute growth of demand, intercity truck ton-miles almost tripled between 1950 and 1976. As for relative change in demand, trucking firms' share of total intercity freight transport rose from 16.3 percent to 22.6 percent during this period.[11]

By all accounts, the demand for highway carrier transportation is of greater than unit elasticity. Estimates of overall price elasticity of demand have varied from -1.15 (Benishay and Whitaker)[12] to -2.023 (Eugene D. Perle),[13] with an intermediate value of -1.841 found by Alexander Morton.[14]

While output per work-hour in highway transportation has risen somewhat more rapidly than for the private domestic economy as a whole since World War II, the rate of increase has been substantially less than for agriculture or for transportation as a whole. Between 1947 and 1965 the annual rate of growth of labor productivity was 2.6 in the private domestic economy, 5.1 in agriculture, and 4.4 in transportation.[15] By comparison, labor productivity in motor freight increased at an annual rate of 2.7 percent between 1947 and 1957 and 3.8 percent between 1957 and 1964.[16]

As for resource mobility, the principal asset—the truck— is relatively short-lived, with a useful life that probably does not exceed ten years.[17] Furthermore, there is a lively second-hand market for used equipment as the classified section of any issue of *Transport Topics* will reveal. Finally, trucks are obviously geographically mobile so that the market is extensive, indeed.

It can be concluded, then, that the trucking industry does not exhibit the structural conditions conducive to "excessive competition," defined as a persistent tendency for industry revenues to be less than industry costs. Thus it would appear that only irrational behavior in the form of an overly optimistic assessment of the likelihood of success in the industry could explain competition of the cutthroat, or ruinous, variety. If irrational entry resulted in returns to capital and labor below their opportunity costs, this would be an adverse performance characteristic of the industry.

Recognition of the foregoing possibility does not establish its existence, however, or even its likelihood.[18] A truck driver might prefer self-employment with imputed wages of less than he would earn as an employee. If so, his decision can scarcely be judged "irrational."

Finally, the possibility of irrational entry into motor freight transport establishes no prima facie case for entry controls as a device to forestall it. In a world in which the future is uncertain, all industries may be subject to excess or deficient capacity at frequent intervals, whatever their market structure. Where persistent excess capacity is the consequence of an overly optimistic appraisal of the prospects of success, the most appropriate solution would appear to be the provision of information on the prospects and pitfalls, the opportunities and the risks, of entering the industry.

Given the inherent structural and behavioral characteristics of the trucking industry, the long-run average rate of pure profit in the industry should approach zero. Only "excessive competition" induced by irrational entry would appear to raise some doubt as to the validity of that prediction. If "irrational" means some action not consistent with the maximization of net revenue, the designation is presumptuous for its failure to incorporate noneconomic objectives into the decision calculus. On the other hand, if it is intended to mean that individuals will dismiss information which would prevent them from acting in a manner contrary to their own perceptions of their welfare, then "irrationality" is by no means confined to potential entrants into the trucking industry. In an imperfect world there may be no remedy for such defects in mankind.

In consumers' goods industries product design and the frequency of changes therein may be dictated by the same considerations as persuasive advertising. Such expenditures may be deemed "promotional" in nature, motivated primarily by the ignorance, vanity, and fears of prospective customers. Since purchasers of truck services are not likely to be influenced by such appeals, variations in the quality of service should be largely a response to the preferences expressed by customers rather than attempts by the sellers to modify and shape those preferences. As a consequence, variety in the quality of service available to the customer of the trucking industry probably enhances economic performance.

A final performance criterion is "progressiveness" in methods of producing an industry's goods or services. As noted earlier, output per work-hour has tended to increase more rapidly in trucking than in the private domestic economy as a whole, but less rapidly than in agriculture and other segments of the transportation sector. Such a test of progressiveness is probably of dubious validity, since the appropriate measure would seem to be how well or poorly an industry performed relative to its opportunities.

An industry dominated by small firms in which innovations are subject to rather easy and immediate imitation is unlikely to engage in significant research and development activities. On the other hand, the cost-reducing innovations made available by the suppliers of such an industry can be expected to spread rapidly. In the trucking industry the low concentration, the ease of entry, and the relatively short life of the vehicle would lead one to predict that innovations promising to reduce operating costs would be adopted in short order by the industry. No better performance could reasonably be demanded.

Conclusions

Highway freight transport is inherently a market structure of low concentration, ease of entry, and variations in service quality limited to customers' preferences. The conduct of trucking firms can be expected to be both noncollusive and nonpredatory. Even though some trucking firms administer rather than negotiate prices, and even though trucker-shipper contracts establish freight charges for an extended period of time, the inability of the sellers to control supply should occasion only minor departures from a competitive level of price. Seasonal variations in the demand for highway transportation should induce associated fluctuations in truck rates.

The inherent economic performance of the trucking industry should be exemplary. If costs are virtually constant over a wide range of firm sizes, departures from minimum efficient scale, particularly by firms exceeding this size, should not result in appreciably greater costs. Except for irrational entry, excess capacity should not constitute a significant problem for the trucking industry. The relatively short life of tractors and trailers, together with the active second-hand market and the geographic mobility of this equipment, should insure against excess capacity. Insofar as irrational entry is concerned, it is more likely to be the rationalization of truck operators who prefer the security of a less competitive market than the plausible outcome of freedom of entry into motor freight transport.

Variations in service quality are more likely to be an industry response to consumer preferences than a seller-initiated alternative to price competition. Variety in the service available is not inconsistent with a competitive market and should achieve a more precise satisfaction of customers' wants than a homogeneous output.

The inherent structure of the trucking industry renders research and development expenditures a remote prospect within the industry. Nevertheless, this same structure should insure the rapid adoption of innovations generated by the suppliers of inputs to the industry.

In short, if competition unfettered by economic regulation of entry, prices, and service cannot accomplish acceptable economic performance in motor freight transport, then there would seem to be little hope that it would achieve it in any industry. To state the proposition differently, if unregulated highway freight transportation is inconsistent with satisfactory performance, then either monopoly restraints are inescapable or else all industries require public utility-type regulation to fulfill performance criteria.

CHAPTER 4

Social Costs of Regulation

It is no secret that government regulation is not generally held in high esteem by the business community. There is one kind of regulation, however, which has earned the dogged support of at least one segment of that community. Specifically, the regulated highway carriers of freight are ardent proponents of continued economic regulation of the trucking industry. Virtually every issue of *Transport Topics,* the weekly news publication of the American Trucking Association, contains one or more accounts of the activities of the "deregulators" who seek to plunge the industry into chaos and confusion.

There are a number of reasons for believing that economic regulation of the trucking industry increases the social costs of freight transport while conferring meager benefits in the process. This chapter explores the rationale for such a prediction and endeavors to measure the costs and benefits attributable to the regulation of the trucking industry in the United States.

Costs of Truck Regulation: A Priori Considerations

A priori reasoning would suggest that inefficiencies engendered by economic regulation of motor freight transport have their genesis in

Reprinted with permission from John Richard Felton, "The Costs and Benefits of Motor Truck Regulation," *Quarterly Review of Economics and Business* 18, no. 2 (Summer 1978):7–20.

entry controls, rate regulation, and limitations on the activities of exempt agricultural and private carriers. Each of these sources of prospective cost enhancement will be considered in turn.

ENTRY CONTROLS. To engage in the interstate highway transportation of freight other than unmanufactured agricultural commodities, a prospective for-hire highway carrier requires the prior approval of the Interstate Commerce Commission. There is little reason to believe, however, that merely limiting entrance into the industry would increase carrier costs or even the rates for carrier services. First, there are some 16,000 interstate common carriers in the United States.[1] Second, despite extensive market segmentation by commodity and origin-destination pairs, trucking company resources are inherently very mobile; the unspecialized nature of a large percentage of the vehicles plus their geographic mobility make intermarket transference an ever-present possibility. Third, unlike highway carrier regulation in some European countries, American regulation does not limit individual firm investment; therefore, an increase in the size of existing firms is an alternative to the entrance of new firms. Fourth, empirical studies, almost without exception, have concluded that highway freight transportation is an industry of constant returns to scale.[2] Consequently, the growth of existing firms should not occasion higher costs.

For economic regulation to attenuate highway carrier competition, it must supplement restrictions on entrance into the industry with restrictions on entrance into particular markets. This it accomplishes by limiting the commodities a carrier may transport; the points, terminal and intermediate, it may serve; and the route or routes it may traverse. An unintended side effect, however, is to increase carrier costs by reducing the average number of tons per load and increasing the circuity of truck movements.

RATE REGULATION. As if entry controls were insufficient to curtail the inherent competitiveness of the trucking industry, Congress also saw fit to legalize motor carrier rate bureaus, as well as to confer upon the Interstate Commerce Commission the authority to establish the minimum rates carriers might charge for the performance of transport services. While such cartelization in conjunction with entry controls may generate some monopoly profits for the holders of operating authority, it is even more likely to promote nonprice competition in the form of more frequent scheduling of truck departures. This, of course, will exacerbate further the problem of inefficient truck utilization.

Restrictions on Exempt Agricultural and Private Carriers

Economic regulation may also increase highway freight transport costs by virtue of the restrictions on for-hire carriage by exempt agricultural and private trucks. Pursuant to regulations of the Interstate Commerce Commission, these exempt and private carriers are foreclosed from the transportation of regulated commodities on a for-hire basis. A company may not even transport commodities for a wholly owned subsidiary if the latter is a legally separate corporation.

The predictable result of such restrictions on the operations of exempt and private carriers is a greatly reduced ability to secure balanced two-way traffic. This is precisely what Miller found in his study of the effect of regulation on the ability of private carriers to obtain backhauls. Thus, he points out, "if the private vehicles [of the closed, unrefrigerated van type] could be brought up to the level of performance of the ICC regulated vehicles, it would be possible to obtain an increase in total loaded vehicle miles of 17.1 percent without any significant increase in line haul costs."[3]

Costs of Truck Regulation: Effect on Rates

The first step in the estimation of costs induced by regulation of truck transportation is the determination of the effects of regulation on for-hire carrier rates. To the extent that higher rates are attributable to monopoly profits, however, it will be necessary to deduct such income transfers in computing the cost increase. On the other hand, it will also be necessary to add the costs regulation imposes on private and exempt carriers, as well as the direct costs incurred by the regulatory authority.

A number of attempts have been made to measure the impact of economic regulation on highway carrier rates. In the wake of two U.S. Supreme Court decisions holding fresh and frozen poultry and frozen fruits and vegetables to be exempt agricultural commodities, the Department of Agriculture made several "before and after" studies of truck rates.[4] Following deregulation, fresh poultry rates declined by an average of 33 percent and frozen poultry rates by an average of 36 percent. While the rates on frozen fruits and vegetables declined less extensively, an average of 19 percent, there was a contemporaneous increase in rail rates on frozen fruits and vegetables of 6 to 14 percent. At the same time "stop off" charges of $5 to $15 per stop that were common prior to deregulation were either eliminated entirely or substantially reduced.[5]

In contrast to the "before and after deregulation" study of the USDA, Farmer[6] undertook a cross-sectional analysis of the costs and revenues of 25 exempt agricultural carriers in comparison with 171 common and contract carriers. The regulated carriers' costs and revenues exceeded those of exempt carriers by 66 ⅔ percent or more. A part of the explanation presumably resided in the 40 percent or more greater average tonnage of the exempt carriers.

Sloss[7] endeavored to measure the effect of regulation on rates by comparing Canadian provinces regulating truck rates with those that did not. After having isolated the regulatory effect, he proceeded to compute average revenue per ton-mile disparities between the two groups of provinces. To accomplish this he incorporated into his multiple-regression equations average length of haul, average net weight per loaded vehicle, average fuel tax per gallon, average license cost per truck or per tractor per year, and average annual wage per employee. The obvious difficulty with this methodology is that two of these variables, namely, average length of haul and average net weight per load, may themselves be adversely affected by regulation. Thus the residual rate differences may understate significantly the effect of regulation on truck rates. Perhaps this explains why Sloss found that regulation in Canadian provinces raised rates by only 6.7 percent,[8] a value several orders of magnitude lower than the USDA and Richard Farmer estimates.

Finally, Moore[9] made a comparative study of trucking regulation in five European countries to develop a rough measure of the effect of regulation on truck rates in the United States. He found that truck rates per ton-mile in West Germany, where the stringency of truck regulation rivals that of the United States, were about on a par with our own. On the other hand, the rates in Great Britain, Belgium, the Netherlands, and Sweden, countries with substantially less highway carrier regulation than the United States, were approximately 43 percent lower.[10] Admittedly, labor costs are somewhat higher in the United States than in Europe, but this is probably offset by the higher fuel costs and generally less satisfactory operating conditions present in Europe.

On the basis of these studies it would not be unreasonable to conclude that economic regulation of for-hire truck transportation in the United States had increased rates by at least one-third and conceivably by one-half or more. Inasmuch as the operating revenues of Class I and Class II ICC-regulated trucking firms in 1976 totaled some $22 billion,[11] it follows that regulation of entry and rates of interstate for-hire highway carriers of freight may have increased the freight bill by $5.5 billion to $7.3 billion per year.

Though it would be inappropriate to maintain that the foregoing studies provide a definitive measure of the impact of economic regulation on highway carrier rates, all of them indicate that the effect is not inconsequential, and the USDA, Farmer, and Moore studies suggest that regulation has occasioned a very sizable increase in truck rates. Furthermore, even though there may be some dissimilarities in the inherent structural and operational characteristics of agricultural and nonagricultural carriers for which these analyses do not account, both the USDA and Farmer studies incorporate a downward bias of the effect of regulation on rates. This arises from the inability of agricultural carriers to transport nonagricultural commodities in backhaul. Obviously, this disability tends to increase the cost of exempt commodity transport and to understate the reduction in rates that would occur with deregulation.

Moore's method of measuring the extent to which regulation had increased rates in the United States also tends to underestimate regulatory effects. By considering trucking in Great Britain, the Netherlands, Belgium, and Sweden as "unregulated" because the regulation in these countries was less extensive than in Germany and the United States, his work may well have understated the impact of regulation on highway carrier rates.

It is difficult to determine to what extent the foregoing estimates of regulatory effects are equally applicable to all segments of the regulated trucking industry. Thus, to the extent that carriers utilize highly specialized equipment, backhaul opportunities decline and deregulation may not yield a reduction in rates comparable with that possible in the transportation of general freight by ordinary vans. Despite the fact that regulation of specialized carriers may nonetheless increase rates through service competition, circuitous routing, and inability to serve intermediate points, a very conservative estimate of the impact of deregulation on truck rates would exclude specialized and household carriers from the calculation. Thus only common carriers of general freight have been included in the ensuing social cost calculations.

In 1976 Class I and Class II common carriers of general freight had revenues of $14,030.2 million.[12] If regulation increased the rates of these carriers by one-third to one-half, then the rates were from $3.5 billion to $4.67 billion higher than they would have been in the absence of regulation.

Costs of Regulation: Other Effects

To the extent that economic regulation has succeeded in generating monopoly profits for trucking companies, it has induced a greater increase in rates than in costs. Since monopoly profits are transfer payments rather than social costs, they should be subtracted from the estimated increase in truck rates in any final assessment of the costs of regulation.

Class I and Class II carriers of general freight had intangible assets of $525.9 million in 1976.[13] These assets represented payments to the previous certificate holders by the acquiring firms. On the reasonable assumption that such assets constitute the capitalization of the monopoly profits accruing to the holders of certificates restricting the entry of potential competitors, a rough estimate can be made of monopoly profits in the regulated trucking industry. If monopoly profits are capitalized at, say, 15 percent, then intangible assets of $525.9 million would presuppose monopoly profits of $78.9 million per year. For a number of reasons this estimate is probably low. First, some carriers' operating rights date from the passage of the Motor Carrier Act of 1935, so there has never been any occasion to incorporate intangible asset values into their balance sheets. Second, some transfers of operating authority certainly occurred some time ago, so that the present value of operating rights may exceed by some substantial margin the transfer price. Third, some intangible asset values may have been written off. Thus Moore estimates that trucking companies have probably amortized about 20 percent of their intangible asset values.[14] Fourth and finally, the appropriate capitalization rate might be somewhat more than the 15 percent rate assumed in these calculations.

It is also possible that monopoly profits have been dissipated, at least to some extent, in the form of higher wages. If the Teamsters Union has been able to divert to its members some of the excess profits generated by regulation, the sum transferred from truck owners to teamsters as well as residual excess profits should be deducted from the increase in truck rates attributable to regulation to calculate the true social costs. Thus Annable has contended that the Teamsters Union "has been able to expropriate the excess profits which accrue to the cartel."[15]

Neither the theoretical nor the empirical basis of this proposition is very convincing. The teamsters would be able to "expropriate the excess profits" only if the ICC were unwilling to permit carrier rate increases in the face of wage increases achieved by the union. As for the general association of monopoly and wage rates, Schwartzman, who compared "average annual earnings in Canadian monopolistic industries with those in matched United States industries which are competitive, or less monopolistic,"[16] discovered "little ground for believing that monopolistic firms either exploit their employees or distribute excess profits to them."[17] Furthermore, Annable himself concedes that "a dual wage structure, that is, a rate in for-hire motor carriage higher than exists in the private segment of the industry in the same area . . . is not employed in motor freight."[18]

If, on the other hand, higher wage rates resulting from the bargaining activities of the Teamsters Union are passed on to shippers and receivers, it does not follow that the teamsters would be any less successful in organizing and raising wages in an unregulated trucking industry. If so, no additional deductions need be made from regulated carrier revenues in calculating the social costs of regulation.

The fact that the teamsters are strong supporters of continued government regulation is not convincing proof that wages would be lower or even that the teamsters believe they would be lower after deregulation. Even though the teamsters could achieve equally high wage rates in a competitive trucking industry, there might, as Moore[19] has pointed out, be fewer jobs because of greater efficiency. Also, deregulation might lead to an influx of owner-operators and thus to a substitution of entrepreneurs for employees.

Even if the estimated $78.9 million of monopoly profits is too small by a factor of two, the deduction from the social costs of truck regulation is very small. If economic regulation has increased truck rates by at least $3.5 billion per year, $79 million is a 2.25 percent deduction and even $158 million is only 4.5 percent.

COSTS OF REDUCED VOLUME OF REGULATED TRUCK FREIGHT.
While regulation may well have increased the costs of transporting the current volume of general freight traffic by some $3.5 or more billion, it has also imposed some additional costs by reducing the volume of traffic transported. On the very reasonable assumption that motor freight transportation is a constant-cost industry and that Benishay and Whitaker's estimate of -1.15[20] is the best available for the elasticity of demand for truck transportation,[21] the calculation of welfare loss is quite straightforward. In 1976, Class I and Class II common carriers of general freight accomplished 98 billion ton-miles of transportation and earned $14 billion in operating revenues or average revenue of $0.143 per ton-mile. If regulation increases rates by one-third or more, average revenue in the absence of regulation would have been at least $0.036 per

ton-mile lower.[22] With a linear demand curve and an arc elasticity of demand of -1.15, a reduction of rates to an average of \$0.107 per ton-mile (\$0.143 $-$ \$0.036) would have generated an additional 15 billion ton-miles of traffic or a welfare gain of \$270 million.[23] See Figure 4.1. This must be added to the costs of regulation.

COSTS OF UNDERUTILIZING PRIVATE TRUCKS. In any complete reckoning of the social costs of truck regulation, it is also necessary to consider the impact of regulation on private carriers. Inasmuch as private carriers may not legally engage in for-hire transportation of any commodity other than an unmanufactured agricultural one, their costs per ton-mile will increase from their inability, typically, to obtain balanced two-way loads. A 1969 survey by Comsis Corporation revealed that privately owned and operated tractor-trailer vans were empty 31.4 percent of the time, implying an empty backhaul 62.8 percent of the time, while similar vehicles transporting regulated commodities were empty 19

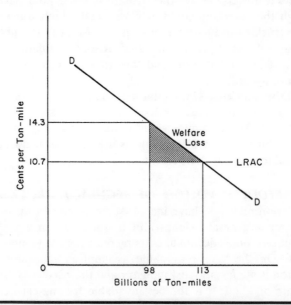

Fig. 4.1. Welfare loss from reduction in the number of ton-miles of commodities transported by ICC-regulated Class I and Class II common carriers of general freight from 98 to 113 billion ton-miles in 1976, occasioned by regulatory induced increase in rates from 10.7 cents per ton-mile to 14.3 cents per ton-mile.

percent of the time, equivalent to a 38 percent empty return experience.[24]

Private vans produced some 8,095 million truck miles in 1972.[25] If they had been able to achieve the same utilization as regulated ones, private trucks could have accomplished the same volume of traffic in 1972 with 1,435 million fewer vehicle miles.[26]

The value of this saving is dependent upon private carrier costs per vehicle-mile. In 1975 common carriers of general freight earned revenues of $1.77 per intercity vehicle-mile.[27] If economic regulation elevated rates as much as 50 percent over social costs, then private carrier costs of transporting general freight must have been at least $1.18 per vehicle-mile. For 1,435 million vehicle-miles, the cost comes to $1,693 million.

DIRECT COSTS OF REGULATORY AGENCY ACTIVITIES. Finally, there are the costs incurred by the Interstate Commerce Commission, itself, in regulating the trucking industry. Fully 90 percent of the workload of the ICC is accounted for by cases involving motor carrier operating authority, finance, rate investigations and suspensions, and complaints.[28] Even though other activities of the ICC were continued, presumably much, say 50 percent, of the present budget of $50 million per year[29] could be saved if economic regulation of the trucking industry were eliminated.

AGGREGATE COSTS OF TRUCK REGULATION. It is now possible to aggregate the social costs of motor freight regulation by considering the foregoing elements of social cost:

Item	Social cost estimate (millions)
Increase in rates of carriers of general freight	$3,481
Less monopoly profits	158
Added social costs of existing volume of general freight transported by regulated carriers	$3,323
Welfare loss attributable to general freight not transported by regulated carriers	270
Increased cost to private carriers from inability to secure backhauls comparable with regulated carriers of general freight	1,693
ICC costs of regulating highway carriers	25
	$5,311

An annual saving of $5.3 billion constituted 0.4 percent of the 1976 national income of $1,348 billion or $25 per year for every man, woman, and child in the United States. Furthermore, there are several reasons for believing this estimate to be on the low side: (1) each constituent of total social cost was conservatively estimated; (2) regulated carriers other than ICC-regulated Class I and Class II common carriers of general freight and trucks other than general-purpose vans were excluded from the computation;[30] and (3) exempt carriers, although they face much the same difficulties as private carriers in obtaining backhauls, were also omitted from the estimates of regulation-induced costs.

Benefits of Truck Regulation

The monopoly profits generated by truck regulation are only a "benefit" if a redistribution of income from final consumers to the owners of regulated trucking firms is deemed to enhance economic welfare. There are probably very few individuals outside the regulated trucking industry who would give assent to such a proposition.

ICC'S ESTIMATE OF BENEFITS. The only comprehensive, quantitative assessment of the benefits of trucking industry regulation was completed recently by the Bureau of Economics of the Interstate Commerce Commission. The bureau notes that if motor carrier rates had risen to the same extent between 1969 and 1975 as wholesale prices generally, motor carrier revenues would have been higher in 1975 by some $3,735 million.[31] It is the bureau's contention that this suppression of rate increases is a direct benefit of regulation. Such a "post hoc, ergo propter hoc" argument does not merit serious consideration.

In addition to the benefits attributable to rate-level suppression, the bureau contends that additional benefits accrue from the increased efficiency of the industry in a regulated environment. Based on Daryl Wyckoff's finding that after deregulation truckload rates in Great Britain declined by 10 percent while less-than-truckload rates rose by 40 percent, the bureau maintains that a similar impact in the United States would increase the total highway carrier freight bill by some 20 percent or $3.8 billion in 1975 prices.[32]

While the bureau might reasonably contend that the reported increase in motor carrier rates in Great Britain after deregulation confirms the bureau's estimate of the extent to which regulation suppressed rates in the United States, the bureau treats the "costs" of deregulation and the "gains" of regulation as additive. It is certainly difficult to avoid the conclusion that the bureau is engaged in double counting.

In addition to the foregoing "benefits," the bureau calculates that regulation has reduced carrier financing costs by some $25 million per year (more double counting) and consignee inventory costs by another $59 million.[33] Altogether, the bureau concludes that economic regulation of the trucking industry has conferred benefits of some $7,634 million. Inasmuch as both the costs of regulation, discussed earlier, and the bureau's computation of the benefits of regulation depend for their validity upon the presumed effect of regulation upon truck rates, clearly they cannot both be correct.

SERVICE BENEFITS. Perhaps the most frequently alleged benefit of truck regulation is that it improves the quality of service, especially for rural and other isolated shippers and for those who wish to ship relatively small loads. The argument is that regulation, by allowing truck revenues in excess of costs on some traffic, permits the subsidization of small shipments and the provision of service to areas of low traffic density. As Alfriend, a consultant to a number of motor freight rate bureaus, has declared,

> It is necessary to subsidize the traffic of shippers and receivers located at points that do not generate sufficient traffic to make adequate service economically feasible at rates they can afford to pay. Otherwise those shippers and receivers would not have adequate service and the growth and dispersion of industry throughout the nation would be drastically retarded.[34]

Regardless of the merits of the policy of subsidizing small and isolated shippers so as to promote geographic dispersion of economic activity, it is doubtful that the existing regulatory process contributes to that objective. In the first place, the mere fact that regulation permits carriers to secure monopoly profits in the transportation of some commodities, in some quantities, and to and from some locations does not motivate them to dissipate those profits by serving small, isolated shippers at a loss. It could be argued that, whatever their motivation, regulated trucking companies are required to serve such shippers by virtue of their common carrier status. The truth seems to be that where there is a will, there is a way to avoid these obligations. Gifford has enumerated a number of avoidance techniques employed by trucking companies, including cancellation of agreements with interlining carriers, tariff restrictions, rate increases, embargoes, and onerous packaging requirements.[35]

Second, the commodity, route, and intermediate point restrictions imposed on regulated carriers restrict their ability to provide that flexibility of service that would benefit small and isolated shippers in particular. In order to overcome some of the limitations on operating authority, growth through merger is a widespread phenomenon in the regulated motor freight industry. Unfortunately, whatever gains in flexibility may accrue to a carrier by virtue of some expansion of operating authority may be more than offset by the inflexibility associated with increasing firm size. As R. L. Banks and Associates concluded after a study of nine Class I and Class II common carriers serving primarily small communities,

> The overwhelming impression after interviews with carrier management, as somewhat supported by comparative data, is that small carriers succeed because they are specialists in serving markets requiring the kind of attention which appears to be uneconomical for large carriers to offer. In essence, small carriers appear to be better equipped to handle shipments in small markets because their pickup-and-delivery service, as well as terminal operations, are geared for small LTL shipments, their managements maintain close relations with customers, tight control over their organization and pay close attention to changing market conditions.[36]

Third, regulation makes private transport a less feasible alternative for small than for large shippers. Despite the inability of private carriers to transport nonagricultural commodities, the large shipper may be able to achieve sufficiently high utilization to justify resort to operation of his own fleet. Small shippers, however, are more likely to find that their shipment sizes are too small, their shipment schedules are too irregular, and their shipment destinations are too scattered to warrant private carriage in the absence of an opportunity to engage in supplemental for-hire transport.

Fourth, isolated areas whose principal exports are agricultural in nature are handicapped by the inability of exempt haulers of agricultural commodities to transport nonagricultural commodities in backhaul. That inbound regulated carriers may transport agricultural commodities as a backhaul from the rural area may well prove an inadequate alternative.

All in all, the proposition that regulation is the sine qua non of adequate truck service to small shippers and out-of-the-way locations is unconvincing. The increase in the social costs of motor freight transportation that appears to be occasioned by the existing regulatory process is so great that it is difficult to imagine that even internal subsidization of the magnitude alleged by the supporters of regulation would offset the higher costs affecting to some greater or lesser extent all users of truck transportation.[37]

Conclusions

The Bureau of Economics of the ICC may have identified one benefit from economic regulation of the trucking industry. If rate regulation promotes nonprice competition in the form of more frequent scheduling, it is possible that some inventory savings may accrue to consignees. Such an outcome is not certain, since the greater flexibility and carrier utilization possible in an unregulated highway transport market might produce equally frequent and speedy service. Even if the full $59 million in inventory savings estimated by the Bureau of Economics is realized, however, this is a meager benefit to counteract a $5.3 billion additional social cost attributable to the continuation of economic regulation.

CHAPTER 5

Rate Inflexibility and the Backhaul Problem

Backhaul operations by a regulated carrier are controlled by the Interstate Commerce Commission. There are limitations on the commodities the carrier may transport, the routes it may traverse, the intermediate points it may serve, and the rates it may charge. Rate regulation appears to have a dual effect: (1) the absence of rate competition promotes nonprice competition in the form of more frequent service and consequently less use of capacity, and (2) ICC refusal to approve lower rates in the face of spatial imbalances in traffic exacerbates the problem of reduced or empty backhauls. Both operating authority limitations and rate regulation contribute to the problem of unbalanced two-directional truck traffic, but either variety of regulation could presumably be abolished without eliminating the other. Furthermore, in the absence of rate regulation, a substantial reduction in the extent of empty or near-empty backhauls might be achieved, even though the use of capacity in both directions might still be reduced by restrictions on operating freedom.[1] It is the effect of rate regulation upon the relative volume of forward and backhaul traffic that is the subject matter of this chapter.

Reprinted with permission from John Richard Felton, "Impact of ICC Rate Regulation upon Truck Back Hauls," *Journal of Transport Economics and Policy* 15, no. 3 (Sept. 1981):253–67.

ICC Policy on Backhaul Rates

There is no specific statutory provision to preclude the ICC from adjusting relative forward and backhaul rates in the face of spatial traffic imbalances, but it has regularly denied motor carriers the opportunity to enhance net revenues in this manner. Thus in a 1954 proceeding the commission declared: "The fact that the concerned movement is a back haul and involves little additional operating cost is not a factor which overcomes the failure to show that the proposed rates would be themselves compensatory."[2]

The insistence that backhaul rates be "compensatory," independent of the revenue generated on the forward haul, makes it clear that the commission has failed to grasp the economic implications of the joint products. Refusing to recognize that joint costs are inherently incapable of assignment to forward and backhauls, the commission has developed a measure of applicable backhaul costs that charges the backhaul with a pro rata share of the line-haul costs incurred during the round trip. ICC Hearing Examiner Jair S. Kaplan has described the method of calculating the line-haul costs chargeable to the backhaul as follows:

> In its practical application, Highway Form B, for example, determines first line-haul costs per vehicle mile, without regard as to whether the vehicle is fully or partially loaded, or empty. The line-haul expense is then divided by the average load for the entire round trip to determine the line-haul costs per hundred-weight mile which, in turn, may be multiplied by the one-way distance in order to obtain the line-haul costs per 100 pounds for the movement involved.[3]

The persistence with which the ICC adheres to the fiction that forward and backhaul cost allocation is a meaningful enterprise no doubt stems from its generally protectionist attitude toward regulated carriers. On numerous occasions the ICC has expressed the fear that if carriers were permitted to reduce rates whenever it would augment their net revenues, the "added traffic" theory as the commission calls it, it would lead to destructive competition among the carriers. In one of its early decisions the commission explained its rejection of reduced backhaul rates in this way:

> An unbalanced condition of truck traffic, because of the number of operators, is apt to be somewhat of an individual

matter. That is to say, the traffic of one truck operator may preponderate in one direction, whereas that of a competing operator may preponderate in the other. As between operators, therefore, the application of the ["added traffic" theory] might well result in a break-down of the rates in both directions.[4]

If there is excess capacity in both directions, the industry is not in long-run equilibrium, and efficiency dictates a reduction in the number of vehicles operating in this particular locale rather than the preservation of that capacity through higher rates. Even Locklin, who is generally favorable toward the commission's protectionist policies, conceded that if two carriers are burdened with empty backhauls in opposite directions, there must be excess capacity, and that the commission "should not underwrite excess capacity by excessive rates."[5]

While the great preponderance of ICC decisions involving reduced backhaul rates have required those rates to cover their pro rata share of joint line-haul costs per hundredweight, in a few cases a narrowly divided commission has approved a method of joint-cost allocation in which line-haul costs are apportioned on the basis of the relative magnitude of forward and backhaul traffic.[6] Finally, it even approved a "noncompensatory" backhaul rate in a case in which the reduced rate would not harm either regulated carriers or shippers.[7] Despite these anomalies, the general thrust of commission policy has clearly been to encourage the preservation of excess capacity by preventing rates from falling to a competitive level.[8] As the commission declared in rejecting a rate reduction the carrier maintained would increase its net revenue, "there is no showing that the defendants could not in fact effectively compete for the instant traffic at higher rates."[9]

Economics of Backhaul Pricing

Round-trip truck movements, as noted above, are joint products, and their production involves "joint costs." Joint costs are the result of producing two or more outputs in fixed proportions.[10] In view of the unchanging output ratios, some costs are nonallocable even in the long run. By way of contrast, if the output proportions are variable, all costs are assignable to the various kinds of output in the long run, even though there may be inseparable "common costs" in the short run.

It is perhaps obvious that for each outbound truck movement, there is a corresponding inbound truck movement; the ratio is fixed and unchanging. Though there are no separable costs of an empty backhaul, additional costs are incurred in returning a vehicle loaded rather than empty. Marginal loaded backhaul costs include the additional driving necessary to pick up and deliver a load, the terminal costs associated with the pickup and delivery operations, and the additional line-haul costs (cargo insurance, loss and damage, increased fuel consumption, and possibly an increase in transit time) in moving a loaded, rather than empty, truck.[11]

Figures 5.1 and 5.2 illustrate the determination of forward and backhaul truck rates in a purely competitive market under different relative demands for forward and backhauls.[12] The demand for transport from City A to City B (D_f) is assumed to be greater than from City B to City A (D_b).[13] Only one commodity is transported in each direction; or alternatively, all commodities moving in a particular direction are as-

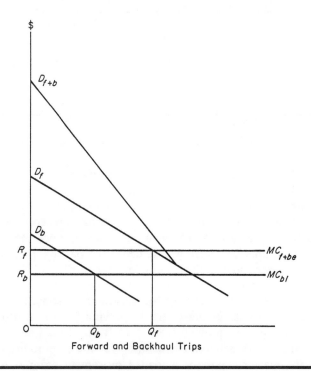

Fig. 5.1. Competitive forward and backhaul rates: Some empty backhauls.

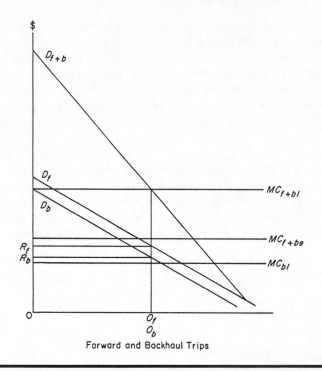

Fig. 5.2. Competitive forward and backhaul rates: No empty backhauls.

sumed to impose equal separable costs on the carrier. Marginal costs of the forward haul plus empty return (MC_{f+be}) are assumed to be constant, a reasonable assumption over the long run in an industry in which scale economies appear to be so insignificant.[14] The marginal costs of a loaded backhaul (MC_{bl}) are also assumed to be constant, since the additional cost of picking up, transporting, and delivering backhaul traffic should be directly proportional to the volume of that traffic.

Figure 5.1 depicts the competitive solution when marginal loaded backhaul costs equal the demand for backhauls at some quantity (Q_b) smaller than the total number of trucks moving from A to B (Q_f). The total number of trucks moving from A to B, in turn, is determined by the point of equality between the demand for the commodity transport (D_f) and the marginal cost of a loaded movement from A to B plus empty backhaul (MC_{f+be}). Under those circumstances, all the joint costs will be borne by the shippers whose products move from A to B, while shippers whose goods are moving in the opposite direction will pay only the separable, that is, marginal, loaded backhaul costs.

Figure 5.2 illustrates the competitive solution when the demand for backhauls (D_b) exceeds marginal loaded backhaul costs (MC_{bl}) at the number of forward hauls at which the demand for forward hauls (D_f) would equal the marginal cost of a loaded movement from A to B plus empty backhaul (MC_{f+be}). There are no empty backhauls, and the number of loaded round-trips ($Q_f + Q_b$)/2 is determined by the intersection of (D_{f+b}) and (MC_{f+bl}). Thus a portion of the joint cost will now be borne by shippers whose goods move from B to A.

To what extent would the competitive model fit the trucking industry if Congress and states were to free it from rate regulation? Without regulation, truck rates might be established in any number of ways.[15] Larger firms in particular might promulgate rate schedules they would modify from time to time on the basis of changes in cost and demand.[16] Smaller firms would be more likely to negotiate the rate for each shipment. In some cases the carrier and the shipper might negotiate a long-term contract. Finally, particularly the larger shippers might establish the rates they would pay for various shipments to various destinations.

Despite the irreconcilability of the purely competitive model with administration of rates by carrier or shipper, the inherent structure of the industry, negligible economies of scale, low entry barriers, ease of intermarket transference of operations, and minimal product differentiation militate against any substantial departure from a purely competitive price, as noted in Chapter 3. In other words, despite the formal inconsistency of a market-determined and an administratively determined price, administratively determined prices in a trucking industry free of rate regulation are not likely to depart very far or for very long from the prices that would obtain if carriers abstained from any quotation of their rates of charge.

Backhaul Pricing in Great Britain and Australia

If, in the absence of regulation, the trucking industry would indeed conform to the competitive model, it might be instructive to study backhaul pricing in Great Britain and Australia, two countries in which economic regulation has always been much less extensive than in the United States. Thus the trucking industries in these countries have never been subject to rate regulation, and such entry controls as existed have always tended to be less detailed.

It would be most helpful if information were available on the relative demands for forward and backhaul shipments on a number of routes, together with the costs incurred by vehicles when moving loaded and empty. Data on rates of charge by direction could then be compared with the associated costs to determine the extent to which predictions of the competitive model were verified by empirical results. Unfortunately the data necessary for such a definitive test of the model are lacking, so evidence of a less convincing nature must suffice.

GREAT BRITAIN. A system of licensing did operate to restrict entry into the British trucking industry for the thirty-five years following the Road and Rail Traffic Act of 1933, but professional carriers were not subject to rate regulation or to the kind of commodity, route, and point restrictions that have segmented American markets and aggravated the problem of return loads.[17] Great Britain should constitute an appropriate laboratory in which to determine the inherent responsiveness of rates to spatial imbalances in highway freight traffic, yet it is difficult to perform this task because of the paucity of data on actual rates of charge. While some of the larger carriers, including the governmentally owned British Road Services (BRS), do publish rates, there is no British equivalent to the Elkins Act of 1903 to compel adherence to them. Thus published rates appear to be maximums only, with actual rates subject to negotiation on the basis of shipment weight, distance, commodity characteristics, season, direction, and so on.[18]

For a brief period, however, published rates and actual rates may have coalesced: that is, in 1953 and 1954, when the BRS conducted a very substantial portion of the long-distance trucking operations in Great Britain. Owing to its dominant position, BRS was able not only to publish rates but also to abide by them with reasonable fidelity. Walters has observed:

> At these [fixed] rates, quantities of traffic on offer varied considerably from day to day; one day the outward trip would be full, another the homeward journey would be at capacity. . . . In practice, much of the traffic of the group was nearly balanced . . . but in a few hauls, noticeably those to non-industrial towns, [some lack of balance was present].[19]

Since a trucker cannot predict the day-to-day balance of traffic that will follow various rate levels, it is reasonable, as Walters has noted, to establish rates so as to take "account of the chances of being full up on each stage of the round-trip."[20]

Evidence of a high degree of balance in road freight traffic is also provided by Chisholm and O'Sullivan in their study of freight flows.[21] A linear regression of tonnage transported by road from seventy-eight zones in Great Britain on tonnage destined for these zones yielded a coefficient of determination (R^2) of 0.94. The origin-destination tonnages for each zone were so nearly equal that their conclusion is self-evident: "there is no systematic net transfer of goods from some regions of the country into others."[22]

How far differential rates for forward and backhauls have promoted zone-by-zone equality of import and export tonnage, and how far these differential rates have enabled carriers to achieve balanced two-way movements, is unfortunately not established by the Chisholm and O'Sullivan study. The absence of a net movement of commodities from one zone to another over the course of a year is consistent with imbalances at particular seasons, or over particular routes, or with the compatibility of commodities for shipment in a particular truck.

The most significant evidence on the effect of the direction of movement on rates was, perhaps, developed by Bayliss and Edwards in their analysis of charges to shippers for commodities transported by road.[23] Employing a multiple regression equation in log-linear form, they found that twenty variables, all of which were significant at the 5 percent level, collectively explained 90 percent of the variation in road charges. Of the twenty origins and destinations represented by the ten planning regions included in the analysis, two origins (Yorkshire and Scotland) and four destinations (Northern, East Midland, East Anglia, and North Western) were significant at the required 5 percent level. The weight of the consignment dwarfed in significance the other variables, accounting for more than 80 percent of the variation in freight charges. The slope coefficients of the origin-destination variables were lower than those for length of haul, type of truck, identity of the carrier, and five out of six of the commodities transported. Bayliss and Edwards conclude:

> There does appear to be a little, but certainly not conclusive, evidence that the region of origin or destination does have an influence in road haulage rates. But definite conclusions could only be drawn if it were possible to take many more regions; combinations of regions; and isolate the influence of haul and consignment of size as between regions.[24]

The relatively minor influence of regional origin-destination patterns on rates does not, of course, demonstrate that directional rate differences are unimportant in reducing empty-return loads on particular routes. Furthermore, even if rate differentials as between forward and backhauls are of relatively minor importance in Great Britain in reducing spatial traffic imbalances, this may stem from the absence of the kind of entry controls that have fragmented American markets for highway transport.[25]

AUSTRALIA. In Australia economic regulation of intrastate trucking operations is a matter within the jurisdiction of the separate states. Before 1954 the states also regulated the interstate operations of motor freight carriers pursuant to whatever statutory provisions governed intrastate transport. In 1954, however, the Judicial Committee of the Privy Council held that state regulation of interstate trucking infringed upon the power of the national government. For more than a quarter of a century now, interstate trucking has been free from state and federal regulation. Furthermore, such regulation as does exist has been for the purpose of protecting railroads from intermodal competition and does not appear to have reduced competition among the firms engaged in trucking operations.[26]

Joy,[27] Kolsen,[28] and Nelson[29] are all in agreement that in the large interstate markets a condition approximating pure competition prevails. They all note the sensitivity of rates to variations in the demand for transport, and Joy observes: "Full loads in each direction [on the Melbourne-Sydney route] are normal."[30] The ability to achieve balanced two-way loads is attributable, as Joy observes, in part to rate flexibility but also to voluntary delays while awaiting return loads:

> The distances between Australian capitals are too long to justify running empty on the off-chance of finding a load, and even owner-drivers with heavy hire-purchase commitments usually prefer an involuntary rest to operation at a rate too low to provide an adequate "wage," or surplus over short-run direct costs such as fuel and road tax.[31]

D. C. Ferguson has developed a model to explain the effect of spatial traffic imbalances upon rates and has applied it to wool transport in Australia.[32] He visualizes three possibilities:

1. If the demand for transport in both directions has the same elasticity, the rates will be identical.

2. If the demand for transport on the return trip is sufficient to defray only the additional costs incurred in returning loaded (or partially loaded), the rate for the forward-haul must cover the loaded costs of the forward haul plus the unavoidable costs of an empty back-haul.

3. If the demand for transport on the return trip, while more elastic than for the forward haul, is nevertheless sufficient to defray more than the additional costs incurred in running loaded rather than empty, the rate for the forward-haul will lie somewhere between the lower and upper limits represented by possibilities 1 and 2.[33]

Ferguson then applied the model to nineteen routes, which he classified as primary, secondary, and tertiary on the basis of backhaul potential. Intercapital routes, where transport demand was assumed to be roughly equivalent in both directions, were classified as primary; routes between country centers, where transport demand for return loads was assumed to be insufficient to cover more than the avoidable costs of return loads, were classified as tertiary routes; and routes between country centers and capital cities located in other states, where demand was sufficient to defray more than the unavoidable costs of an empty return, were classified as secondary. As the cost of a semitrailer truck, loaded in both directions, was calculated to be 40 cents per mile, but only 33 cents per mile if empty, Ferguson estimated forward-haul rates at 40 cents per mile on primary routes, 73 cents per mile on tertiary routes, and 56 cents per mile (midway between the rates on primary and tertiary routes) on the secondary routes.[34]

The route-by-route actual and estimated forward-haul rates for the transport of wool in Australia about 1970 are set forth in Table 5.1. The correlation between actual and predicted rates, 0.97, would appear to be extraordinarily high in view of the crudeness of the model. The implicit assumptions include:

1. Costs are uniform throughout the country.
2. Competition is sufficiently effective, even in the short run, to drive rates to the level of long-run average costs.
3. A threefold classification of routes is sufficient to allow for all the variations in relative demands for forward and backhauls on various routes.

All in all, Ferguson's study provides strong support for the proposition that rates and output in an unregulated setting approximate those of

Table 5.1. *Comparison of Actual and Predicted Forward-haul Truck Rates per Bale of Wool on Various Australian Routes, Circa 1970*

From	To	Mileage	Route Classification	Actual Rate per Bale ($)	Predicted Rate per Bale ($)	Deviation of Predicted from Actual ($)
Adelaide	Melbourne	470	1	2.10	2.09	-0.01
Adelaide	Sydney	913	1	4.00	4.06	+0.06
Adelaide	Geelong	454	1	2.50	2.02	-0.48
Brisbane	Sydney	653	1	2.80	2.90	+0.10
Brisbane	Melbourne	1,092	1	4.50	4.85	+0.35
Brisbane	Newcastle	547	1	2.80	2.43	-0.37
Portland	Adelaide	368	2	2.50	2.29	-0.21
Inverell	Brisbane	263	2	1.50	1.64	+0.14
Glen Innes	Brisbane	237	2	1.50	1.48	-0.02
Warialda	Brisbane	261	2	2.00	1.62	-0.38
Delunga	Brisbane	255	2	2.00	1.59	-0.41
Bingara	Brisbane	282	2	2.00	1.75	-0.25
Barraba	Brisbane	320	2	2.20	1.99	-0.21
Brisbane	Dalby	136	3	1.35	1.10	-0.25
Brisbane	Roma	304	3	2.85	2.47	-0.38
Brisbane	Texas	191	3	1.80	2.55	-0.25
Brisbane	St. George	326	3	3.10	2.64	-0.46
Brisbane	Goondiwindi	228	3	2.15	1.85	-0.30
Brisbane	Dirrandandi	376	3	3.35	3.05	-0.30

Source: D. C. Ferguson, "Joint Products and Road Transport Rates in Transport Models," *Journal of Transport Economics and Policy* 6, no. 1 (Jan. 1972):74.

the purely competitive model. Relative forward and backhaul rates will depend on relative demands, and forward and backhaul rates, together, will approximate the sum of the separable and joint costs.

Welfare Loss from Empty Backhaul

Of the 15,783 million truck miles generated by for-hire carriers of intercity motor freight in the United States in 1976, more than 6,000 million were probably accomplished by ordinary vans, the vehicles offering the greatest opportunity for enhanced utilization of equipment.[35] If ordinary vans accounted for the same percentage of total intercity truck miles in 1976 as in 1972, that is 39.3 percent, then 6,202 million intercity truck miles were produced by such vans in 1976.[36]

According to an ICC survey of truck operations on the interstate highway system in 1976, the mean trip length of a sample of loaded and partially loaded ICC-regulated trucks of all types was 324 miles.[37] Since loaded and partially loaded vans operated by carriers of all types (ICC regulated, private, and exempt) moved an average of 261 miles per trip, compared with a 260-mile average for all trucks, an average trip of 324 miles for all loaded or partially loaded ICC-regulated vans would appear to be a reasonable estimate.

To estimate the average length of trip of empty ICC-regulated vans is more difficult. Empty ICC-regulated trucks of all types had a mean trip length equal to only 44 percent of that of the nonempty trucks. On the other hand, empty vans operated by carriers of all types had a mean trip length of 60 percent of the loaded or partially loaded ones. For these reasons, it will be assumed that empty ICC-regulated vans had an average trip length of 162 miles, 50 percent of the trip of the nonempty ones.

In order to allocate total ICC-regulated van miles to empty and nonempty vehicles, it is also necessary to know the percentages of miles attributable to empty and loaded vehicles. The ICC survey found that 12.2 percent of ICC-regulated van miles were empty.[38] If, therefore, 87.8 percent of the total truck miles were effected by loaded trucks traveling an average of 324 miles and 12.2 percent by empty trucks moving an average of 162 miles, then regulated vans made 16.8 million loaded trips and 4.7 million empty ones. This implies a total of 10.8 million backhauls [(16.8 million + 4.7 million) ÷ 2], or 6.1 million loaded and 4.7 million empty backhauls.

If the ratio of the revenues generated by ICC-regulated vans to the revenues of all common carriers of general freight is the same as the ratio of their vehicle-miles (6,202 million to 7,564 million), then ICC-regulated vans earned $10,890 million, or 82 percent of the $13,280 million earned by common carriers of general freight in 1976.[39] With a total of 16.8 million loaded trips, this would amount to $684 per loaded trip.

If backhauls were loaded rather than empty, presumably loaded backhaul miles per trip would rise to the neighborhood of forward miles per trip. As a consequence, additional line-haul costs would be incurred in making pickups and deliveries at points different from the forward-haul pickup and delivery points. In 1976 regulated carriers of general freight incurred line-haul costs of $5,700 million for 7,564 million vehicle-miles, or $0.754 per vehicle-mile. If backhaul trips were to increase in length from 162 to 324 miles on average, regulated vans would incur an additional $122 in line-haul costs by virtue of the increased length of haul. Furthermore, if the line-haul costs of a fully loaded vehicle were found to be as much as 15 percent greater than those of an empty one,[40] the line-haul cost of moving a loaded van 324 miles rather than an empty one 162 miles might increase to as much as $140, that is, by an additional $18.

If terminal costs rise proportionally with the number of loaded trips, it is merely necessary to divide each element of cost by the number of loaded trips. These calculations are set forth in Table 5.2. With aver-

Table 5.2. Calculation of Additional Terminal and Line-haul Costs of Regulated Empty Vans Transporting General Freight in Backhaul, 1976

(1) Cost Item Terminal	(2) Total, All Truck Types $ million	(3) Applicable to Vans (2) × 0.82 $ million	(4) Cost per Loaded Backhaul Trip (2) ÷ 16.8 million $
Pickup and delivery	2,966	2,432	145
Billing and collecting	343	281	17
Platform	1,562	1,281	76
Terminal	1,310	1,074	64
Maintenance	218	179	11
Traffic and sales	422	346	21
Insurance and safety	121	99	6
General and admin.	676	554	33
Total, terminal			$373
Line-haul costs			140
Total Additional cost per loaded backhaul trip			$513

Sources: *Trinc's Blue Book of the Trucking Industry* (1977), S-3 and calculations by the author.

age revenues of $648 per loaded trip and additional costs of loaded backhaul trips of $513, there are obvious opportunities for expanding loaded backhauls through rate reductions.

Assuming a linear demand curve and an elasticity of demand of −1.15 within the relevant range,[41] a reduction in backhaul rates from an average of $648 per trip to $513 per trip would eliminate 2.7 million or 57.4 percent of the 4.7 million empty backhauls[42] and yield a welfare gain of $182 million.[43] In Figure 5.3, D_b, the demand for truck transport for backhaul trips of general freight, has an arc elasticity of −1.15 between 6.1 and 8.8 million trips, the point at which $D_b = MC_{bl}$.

If the backhaul rates of regulated carriers of freight in ordinary vans fell to the level of the additional costs of a loaded rather than an empty return, presumably some commodities would be shipped which would not otherwise have been transported at all. Clearly this constitutes a welfare gain.

On the other hand, a reduction in the backhaul rates of regulated vans would presumably divert some traffic from other carriers, the main losers probably being private (own-account) operators. Private carriers,

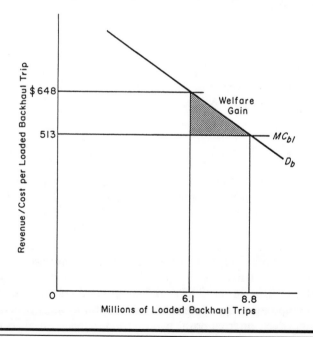

Fig. 5.3. Potential welfare gain from competitive backhaul rates.

because of their inability to transport commodities on a for-hire basis, would relinquish some traffic to regulated vans. If the opportunity cost of the resources no longer devoted to private carriage is equal to the demand price for the additional backhauls now transported by regular carriers, that traffic diversion is equally a welfare gain.

There are two main reasons for believing that the foregoing estimate understates the welfare loss associated with inflexible backhaul rates: (1) trucks other than ordinary vans represent some foregone backhaul opportunities, and (2) partially loaded vehicles might be more fully loaded. Both these sources of underestimation are worthy of comment.

OTHER UNSPECIALIZED TRUCKS. The extent of empty miles by trucks transporting regulated commodities in various types of equipment is set forth in Table 5.3. Even though ordinary vans constituted some 57.7 percent of all regulated trucks and presumably accounted for more than 50 percent of all truck miles and vehicle round-trips, refrigerated vans and flatbed trucks are sufficiently unspecialized to respond to reduced backhaul rates and sufficiently numerous to add significantly to the estimated welfare gain.

EMPTY TRUCK CAPACITY. The percentage of empty regulated-truck capacity is also set forth in Table 5-3. For ICC-regulated carriers, as a whole, 16.2 percent of all truck *miles*,[44] and 22.8 percent of all truck *capacity*[45] was empty. Flexible backhaul rates might have added appreciably to the number of vehicles partially loaded.

Conclusions

A potential welfare gain of $182 million per year from the abandonment of the ICC's policy of maintaining high and inflexible backhaul rates may seem meager in an industry in which annual revenues exceed $20 billion. Even if the estimate is too low by a factor of two or three, the welfare gain is less than 3 percent of industry revenues.

High and inflexible backhaul rates, however, are only one consequence of rate regulation. The elimination of rate controls should improve utilization by promoting peak-load pricing and by discouraging nonprice competition. The potential contribution of market-determined rates to improved intertemporal use of truck capacity and to reduced service competition is eminently appropriate for further research.

A far more important source of gain than the deregulation of

Table 5.3. *Extent of Empty Miles and Capacity of ICC-regulated Trucks, 1976*

Type of Truck	No. of Trucks in Sample	Percent of Empty Truck Miles	Percent of Empty Truck Capacity
Van	3,909	12.2	20.9
Refrigerated van	1,008	11.0	15.9
Flat or lowboy	1,332	16.6	20.6
Tank	529	41.0	44.9
Total	6,778	16.2	22.8

Source: Interstate Commerce Commission, *Empty/Loaded Truck Miles on Interstate Highways During 1976* (Washington 1977), 6, 8, 12, 14.

highway carrier rates undoubtedly lies in the relaxation of entry controls. Circuitous routes, bypassed intermediate points, commodity restrictions, unnecessary interlining, and uneconomical mergers tend to increase the costs of the regulated trucking industry. The prohibition against for-hire carriage of nonagricultural commodities by private and exempt agricultural carriers is another important cost of regulation. Chapter 4 estimates the social costs of regulation to be in excess of $5 billion per year. It is not, then, that the total welfare loss from economic regulation of trucking is small, but merely that the portion of the loss that arises from high and inflexible backhaul rates does not loom large in comparison with all other sources of social cost.

CHAPTER 6

Regulatory Rigidity and Seasonal Variations in Demand

One of the characteristics of a service industry distinguishing it from one producing a commodity is that production and consumption occur simultaneously. Since a service such as transportation must be produced at the time it is consumed, seasonal or other irregularities in consumption cannot be overcome by inventory accumulation and decumulation. Intertemporal disparities in the output of transportation and other services can, however, be reduced through a system of peak-load pricing. Such a system of pricing occurs automatically in a competitive industry and may occur by design in a regulated one. The telephone industry has utilized time-of-day pricing for some few years, and the electric light and power industry has increasingly used seasonally variable rates to improve plant load factors, especially for large customers.

A segment of the for-hire trucking industry, the carriers of agricultural commodities, operates in competitive markets with freely fluctuating rates in response to seasonal variations in transport demand. On the other hand, even the somewhat limited peak-load pricing that characterizes the public utility sector has no counterpart in the regulated portion of the trucking industry.

Reprinted with permission from John Richard Felton, "Seasonal Variations in Demand and the Economic Regulation of Trucking," *Logistics and Transportation Review* 16, no. 3(1981):243–63.

The ability of the regulated sector of the trucking industry to respond to seasonal fluctuations in demand is affected not only by the inflexibility of rates but also by entry controls limiting the commodities a carrier may transport, the points it may serve, and the routes it may travel. As a consequence, the opportunity to mitigate seasonal fluctuations in the demand for transportation service by altering the commodity mix or shifting the locale of operations tends to be foreclosed to some greater or lesser extent.

The effects of rate regulation and entry controls upon the ability of regulated for-hire highway freight carriers to respond to intertemporal variations in the demand for transport service is the subject of this chapter. First, however, it is appropriate to consider the possibilities of rate and capacity adjustment present in an unregulated environment.

Unregulated Truck Rate and Capacity Adjustments

Were it not for the existence of joint products, the provision of trucking service in an unregulated setting should conform to the traditional model of a purely competitive industry.[1] Price should equal marginal cost in the short run, and industry capacity should tend toward a level equating price and average cost in the long run. When two or more outputs are produced under conditions of joint supply, however, the separate marginal costs of these products are indeterminate, and the long-run tendency is merely for the *collective* revenue from such joint products to equal the total costs of producing them.[2]

The crucial element in joint supply would appear to be the inability of the seller to adjust productive capacity in consonance with the different demands for the joint products. As Wallace has observed, "It is impossible to increase or decrease the amount of capacity available for sale in one market without changing in the same proportion (and the same direction) the facilities available for serving another market."[3]

The determination of trucking rates and individual firm output in the short run under purely competitive conditions is set forth in Figure 6.1. A large number of trucking firms, no one of which can affect the rate of charge, is assumed to be engaged in transporting a single homogeneous commodity from A to B with no backhaul. The demand for truck service is lower during the period January through June (D_1) than during July through December (D_2), but it is constant throughout each of these six-month periods. Finally, D_1 and D_2 are assumed to be independent.

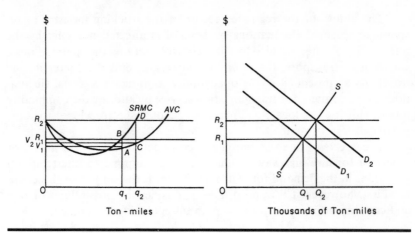

Fig. 6.1. Determination of peak and off-peak trucking rates and individual trucking firm output in the short run under purely competitive conditions.

In the short run, the firm will provide that volume of truck service that will equate firm ton-miles with the industry-established truck rates, provided that such rates equal or exceed the firm's variable costs. In Figure 6.1, the trucking company accomplishes q_1 ton-miles between January and June and q_2 ton-miles between July and December, pursuant to rates R_1 and R_2, respectively. In the long run there will be a tendency for industry capacity to expand or contract so that the trucking firm's quasi rents, $R_1 V_1 A B$ plus $R_2 V_2 C D$, equal the annual capital cost of capacity at an output of OQ_2.[4]

Suppose the assumption as to the constancy of demand for transport service over an entire six-month period be dropped. Under such circumstances demand would be subject to continuous variation and truck rates would presumably vary continuously too. Removal of the assumption of a constant demand also makes it desirable to drop the assumption of the independence of demands for different time periods. Thus the quantity of truck service demanded at time t_1 is dependent not only upon the rate at t_1 but also upon the rates at adjacent times.[5] Intertemporal demand interdependence would tend to reduce the divergence between peak and off-peak rates and outputs. With reference to Figure 6.1, the interdependence of D_1 and D_2 should increase the magnitude of R_1, D_1, and Q_1 and decrease the magnitude of R_2, D_2, and Q_2.

Seasonal Variations in Demand for Agricultural
Commodity Transport

Perhaps the most vociferous and united opponents of truck regulation during the hearings prior to the passage of the Motor Carrier Act of 1935 were the farm organizations.[6] While they were unsuccessful in blocking passage of the act, they did succeed in obtaining the only extensive exemption from its provisions. The principal argument in support of exempting the transportation of agricultural commodities was that the perishability characterizing some agricultural products and the seasonality characterizing virtually all of them require flexibility in transport operations. Regulation was regarded, even by some of its supporters, as likely to impart some inflexibility into highway freight transport.[7]

In his study of the function of truck brokers in the transportation of exempt agricultural commodities, Hunter listed the minimum and maximum truck rates on a number of agricultural commodities from various origins to nine major markets in 1959.[8] The smallest variation in truck rates, 120 to 125 cents per cwt. (4.1 percent), occurred in the movement of chickens from Chicago to New York; the greatest variation, 50 to 130 cents (88.9 percent), occurred in the shipment of potatoes from Wyoming, Delaware, to Miami.[9]

Since the Hunter study does not set forth rates for different times of the year, it is not possible to distinguish the separate influence of seasonal and locational (forward haul and backhaul) factors on annual rate variations. There are two reasons, however, for believing that spatial considerations are more important than temporal ones in accounting for truck rate variations:

1. Interdependence in the demands for peak and off-peak transport will tend to reduce disparities between peak and off-peak rates. Since, on the other hand, the demands for forward and backhauls are completely independent of one another, there will be no similar tendency for directionally flexible rates to narrow the gap between forward and backhaul rates.
2. The avoidable costs of off-peak transport are likely to be substantially greater relative to peak costs than the avoidable costs of backhauls relative to forward hauls. An outbound vehicle must return to its base before it can make a subsequent outbound trip; therefore, the great bulk of the vehicle operating expense incurred returning to its base is unavoidable. By way of

contrast, truck line-haul costs are clearly avoidable during off-peak, as well as peak, periods of transport demand.

Some evidence of the greater influence of spatial than temporal factors in truck rate variations can be gleaned from a comparison of rate variations in the transportation of potatoes to different markets. Of the nine major markets receiving agricultural commodities in 1959, eight were recipients of potatoes. The truck rates on potatoes to Miami and Jacksonville from six origins in the Middle Atlantic states varied by an average of 78.9 percent over the course of a year. By way of contrast, the rates on potatoes to Chicago, Atlanta, Dallas, Los Angeles, New York, and Philadelphia from a wide range of origins varied by an average of only 20.2 percent. Since similar seasonal factors would appear to be operative irrespective of destination, the far greater rate variation to the Florida markets suggests that potatoes are primarily a backhaul from the transportation of citrus products to the Middle Atlantic states.

Evidence of seasonal truck-rate variations, as well as of seasonal truck capacity adjustments, has been provided by Miklius. He notes that "rates on fresh fruits and vegetables from California are about 10 to 15 percent lower during the winter for similar commodities moving the same distances than they are at the summer peak [and that] 26 percent of the EMC [exempt motor carriers] truckers interviewed during July 1965 state that they shifted to other markets during the off-peak months. . . . "[10] The off-peak differential reported by Miklius is about one-half the rate variation in California produce shipments found by Hunter in 1959. Specifically, Hunter calculated the minimum truck rates of nine fruits and vegetables transported to four major markets as averaging 22.9 percent below the maximum rates.[11] The greater variation found by Hunter is presumably attributable in part to his inclusion of both seasonal and haul influences on price.

Seasonal Variations in Demand for Truck Transport in Australia

Prior to 1954 the individual Australian states regulated interstate as well as intrastate trucking operations. While the federal government presumably had the constitutional authority to regulate interstate highway transportation, it did not see fit previously nor has it attempted subsequently to do so. In 1954 the Judicial Committee of the Privy Council held that state regulation of interstate trucking was an unconstitutional interference with the powers of the federal government.[12] Within the next two decades South Australia and New South Wales repealed the statutes regulating intrastate trucking, and Nelson has recently reported that deregulation is "knocking on the door in Victoria, Queensland and Western Australia."[13]

The deregulation of interstate truck transportation in Australia was followed by a period of excessive competition and rate instability. Within three years, however, stable conditions returned but with a previously unheard-of flexibility. Ten years after the termination of interstate regulation the bulk of interstate traffic was carried by 2,000 owner-operators, the majority subcontracting with larger firms on a more or less permanent basis. Not only did rates fluctuate with seasonal variations in demand but also truck operators tended to shift locations pursuant to these intertemporal changes in transport demand. As Joy has commented:

> Although the majority of owner-drivers operate where market forces produce the most profitable (in the short-run) rates, a sizable minority operates on regular routes and for the same principal in each direction. . . . Off the inter-capital routes, rates fluctuate freely, ensuring that seasonal demands are met with adequate capacity. This means that, in the event of a shortage of work between Melbourne and Sydney, owner-drivers will look elsewhere for traffic rather than "cut each other's throat" for the remaining inter-capital work.[14]

More recently, Nelson noted that the route between Sydney and Melbourne was served by some 2,000 owner-operators, accomplishing about 60 percent of the total truck ton-miles on the route.[15] Some 1,800 of these drivers subcontracted with 5 freight forwarders on a permanent basis while the remaining 200 operate on an "anywhere-for-hire" basis. As Nelson has observed:

> These tramp operators . . . shop for full loads at good rates when there is an excess of traffic to be hauled and at lower rates when traffic falls off temporarily. Equipment is laid up or transferred to other routes when traffic is slack and rates are low. . . .[16]

The combination of rate flexibility and intermarket equipment mobility apparently accomplishes the required adjustment of capacity to demand without any significant dislocations. If supply and demand equilibrium can be achieved with the shifting of only 10 percent of the owner-operators and these operators account for 60 percent of intercapital traffic, it follows that a 6 percent equipment shift over the course of a year will yield high vehicle utilization. In short, freedom from rate controls and entry, route, commodity, and point restrictions minimizes the extent to which truck operators find it necessary to shift the locus of transport operations in response to seasonal variation in transport demand.

Inhibitions to Adjustment to Seasonal Variations in Regulated Trucking: Rate Regulation

The Motor Carrier Act of 1935 requires that highway carriers publish as well as abide strictly by their tariffs and that they announce at least thirty days in advance any changes in their rates. The Interstate Commerce Commission may also suspend rates for as long as seven months while it investigates their legality. As a consequence, the unresponsiveness of regulated truck rates to seasonal fluctuations in demand is an integral part of the regulatory process.

In addition to the rate inflexibility imposed by statute, rigidity is also imparted by the operations of rate bureaus. These bureaus operate as price-fixing cartels to maximize industry joint profits. While the Reed-Bulwinkle Act of 1948 guarantees to carriers the right of independent action, the publication and adherence requirements discourage such action since a carrier cannot legally offer secret rate reductions.

Assuming, however, that highway carriers were not subject to rate regulation, what effect would its absence have upon the efficiency of truck operations? Frederick J. Beier has recently completed a study of the potential impact of off-peak rail rates on railroads and shippers, but he notes that "the analysis methods used are generally applicable to any freight mode."[17] Whatever the prospective benefits of seasonal rates in the trucking industry, Beier concludes that off-peak rates in the railroad industry hold little promise for increasing carrier net revenues or improving railroad operating efficiency. After listing the characteristics of commodities which render them susceptible to demand-sensitive pricing (seasonal fluctuations in the *demand for transportation* and not merely in the *supply and/or demand for the commodity*, a high ratio of transport costs to delivered price of the commodity, and suitability for storage at relatively low cost), Beier contends that relatively few commodities, primarily grain, fulfill all three criteria.[18] Furthermore, after finding a rather weak correlation between rail carloadings of wheat and corn and the prices of these grains at different times of the year, he concludes that only corn exhibited a price pattern which would render off-peak rail rates effective.[19] Even with respect to corn, it would be necessary for railroads to offer off-peak rail discounts of 20 percent or more to offset the additional storage costs the shipper would incur by holding corn rather than shipping it during the trough of grain carloadings.[20] Finally, Beier points out that carriers generally may lack the capacity to carry the additional traffic necessary to offset the adverse revenue effects of off-peak rate reductions and that discounts of the magnitude required to induce off-peak traffic shifts may depress rates below variable costs.[21] All in all, he sees little likelihood that railroads will be able to utilize off-peak rates to improve efficiency or enhance profitability.

For a number of reasons, Beier's argument fails to be convincing. First, a high transportation-cost/commodity-price ratio may be a necessary condition of high elasticity of demand for transportation but it is not a necessary condition of high elasticity of demand for transportation by a particular mode.[22] As a consequence, peak-load pricing for commodities with a low transportation-cost/commodity-price ratio may be effective where inter-modal competition is present.

Second, Beier equates realized price movements with expected ones. Thus he contends that "wheat would be unaffected by off-season rates" because "wheat prices declined throughout the year." He observes that wheat prices during the off-peak period are higher than during the remainder of the year, but he does not concede that shippers would take advantage of off-peak rates. As a matter of fact, had they been able to predict the actual course of prices, shippers would have been better off shipping during the trough of carloadings rather than storing wheat until later even at existing inflexible rates!

Third, Beier assumes that the justification for seasonal rate variation resides in the interdependence of peak and off-peak demand. No one, however, has ever suggested that forward-haul/backhaul rate variation was advantageous only if there was cross-elasticity of demand between outbound and inbound commodity movements. In both situations carrier capacity is a joint product whose efficient utilization requires demand-responsive pricing. Demand interdependence merely adds to the effectiveness of seasonal rate variations in minimizing intertemporal fluctuations in capacity utilization.

Geographic and Commodity Restrictions

Whatever may be the limitations on seasonal rate variations as a mechanism for improving truck utilization, geographic and commodity restrictions on regulated carriers operate rather directly to reduce the ability of trucks to adjust to seasonal changes in transport demand. Operating authorities limiting the holder to particular origins, destinations, intermediate points, routes, and/or areas inhibit carrier adaptability.

Some impression as to the severity of the geographic restrictions can be garnered from a preliminary inventory of motor carrier authorities (IMCA) compiled by the Bureau of Economics, Interstate Commerce Commission, in the early 1960s. While this information was never released, extensive reference to the Bureau of Economics' findings are contained in Ralph Nader's Study Group Report on the Interstate Commerce Commission. With respect to geographic constraints, the Nader Report comments:

> The IMCA profile concludes that [of] the 91,335 grants of authority, 31,645 or 34.6 percent were restricted. But the study employs the term "restriction" in a technical and misleading way. Specifically, IMCA "restrictions" refer to basic limitations in equipment, service, tacking and interchange, operation, auto-carriers, and certain miscellany. *Supposedly* unrestricted carriers . . . are in fact further restricted by routing (including terminal and intermediate points serviced). . . . Of the 88,483 grants to regular and irregular common carriers, 14,150 or 16 percent are fundamentally unrestricted as to both routing limitations and generic restrictions.[23]

Even the 16 percent of the carriers that are free from routing and technical restrictions are presumably not free to shift the locus of their activities from one geographic area to another. Thus no regulated carriers in this country are unrestricted, in the sense the Australian carriers are, to shift their entire operation in response to seasonal fluctuations in the demand for transport.

Commodity limitations constitute additional constraints on a carrier's ability to adapt to changing demands. With just two commodities and in the limiting case, carrier "X" would transport only "widgets" for which a transport demand existed from January through June, and carrier "Y" would transport only "gizmos" for which a transport demand existed from July through December. If the same vehicles were suitable to transport both widgets and gizmos and the truck capacity requirements were the same for both commodities and no interchange of equipment took place, the commodity restrictions in this case would necessitate a complete duplication of equipment. While the relaxation of these assumptions would for the most part reduce the extent of excess capacity, the two-commodity assumption has the opposite effect. The greater the number of commodities, the greater the potential excess capacity attributable to noncoincident seasonal peaks in the demand for transportation of different commodities.

The Nader Study Group also comments on this aspect of the Bureau of Economics' inventory of motor carrier authorities:

> But even certificates without "restrictions" and "writing restriction," the so-called 16 per cent fundamentally unrestricted are severely limited by commodity descriptions. Obviously carriers with the same restrictions, operating on similar routes or in the same areas, are not competitive unless authorized to carry the same commodities. . . . Grants of authority are ludicrously narrow: a survey of specific commodity restrictions reveals that one carrier is limited to "*exposed* film," another to "*unexposed*" photographic paper. Carriers have certificates restricted to flexible pipe or plastic pipe or lead pipe, *ad infinitum*.[24]

To some extent, the adverse effect of narrow commodity definitions is mitigated by multiple grants of authority to individual carriers and the practice in some grants of specifying commodities in "clusters." Thus, as of December 31, 1964, the 13,901 Class I, II, and III ICC-regulated trucks with permanent authority held an average of 6.6 grants per carrier. As for commodity clustering, some 295 authorities of a sample of 1,305 in the IMCA study, or 22.6 percent, included clusters, with the average cluster consisting of 3.45 commodities.[25]

While multiple grants of operating authority and commodity clustering may offset somewhat the reduction in truck utilization associated with different seasonal transport peaks by different commodities, the combined impact of rate and geographic and commodity limitations must be substantial. Presumably, these impacts could be lessened to some considerable extent by short-term leasing. Thus during off-peak periods carriers with excess capacity attributable to regulatory constraints could lease equipment to other trucking firms.

The extent to which intercity truck common and contract carriers subject to ICC regulations employ leasing is set forth in Table 6.1. Truck-leasing agreements without drivers tend to be of a long-run nature, negotiated for reasons other than reducing seasonal fluctuations in transport demand. Since some leasing agreements with drivers may also be long run, the vehicle-miles with driver constitutes an upper limit to leasing as a device to counteract seasonality in truck utilization.

Table 6.1. *Extent of ICC-regulated Truck Leasing in Intercity Operations, 1976*

Type of Intercity Carrier	Vehicle-Miles (in millions) and Percent of Total					
	All Vehicle-Miles		With Driver		Without Driver	
	Number	Percent	Number	Percent	Number	Percent
General freight	7,564	100	757	10.0	1,086	14.4
Special carriers:	8,166	100	3,268	40.0	1,424	17.4
Common	7,060	100	2,978	42.2	1,297	18.4
Contract	1,106	100	290	26.2	127	11.4

Source: *Trinc's Blue Book of the Trucking Industry, 1977 Edition* (Washington: Trinc's Transportation Consultants, 1977), S-3, S-6.

Table 6.1 also reveals that short-term leasing is much more extensive among specialized than general freight carriers, particularly those engaged in common carriage. This suggests that "specialization" is more likely to inhere in the commodities transported than in the vehicles employed.

To what extent can short-term leasing overcome the rigidities occasioned by rate, geographic, and commodity regulation? It is clear that leasing cannot negate the inflexibilities attributable to rate regulation. With geographic and commodity regulation, short-term leasing may enable the *regulated carriers* to adjust capacity to a marked degree in response to variations in demand, but this may merely shift the burden to owner-operators and private carriers. According to the 1972 Census of Transportation, the trucks, excluding pickups and panels, owned by for-hire carriers averaged 41,700 miles that year.[26] Despite the fact that ordinary vans are among the more heavily utilized truck types (so that the ordinary vans owned by for-hire carriers undoubtedly exceeded 41,700 miles on the average), all ordinary vans, including those owned by for-hire carriers, accomplished an average of only 31,500 miles in 1972.[27] Thus private carrier truck utilization may only have been about one-half as great as that of regulated motor carriers.

While short-term leasing arrangements may improve somewhat the adaptation of truck capacity to intertemporal variations in the demand for transport, the regulated carriers are in a strategic position to shift much of the burden of excess capacity to carriers lacking the authority to transport regulated commodities. A regulatory scheme benefitting the possessors of monopoly privileges at the expense of those carriers denied direct access to the market for the transport of nonagricultural commodities has little to recommend it.

Simulation of the Effects of Operating Authority Limitations upon the Ability of the Trucking Industry to Adapt to Seasonal Variations in Demand

During 1976 the Interstate Commerce Commission undertook a study of truck capacity utilization in the United States.[28] More than 13,000 trucks were randomly sampled at different times of the hour, day, week, and month on all 225 segments of the interstate highway system. Trucks were categorized by domicile, type of equipment, and type of fuel. Information was also obtained as to type of carrier; origin and destination; loaded or empty; and, if loaded, the extent of the load and nature of the commodity.

Since regular vans are by far the most versatile vehicle type, the simulation employed here was limited to vans operated by ICC-regulated and private carriers. Exempt carriers were excluded for two reasons. First, these carriers are primarily agricultural commodity haulers that can carry only a narrow range of commodities legally. Their operations could thus be expected to be subject to more pronounced seasonal variations than private or ICC-regulated carriers. Second, since the ICC defined exempt carriers as those not subject to federal regulation or engaged in private carriage, this classification may include carriers subject to state regulation. The inclusion of these carriers in the sample would tend to overstate seasonal variation in truck utilization. The sample frame thus consisted of the 6,175 ICC-regulated and private vans included among the 13,165 trucks sampled by the ICC.

A measure of monthly truck utilization was constructed by weighting each truck sampled by the extent to which it was loaded. The weights used were: $0 = $ empty, $1 = \frac{1}{4}$ full, $2 = \frac{1}{2}$ full, $3 = \frac{3}{4}$ full, and $4 = $ full. These factors were then summed to obtain an *index of truck utilization* for each month. The index is equal to the number of trucks times their average level of capacity utilization.

An *index of seasonal variation in truck utilization* was then calculated as follows:

$$\frac{\text{maximum monthly utilization} - \text{minimum monthly utilization}}{\text{average monthly utilization}}$$

If traffic of a particular commodity group or within a specific region exhibited no seasonal variation, that is, was distributed equally throughout the year, this index would be zero. The higher the value of this measure, the greater is the seasonal variation in truck utilization.

THE IMPACT OF GEOGRAPHIC RESTRICTIONS. Geographic restrictions in motor carrier operating authority can be expected to increase seasonal variation in truck utilization, since such restrictions limit the carrier's ability to shift from one locale to another in response to seasonal fluctuations in demand. It was hypothesized, therefore, that *regional* indexes of seasonal variation in truck utilization would be lower than the indexes of hypothetical *routes* within the region, even though the routes were long and connected major population centers within the region. Should the routes exhibit greater seasonal variation than the regions, this would also provide an indication as to the potential for enhanced truck utilization under a regime of unrestricted geographic mobility of trucking operations.

Seasonal variation indexes for ICC-regulated and private vans were calculated for the six ICC regions and for six routes, one within each region. The six ICC regions are shown in Figure 6.2. They are: (1) New England, (2) Middle Atlantic, (3) Southeast, (4) Northern Midwest, (5) Southern Midwest, and (6) West. Within each region a rather extensive route was constructed by summing end-to-end segments. These routes and their total mileage are:

Region 1 (Route 1): White Plains-New Haven-Providence-Boston-Concord-St. Johnsbury-Canada (location unspecified), 242 miles.
Region 2 (Route 2): Cincinnati-Columbus-Cleveland-Erie-(Interstates 70 and 80), 500 miles.
Region 3 (Route 3): Louisville-Nashville-Chattanooga-Atlanta-Macon-Savannah-Jacksonville-Daytona Beach, 900 miles.
Region 4 (Route 4): St. Paul-Madison (Interstate 90)-Milwaukee-Chicago-Champaign-Indianapolis-Louisville, 696 miles.
Region 5 (Route 5): Council Bluffs-Kansas City-Wichita-Oklahoma City-Little Rock-Dallas, 1,177 miles.

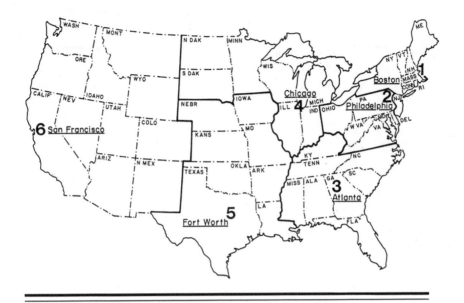

Fig. 6.2. Interstate Commerce Commission regions.

Region 6 (Route 6): Los Angeles-Sacramento-Portland-Seattle-Butte-Canada (location unspecified), 2,178 miles.

Table 6.2 sets forth the seasonal variation in truck utilization for the six regions and six routes, as well as the mean utilization for all regions and routes. In five of the six regions, seasonal variation in truck utilization was markedly less for the region than for the route. Since traffic densities tended to be significantly higher for the routes than for the regions in which they were located, the probable adverse impact on truck utilization of restricting carriers to particular routes is clear. With a route seasonal variation index almost twice as large on the average as the regional index, the potential for improvement in seasonal utilization through greater mobility of trucking resources must be great, indeed.

A final issue is whether the foregoing simulated routes are reasonable representations of actual operating authorities. While the simulated routes do not include any "off-route" origins and destinations, a characteristic of most actual authorities, the routes are probably longer than the great majority of ICC-approved routes and there are no intermediate-points restrictions in the simulated routes. Thus, the simulation model provides an order-of-magnitude indication of the actual impact of route restrictions on the ability of carriers to take advantage of noncoin-

Table 6.2. *Seasonal Variation in Truck Utilization by Region and Route: ICC-regulated and Private Vans*

	No. of Trucks	Seasonal Variation Index	Route Variation Index as a Percent Regional Variation Index
New England:			
Route 1	178	2.623	242.6
Region 1	1018	1.081	
Middle Atlantic:			
Route 2	185	3.078	172.5
Region 2	1220	1.784	
Southeast:			
Route 3	202	2.542	210.4
Region 3	1509	1.208	
Northern Midwest:			
Route 4	220	2.222	226.3
Region 4	1083	0.982	
Southern Midwest:			
Route 5	154	1.119	99.4
Region 5	618	1.126	
West:			
Route 6	158	2.337	229.6
Region 6	727	1.018	
U.S.:			
All routes	1638	2.352[a]	191.0
All regions	6175	1.231[a]	

Source: Compu-Serv Network, "ICC Data," EBCDIC, n.d.

[a]Computed by weighing seasonal variation index by the percentage of all carriers on that route or in that region.

cident seasonal peaks in the transport of commodities within various sections of the country.

THE IMPACT OF COMMODITY RESTRICTIONS. Preliminary analysis of the data indicated that regular vans were being used to transport all fifteen of the commodity groups defined by the ICC. It was hypothesized that, absent commodity restrictions, carriers could participate in the traffic of all commodities and thus minimize seasonal variations in truck utilization. Accordingly, the seasonal variation in the utilization of regular vans by private and ICC-regulated carriers was calculated for each commodity group and for all commodities collectively. Table 6.3 reports the results of these calculations.

Only one commodity group (machinery, equipment, and parts) exhibited less seasonal variation than did commodities as a whole. More specifically, the weighted seasonal variation index of all commodity groups exceeded the all-commodity index by almost 40 percent. In gen-

Table 6.3. *Seasonal Variation in Truck Utilization by Commodity Group: ICC-regulated and Private Vans*

Commodity	No. of Trucks	Seasonal Variation Index	Seasonal Variation Index of Individual Commodity Groups as a Percent of all Commodities
All commodities	6175[a]	0.770	100.0
Machinery, equipment parts	276	0.756	98.2
Agriculture, regulated	768	0.824	107.0
General freight	1665	0.987	116.5
Misc. products of manufacturing	1243	0.94	117.4
Chemicals	165	1.016	131.9
Paper and paper products	318	1.086	141.0
Motor vehicles, parts	211	1.134	147.3
Agriculture, exempt	220	1.351	175.4
Scrap	32	1.398	181.6
Wood and wood by-products	93	1.414	183.6
Household goods	266	1.482	192.5
Building materials	88	1.648	214.0
Primary wood products	209	1.785	231.8
Liquid petroleum products	41	2.727	354.2
Other commodities	103	3.815	495.4
Wtd. average, all commodity groups		1.398	139.1

Source: Compu-Serv Network, "ICC Data," EBCDIC, n.d.
[a]Includes 475 nonresponses to commodity classification question in survey.

eral, the more broadly defined commodity groups, such as general freight and miscellaneous products of manufacturing, were subject to less pronounced seasonal variations in truck utilization than the more narrowly defined commodity groups. Clearly, the elimination of commodity restrictions should enable carriers to achieve better seasonal utilization of vehicles.

Again the question arises as to the extent to which the commodity restrictions employed in the simulation model correspond to reality. Motor carrier operating authorities in general are likely to be much more restrictive than those assumed in the model. Rather than having the authority to transport all commodities within a commodity group, as assumed in Table 6.3, a carrier may have the right to transport only one or a few specific commodities within the group. Therefore, the seasonal variation in the trucking of these fourteen commodity groups no doubt understates the seasonal variation in truck utilization experienced by most operators.

Conclusions

The theoretical argument that freedom from geographic and commodity restrictions will enhance intertemporal utilization of truck capacity is supported both by experience in unregulated markets (exempt agricultural carriers in the United States and unregulated interstate highway freight transport in Australia) and by the results of the simulation model discussed above. While the model suggests that geographic restrictions contribute much more to poor utilization than do commodity limitations, this may be a consequence of the unrealistically broad commodity authorities assumed by the simulation model. Had the commodity groups been more numerous, so as to replicate more closely the commodity restrictions under which trucking companies operate, commodity restrictions might have emerged as of equal or greater importance than the geographic limitations.[29]

Deregulation of the trucking industry would not only eliminate the geographic and commodity constraints of the present system but also introduce rate flexibility as an additional means of improving the utilization of truck capacity over the course of a year. No simulation of a seasonally flexible system of rates has been attempted here, and it remains a topic for further research.

CHAPTER 7

Operating-ratio
Regulation by the States

For more than twenty years the Interstate Commerce Commission employed a 93 percent operating ratio (operating expense divided by operating revenue) as its sole revenue-needs criterion. Chapter 2 treated the history of such regulation at some length. Although the ICC has now adopted a return-on-equity standard for the determination of the reasonableness of truck rates, the overwhelming majority of state commissions still rely on the operating ratio as the exclusive, or at least primary, criterion of approvability.

A survey of state regulatory commission earnings-control standards in the fall of 1978 revealed that of the forty-seven respondents to the questionnaire, three states did not regulate rates but that thirty-five of the remaining forty-four utilized the operating ratio as the exclusive test of the adequacy of earnings. Another seven states reported that the operating ratio was the primary earnings-control standard.[1]

While three states (Florida, Arizona, and Maine) have deregulated the trucking industry within the past few years and several more have taken some steps to relax interstate motor carrier regulation, Freeman and Beilock have declared: "Thirty-five of the forty-eight contiguous

Janna L. Cowen is Associate Professor of Agriculture, University of Wisconsin-River Falls. She received her Ph.D. in Economics from the University of Nebraska-Lincoln in 1979.

Reprinted with permission from Janna L. Cowen and John Richard Felton, "Operating-Ratio Regulation and Truck Leasing Practices," *Logistics and Transportation Review* 21, no. 2(June 1985):145–60.

states continue motor carrier economic regulation similar to the pre-1980 ICC policy."[2] In one respect, moreover, the states apparently continue to regulate the industry in a manner similar to the pre-1970 ICC policy, namely, in the realm of earnings control. Freeman and Beilock note that the "operating ratio, which sets anticipated or realized costs against expected or actual revenues, is normally the most important measure of a proposed rate change's justness or reasonableness."[3] Thus it seems clear that the operating ratio has retained its preeminence in the regulation of intrastate trucking rates.

Earnings-Control Standards and Resource Allocation

Regulation by means of a rate-of-return criterion may induce distortion in input choices tending toward inefficient resource allocation. In the two decades since Averch and Johnson (A-J) first explicitly addressed this issue in a landmark *American Economic Review* article,[4] a voluminous literature on the A-J effect has developed. Averch-Johnson hypothesized that if the rate of return permitted a regulated utility exceeds its cost of capital but is less than the monopoly rate of return, the firm has an incentive to adopt a capital-intensive technology utilizing capital in greater than least-cost proportions. Thus the firm may make investments in which the social costs exceed the social benefits because the private cost of capital is less than the social cost.

Less attention has been paid to the allocative effects of other earnings-control standards although Bailey has suggested that the firm will use too much of the input that enters into the profit ceiling relative to the input that does not.[5] Presumably operating-ratio regulation, that is, determining the adequacy of revenues by reference to the ratio of operating expenses to operating revenues, creates incentives directly opposite those hypothesized by Averch and Johnson. Thus Kahn has suggested that the operating-ratio method would provide firms with an incentive to inflate operating expenses rather than capital investment.[6] To Cherry, however, must go the credit for developing a theoretical model of the firm under operating-ratio constraint.[7] Unlike the authors he believes that trucking industry technology permits extensive substitution of labor for capital. He assumed a uniform cost of capital for all firms in each year of this study and fitted his data, which had been adjusted to remove the effects of leasing, to a transcendental logarithmic production function. He concluded that operating-ratio regulation had led to resource misallocation in the trucking industry. The extent of misallocation may, however, be less than he estimated, if leasing is considered something other than a data-biasing characteristic of the industry. We think such substitution is unlikely, not only because of the nature of the production function, but also because leasing is an alternative means of increasing the operating ratio without any loss in technical efficiency.

Mechanics and Implications of Operating-ratio Regulation

Regulatory commissions usually maintain a one-to-one correspondence between changes in the average operating ratio of groups of carriers involved in a rate proceeding and authorized adjustments in the general level of rates. If the carriers' average operating ratio has increased by 1 percent, they will be granted a 1 percent increase in rates. The firms regulated by means of the operating ratio thus have a clear incentive to inflate the numerators of their operating ratios to justify a rate increase.

In the jargon of motor carrier regulation, interest on debt is a "below-the-line" item that is excluded from operating expenses in the computation of the operating ratio. Wages and other variable expenses are "above-the-line" items on which the firm is allowed a fixed percentage markup. Lease payments, like wages and salaries, are "above-the-line" items. Through leasing, a fixed input can be converted into a variable input. The firm might therefore be expected to utilize the variable inputs in greater than optimal quantities.

Since highway carriers are regulated on an areawide, rather than an individual basis, joint action to increase the operating ratio is a prerequisite to obtaining a rate increase. Virtually all types of regulated common carriers have organized powerful rate bureaus that engage in collective ratemaking and discourage independent action by individual carriers. The rate conferences, which represent the carriers before regulatory commissions, exhibit considerable sophistication.

To illustrate the effect of equipment leasing on a carrier's operating ratio and rate of return on investment, assume that a common carrier has an average annual investment of $1,000,000, of which $800,000 is in revenue equipment. With a capital turnover ratio of four, the carrier's assets would generate $4,000,000 in operating revenues. Assuming no leasing, straight-line depreciation of transportation equipment over a ten-year period, and an initial operating ratio of 93 percent, the carrier's operating expenses would be $3,720,000, including $80,000 depreciation on revenue equipment. Although the carrier would presumably be paying interest on its investment, this would be excluded from operating expenses. The carrier's rate of return before taxes would be 28 percent.[8]

Now assume that the carrier elects to lease its total revenue equipment in an arm's-length transaction. On the assumption that the lessor must not only cover depreciation, but also all merchandising and administrative costs plus a normal profit on the $800,000 investment, a lease charge of 20 percent on the value of the transportation equipment does not appear unreasonable. The annual rental charge would therefore be $160,000.

The carrier's operating expenses would increase by $80,000 ($160,000 less the depreciation taken if the equipment were owned). This increase would be at least partially offset, however, by decreased interest expense. The carrier's operating ratio would increase to 95 percent, indicating a greater revenue need. Its capital turnover ratio would increase from 4 to 20 and its rate of return to 100 percent. Despite this rather startling return on investment (ROI) a regulatory commission using a 93 percent operating ratio would be likely to grant a 2 percent rate increase.

Extensive leasing of transportation equipment by carriers subject to operating-ratio regulation is consistent with the model's predictions. The nature and extent of equipment leasing in the highway carrier industry will be considered in the ensuing section.

Equipment Leasing in the Motor Freight Industry

Extensive leasing of transportation equipment must be considered a significant economic characteristic of the trucking industry. Vehicles may be leased with or without drivers and for time periods ranging from a single trip to virtually the life of the equipment. Leasing arrangements for vehicles without drivers do not come under the jurisdiction of the ICC. Leases of vehicles with drivers are, with certain exceptions, subject to ICC regulation.[9] Equipment, with or without drivers, may also be leased by one authorized carrier to another.

Among the motor carrier statistics published each year by the ICC are total vehicle miles in owned vehicles, in vehicles leased with driver, and in vehicles leased without driver. Table 7.1 sets forth the mean percentages of total vehicle miles in leased vehicles during the period 1954–73 for three groups of Class I carriers: (1) general freight carriers, (2) specialized commodity common carriers, and (3) contract carriers. This period was selected for analysis since the operating-ratio standard of earning regulation was employed by the ICC throughout these two decades.

General freight carriers specialize in less-than-truckload (LTL) traffic of general commodities, usually maintaining a terminal system for

Table 7.1. Mean Percentage of Total Vehicle-miles in Leased Vehicles, 1954–73: Class I Motor Carriers Engaged in Intercity Services

	Percent of Vehicle-miles in Leased Vehicles	Percent of Vehicle-miles Leased with Driver	Percent of Vehicle-miles Leased without Driver
Common carriers of general freight	30.7	7.8	22.9
Common carriers of commodities other than general freight, specialized commodity common carriers	65.3	41.5	23.8
Contract carriers	25.8	14.0	11.8

Source: Interstate Commerce Commission, *Transport Statistics in the United States for the Year Ended December 31, 1954–73*, Part 7: Motor Carriers (Washington: GPO, 1955–74).

the breakdown and assembly of loads. Although they are allowed considerable latitude as to what commodities they may haul, they are closely regulated as to where they may operate. They often hold regular route authorities allowing them to serve a limited number of points along a precisely specified route, often in accordance with a specified time schedule.

The specialized commodity common carriers generally are not so closely regulated as to the routes that they may travel, but their operating authorities limit them to a narrow range of commodities. They usually haul truckload traffic, have minimal terminal operations, and are long-haul carriers. In terms of traffic and operations, contract carriers are similar to the specialized commodity common carriers, but they serve a limited number of customers under specific contractual agreements.

The three groups differ markedly in the mechanics of rate regulation. Contract carriers are not subject to maximum-rate regulation, but must merely file their actual rates with the ICC. If a particular contract carrier rate is protested by a common carrier, the contract carrier must demonstrate that the rate at issue is compensatory. Since contract carrier rates are set by negotiation between shipper and carrier, they are more or less market determined.

Both general freight and specialized commodity common carriers have historically been regulated by means of the operating ratio. General freight carriers, however, are regulated on an areawide basis, coming before regulatory agencies in large groups represented by rate bureaus, while specialized common carriers constitute a small numbers' case by their very nature.[10] Many of the larger specialized commodity carriers publish individual tariffs and group rate actions usually involve significantly fewer petitioners. A priori, specialized commodity common carriers are the group most likely to be influenced by operating-ratio considerations, because carriers can be expected to perceive a clear-cut relationship between rising operating ratios and rate increases.[11]

Table 7.1 reveals marked similarities and differences in leasing practices among the three carrier groups. The percentage of total vehicle-miles leased by specialized commodity common carriers was approximately two and one-half times as large as for contract carriers, while the percentage of total vehicle-miles leased by general freight carriers was only slightly higher than that of contract carriers. When the data are disaggregated into miles leased with and without drivers, however, a different pattern emerges. The percentage of total miles leased without drivers by the two groups of common carriers is almost identical and twice that of contract carriers. General freight carriers lease less with drivers than contract carriers, but specialized commodity common carriers lease nearly three times the percentage of total miles with drivers as do contract carriers. This last contrast is especially noteworthy, because these two groups of carriers are so technologically similar.[12] The two groups may, however, be quite different with respect to business risk. Specialized common carriers, lacking the assurance of the more stable earnings associated with long-term shipper contracts, may lease rather than own vehicles as a means of reducing such risk.[13]

To investigate the question of differential risk, the authors collected data on the earnings of forty-six specialized common carriers and fifty contract carriers, as reported in Trinc's, for the period 1962 through 1973. Utilizing operating revenues divided by net equity in the previous year as a measure of the earnings rate, we found the standard deviation in the average yearly earnings of the specialized common carriers to be 6.566 over the eleven-year span, compared to a standard deviation of 2.694 for the contract carriers as a group. It seemed appropriate, therefore, to explore the influence of earnings variability on leasing.

The absolute deviation in earnings rates for both carrier groups combined was regressed on the percent of total miles leased, with the following results (t-value in parentheses):

$$\text{Percent Leased} = 45.579 + 0.1766 \; ABS \; DEV; \; R^2 = 0.02$$
$$(3.086)$$

The coefficient of leasing is statistically significant but of such small magnitude that earnings instability does not seem to influence leasing to any great extent. Furthermore, the low R^2 indicates that other factors have a far greater impact on leasing than does earnings instability.

Other Factors in the Leasing Decision

In addition to elevating operating ratios to justify rate increases, a number of other explanations have been, or might be, advanced for widespread resort to leasing by the trucking industry. These would include: (1) mitigating seasonal fluctuations in demand, (2) reducing geographic traffic imbalances, (3) conserving working capital, (4) achieving economies of scale in the maintenance of equipment, (5) taking advantage of innovations, (6) exploiting the monopoly power represented by operating rights, and (7) diversion of profits to a subsidiary. Let us consider the presumed relationship between each of these factors and the extent of equipment leasing.

SEASONAL FLUCTUATIONS. The derived demand for highway freight transportation is subject to seasonal fluctuations, and short-term equipment leasing provides carriers with a means of adapting to short-run variations in demand. The inflexibility of regulated freight rates exacerbates the distortion caused by the seasonality of demand, providing additional incentive for leasing.

GEOGRAPHIC IMBALANCES. A regulated carrier may lease from an independent owner-operator to haul a load for which a profitable backhaul does not appear readily available. Just as regulatory-imposed rate rigidity tends to aggravate the problem of seasonal variations, so may commodity and point restrictions, as well as rate regulation, intensify spatial imbalances in traffic.

CONSERVATION OF WORKING CAPITAL. This is the explanation of leasing most frequently cited by industry spokesmen. Presumably, carriers finding it difficult to raise capital for equipment purchases have the alternative of leasing.

ECONOMIES OF SCALE. Taff has pointed out that "full-service" leases, pursuant to which the lessor agrees both to supply and maintain the vehicle may allow smaller carriers to realize economies of scale in the maintenance function.[14]

INNOVATION. Leasing may allow carriers to take advantage of innovations after a shorter interval than would ownership, since they can readily allow leases on old vehicles to lapse and be replaced with more modern versions.[15]

OPERATING RIGHTS. One of the consequences of entry regulation has been the possession of monopoly operating rights by existing carriers. A portion of leasing from independent owner-operators probably represents the exploitation of these rights. Authorized carriers provide the right to serve, while independent truckers provide the actual service for a revenue share which is less than the opportunity cost to the authorized carrier of providing the service.

DIVERSION OF PROFITS. If the carrier leases from an affiliated firm, rather than a third party, the transaction offers an opportunity to siphon off profits to an unregulated entity. The diversion-of-profits motive is a function of maximum-rate regulation whatever the regulatory standard, rate of return, or operating ratio. The regulatory standard merely influences the form it will take, purchase or lease.

Seasonal fluctuations and geographic imbalances in traffic would tend to encourage short-term, rather than long-term leasing. The remaining factors, conservation of working capital, economies of scale in maintenance, taking advantage of equipment innovations, exploitation of operating rights, and diversion of profits are primarily incentives for long-term leasing.

As to the relative importance of the short- and long-term incentives for leasing, the long term are probably much more compelling. Virtually all leasing without drivers is long term, since the carrier must hire drivers for the leased vehicles and this represents the same kind of commitment as to other employees. Leasing with drivers, on the other hand, may involve either trip leasing or long-standing, renewable arrangements with owner-operators.

Data collected by the ICC in its 1976 study of capacity utilization reveal that the great bulk of vehicle leasing with drivers, as well as without drivers, is long term in nature.[16] Of 2,471 ICC-regulated vehicles leased with drivers, 2,117, or 85.6 percent, were leased for periods exceeding thirty days.[17] Inasmuch as some 61.6 percent of all leased vehicle-miles in 1976 were leased with drivers,[18] this suggests that only about 8.9 percent of all leasing was motivated by short-run considerations of seasonality and spatial traffic imbalances.

The very modest role of seasonal fluctuations in demand in influencing leasing with drivers is indicated in Table 7.2. Seasonal varia-

Table 7.2. Vehicle-miles Leased with Drivers as a Percent of Total Vehicle-miles and Total Leased Vehicle-miles, 1976, Compared with Seasonal Fluctuations in Demand, 1978: Specialized Commodity Carrier Groups

Specialized Commodity Carrier Group	Vehicle-miles Leased with Drivers as a Percent of all Vehicle-miles, 1976	Vehicle-miles Leased with Drivers as a Percent of all Leased Vehicle-miles, 1976	Greatest Number of Vehicle-miles in Any Quarter as a Percent of all Vehicle-miles, 1978
Petroleum products	24.6	59.2	26.7
Refrigerated products	62.4	74.6	27.4
Agricultural products	32.4	79.2	30.6
Motor vehicles	40.7	94.2	27.7
Building materials	21.9	46.6	27.8

Sources: *Trinc's Blue Book of the Trucking Industry* (Washington: Trinc Transportation Consultants, 1977), 2–4 and *Motor Carrier Statistical Summary* (Washington, D.C.: American Trucking Association, n.d.), First Quarter 1979, Table VII; Second Quarter 1979, Table VII; Third Quarter 1979, Table VII; and Fourth Quarter 1979, Table VII-B.

tions in demand seem slight, indeed, in relation to the extent of leasing without drivers, either as a percent of all vehicle miles or as a percent of all leased vehicle miles. Furthermore, there seems to be little relationship between the extent of leasing without drivers and seasonal fluctuations in demand among the various commodity groups.

Model

To test the various hypotheses advanced to explain truck leasing practices,[19] a linear regression model in the following functional form was developed:

TOTLEASE = f(TYPE, AFFIL, SIZE, AVHAUL, MAINCST, LABCST + DEBT/EQ)

The variables, together with the presumed relationship between each of the independent variables and TOTLEASE, are as follows:

TOTLEASE = Percent of total vehicle-miles in vehicles leased with or without drivers.

TYPE = Dummy variable (1 if specialized common carrier, 0 if contract carrier). The central hypothesis of this paper is that maximum-rate regulation by means of the operating ratio creates an incentive for specialized common carriers to utilize leasing to a greater extent than contract carriers not subject to maximum-rate regulation.

AFFIL = Dummy variable (1 if affiliated with transportation-related company, 0 otherwise). An equipment affiliate offers a carrier subject to operating-ratio regulation the opportunity to divert profits to the affiliate, provided that the worsening of the carrier's operating ratio can be translated into higher rates.

SIZE = Annual operating revenues. Since contract carriers tend on the average to be smaller than specialized common carriers, carrier size is an appropriate variable in any estimate of the separate influence of operating-ratio regulation.

AVHAUL = Average length of haul. The greater the distance goods are hauled, the greater the adverse impact of spatial imbalances on traffic volume. Leasing, therefore, should be positively associated with the average length of haul.

MAINCST = Maintenance cost per vehicle-mile in owned vehicles and vehicles leased without drivers. If there are economies of scale in the maintenance function, leasing should be positively related to the carrier's cost of vehicle maintenance.

LABCST = Labor cost per mile in owned vehicles and vehicles leased without drivers. The higher a carrier's own labor costs, the more likely it is to exploit the monopoly power conferred by its operating authority by leasing vehicles with drivers.

DEBT/EQ = The ratio of debt to equity capital. Carrier difficulty in raising capital should be reflected in the debt-equity ratio — the higher the ratio, the greater the resort to leasing.

Data on individual specialized common and contract carriers were obtained from Trinc's.[20] The sample consisted of 121 specialized common and 114 contract carriers listed therein. Twenty-nine of the former and 25 of the latter were affiliated with other transportation-related companies. Trinc's compiled the data from the carriers' annual reports to the ICC for 1964, a year in which the commission relied almost exclusively on the operating ratio as an earnings control criterion.

The results (t-values in parenthesis) were as follows:

(1)   TOTLEASE = 20.02 + 14.84 TYPE − 0.79 AFFIL + 0.00 SIZE

$$(2.7176) \qquad (-0.1161) \qquad (1.3737)$$

$$+ \ 0.03 \ \text{AVHAUL} \ + \ 1.13 \ \text{MAINCST}$$
$$(2.5641) \qquad\qquad (3.1193)$$

$$+ \ 0.40 \ \text{LABCST} \ + \ 0.25 \ \text{DEBT/EQ}$$
$$(1.7410) \qquad\qquad (0.5593)$$

$$R^2 = 0.16$$

Not only is carrier type significant at the 1 percent level, but also the magnitude of the coefficient indicates that the influence of operating-ratio regulation is considerable. The results are not as kind to the other explanations of leasing. While maintenance cost is also significant at the 1 percent level and average length of haul comes close, the coefficients are small. As for the remaining variables, none is significant at the 10 percent level, the coefficients are uniformly small, *and the sign of the affiliation variable is the opposite of the one assumed in the theory.*

In order to measure the extent to which the independent variables influenced the kind of leasing adopted, total leased vehicle miles were disaggregated into leasing with drivers (LWD) in equation 2 and leasing without drivers (LW/OD) in equation 3. In particular, it was assumed that to the extent that leasing without drivers is short term in nature, it would increase the importance of the average-haul variable in equation 3 over equation 2. It was also assumed that to the extent that both LWD and LW/OD were long term in nature, carriers with affiliates would elect to lease without drivers so that the coefficient of AFFIL in equation 3 would be positive, notwithstanding the negative sign in equation 1. On the other hand, because labor and maintenance costs are shifted to the owner-operator by leasing with driver, the coefficients of these variables should be positive and higher in equation 2 than in equation 3.

$$(2) \quad \text{LWD} = 7.54 + 7.80 \text{ TYPE} - 5.77 \text{ AFFIL} - 0.00 \text{ SIZE}$$
$$\phantom{(2) \quad \text{LWD} = 7.54} \quad (2.1736) \quad\quad (-1.2968) \quad\quad (0.1209)$$

$$+ \ 0.01 \text{ AVHAUL} + 1.43 \text{ MAINCST}$$
$$(2.5395) \quad\quad\quad (6.0021)$$

$$+ \ 0.53 \text{ LABCST} + 0.40 \text{ DEBT/EQ}$$
$$(3.4810) \quad\quad\quad (1.3893)$$

$$R^2 = 0.31$$

$$(3) \quad \text{LW/OD} = 12.48 + 7.04 \text{ TYPE} + 4.98 \text{ AFFIL} + 0.00 \text{ SIZE}$$
$$\phantom{(3) \quad \text{LW/OD} = 12.48} \quad (1.9274) \quad\quad (0.8008) \quad\quad (1.5817)$$

$$+ \ 0.01 \text{ AVHAUL} - 0.30 \text{ MAINCST}$$
$$(1.2111) \quad\quad\quad (-0.8970)$$

$$+ \ -0.13 \text{ LABCST} - 0.16 \text{ DEBT/EQ}$$
$$(0.5935) \quad\quad\quad (-0.3846)$$

$$R^2 = 0.06$$

Since the coefficient of average haul is no higher when the dependent variable is leasing with drivers than leasing without drivers, it may be that average length of haul is a poor proxy for spatial imbalances in traffic. The length of haul is, after all, merely indicative of the incentive to reduce geographic imbalances rather than a measure of their extent. An even more plausible explanation is that leasing without drivers, like leasing with drivers, is primarily a long-term arrangement. The substitutive nature of LWD and LW/OD is revealed by the highly significant negative correlation of −0.222, which they exhibit.

Despite the general interchangeability of LWD and LW/OD, carriers with affiliates have a clear preference for the latter, as indicated by the negative sign of the coefficient of AFFIL in equation 2 and the positive sign in equation 3. While this variable has the predicted sign in the latter equation, it is not statistically significant.

The disaggregation reveals material differences in the influence of maintenance and labor costs on the type of leasing employed. The signs of these coefficients are as expected in equation 2 and the level of statistical significance exceeds 1 percent. The coefficients, however, are low, indicating a relatively minor impact on leasing with driver.

Either type of leasing tends to increase the operating ratio, so there are no a priori grounds for predicting dissimilar coefficients of TYPE. Since the sum of the TYPE coefficients of equations 2 and 3 equals that of equation 1, the magnitude of each coefficient will be lower and the level of statistical significance reduced as the number of applicable observations declines.

The coefficients and statistical significance of the other variables, SIZE and DEBT/EQ, are little affected by the disaggregation. All in all, the relatively low R^2 in all three equations suggests that some of the proxies may lack validity or that other factors, either unknown or not quantifiable, exert a greater collective influence on leasing than those accounted for by the model.

Allocative and Redistributive Effects of Operating-ratio Regulation

The model of the firm under operating-ratio constraint predicts that if regulation is effective, technical efficiency will be impaired by substitution of variable inputs for capital. The leasing alternative offers motor carriers a type of reaction to the regulatory constraint not available to regulated utilities. The substitution of leased for purchased capital is not factor substitution as envisioned by Averch and Johnson and their many followers. From a technological standpoint, it is irrelevant whether capital is leased or purchased. The input remains the same, and technical efficiency is unaffected by the substitution of leased for purchased capital.

The substitution of labor for capital, also a prediction of the model, will adversely affect technical efficiency. Whether such factor substitution has actually occurred is not known. The relatively simple technology of the highway carrier industry may limit its extent. As a rule, the line-haul portion of freight movement is accomplished by one vehicle and one driver, and varying these proportions is simply not feasible. The area in which carriers might overstaff is terminal operations. The general freight segment of the industry is much more labor intensive than are either specialized common or contract carriers, but this is probably a function of general freight carriers' specialization in less-than-truckload shipments, rather than regulatory response.

Since capital leasing has the same effect on the operating ratio as the substitution of labor for capital, carriers can achieve their objective without resorting to factor substitution. A similar option is not available to public utilities subject to rate-of-return regulation. Although capital can be leased, slavery is no longer legal. Utilities cannot "buy" the labor input, converting a variable into a fixed resource. Therefore, rate-of-return regulation may have a more deleterious effect on technical efficiency than operating-ratio regulation.

Operating-ratio regulation, however, may result in rates for regulated firms that exceed substantially the marginal costs and may impair allocative efficiency. It also results in a redistribution of income from consumers to the regulated industry. Permitted profit rates vary directly with utilization of leased capital. Although lease payments are invariably considered an operating expense, these payments include an element of return to capital. Failure to recognize this on the part of the regulatory agency leads to a transfer of income to the regulated industry from society at large. The single most important issue in rate regulation is the division of income between producers and consumers. Operating-ratio regulation can be expected to result in a division of income unacceptable to almost anyone except the regulated industry.

To what extent do the motor carrier regulatory practices employed in most states today create an incentive for equipment leasing as a means of operating ratio inflation? Freeman and Beilock[21] observe that a state commission's "staff would be unlikely to recommend a suspension of a rate change that complies with the state's publishing format unless it is a major general increase or serious protests are registered" and that, even then, "commissions rely heavily on cost evidence developed by the carriers or rate bureaus in ascertaining whether a rate is just, reasonable, fair and non-discriminatory." In view of the impact of leasing upon the operating ratio, it is clear that individual or small groups of intrastate carriers have an incentive to increase operating ratios, especially if they can accomplish this without increasing total costs and if they have the means to do so through equipment leasing as an alternative to purchase.

CHAPTER 8

Rural Impacts of Economic Regulation: Internal Subsidization

Quite apart from the normative issue the merits of employing the regulated trucking industry as a mechanism of income redistribution in favor of small, isolated communities, there is the positive issue as to whether regulation of rates and entry into the industry has conferred any benefits on the residents of rural areas. Unfortunately, many of the proponents of deregulation have not seen fit to address the issue, presumably on the ground that the potential improvement in the efficiency of resource allocation induced by deregulation was sufficient rationale for its adoption irrespective of the impact upon particular segments of the shipping and receiving public. On the other hand, the opponents of any extensive regulatory reform tend to assume implicitly the right of locationally disadvantaged shippers and receivers to service at less than cost and to maintain through assertion and reiteration that regulation is the sine qua non of adequate service at reasonable rates in the less-densely populated areas.[1]

This chapter seeks to determine whether rural areas are the beneficiaries of economic regulation of the trucking industry. Should the evidence suggest that no such benefits redound to out-of-the-way locales,

Reprinted with permission from John Richard Felton, "The Cross-Subsidization of Rural Areas by ICC-Regulated Trucking Firms," *Nebraska Journal of Economics and Business* 19, no. 4 (Autumn 1980):17–27.

then the normative issue becomes moot. In short, if regulation does not achieve a redistribution of income favorable to rural areas, then the failure of a deregulated competitive trucking industry to confer differential benefits on such areas is no longer a valid argument in support of the existing regulatory system.

Rural Community Benefits from Regulation: Rationale and Critique

The proposition that regulation of the trucking industry contributes to the viability and prosperity of sparsely populated regions is voiced so frequently that a brief summary of the argument will suffice. The operating authorities dispensed by regulatory commissions impose obligations on common carriers to provide some unprofitable service in return for the right to generate excess revenues on other kinds of traffic. Were it not for restrictions on entry, truck operators having no public service obligation would enter the profitable markets, "skimming the cream" and leaving to the common carriers no excess revenues to accomplish such internal subsidization. Deregulation, by nullifying exclusive operating rights, would release carriers from any and all obligations to serve, and communities would suffer losses of service as unsubsidized rates rose to cover the higher costs of serving areas of relatively low traffic density.[2]

The foregoing scenario relies heavily on the formal common carrier obligation to serve all who request service within the area in which a carrier has held itself out to serve. If a carrier cannot "pick and choose" among its eligible clientele, it can presumably be required to accept some business that it would have preferred to reject.

While evidence that shippers and receivers in rural areas were the victims of discrimination vis-a-vis those in urban areas would negate this case for continued regulation, the converse is not necessarily true. Price discrimination is a necessary but not a sufficient condition of internal subsidization. Thus a carrier possessing some monopoly power may maintain different price-marginal cost ratios in the different geographic markets it serves without rendering any trucking service at less than the avoidable costs involved. In short, the receipt of excess revenues from serving customers in more densely populated areas neither motivates the carrier to incur losses in serving less densely populated areas nor guarantees that cross-subsidization will occur.

The obligation to serve is insufficient to assure the subsidization of rural by urban traffic if (1) there is some rate which will cover avoidable costs and the regulatory commission will accede to that rate or (2) the carrier can evade its duty to serve. As Gifford has observed:

> A growing number of motor carriers, seeking to avoid shipments they consider to be unprofitable, resort to the curtailment or abandonment of service by embargoes, rate increases, insistence upon more extensive packaging, and/or by tariff restrictions. The most serious threat to the maintenance of adequate small shipments service appears to be the increasing tendency of inter-lining carriers to cancel through route-joint rate agreements, and their refusal to participate in new agreements.[3]

It is obviously difficult to reconcile the ability of commissions to enforce cross-subsidization with the well-nigh automatic protests existing carriers enter to applications for new operating authority by prospective rivals. No infringement on the rights of an existing carrier appears to be too trivial to preclude intervention by affected carriers. Although some case can, perhaps, be made as to the ability of a commission to require a carrier to transport goods upon which it is incurring deficits, it taxes credulity to believe that trucking firms would protest the loss of such traffic. While owner-operators may be true "Knights of the Road," regulated trucking firms can less plausibly be characterized as "Robin Hoods of the Highway."

Finally, even a showing that rural areas are the beneficiaries of cross-subsidization does not prove that rates from and to rural communities would be higher without regulation. Thus regulation of entry and rates may inflate highway transport costs to such an extent that any rural gains from internal subsidization are more than offset. Operating authorities prohibiting a regulated carrier from serving intermediate or off-route points or from utilizing alternative routes or which restrict the commodities the carrier can transport have an especially severe impact upon the adequacy of service to rural areas. Furthermore, the poorer utilization of truck capacity inherent in such limitations increases the cost of whatever service is available. The transport costs of rural shippers and receivers may also be increased because of the inability of private carriers delivering to such areas to transport other than exempt agricultural commodities on return trips. By the same token, the costs of transporting agricultural commodities from rural areas will reflect the inability of these carriers to transport nonagricultural commodities in backhauls to rural origins. Last, but not least, the excess capacity that exempt agricultural carriers experience on return trips *to* rural areas contributes to the excess capacity that regulated carriers face on trips *from* rural areas. Despite the fact that rural communities typically export much greater annual tonnages than they import, regulated carriers encounter a far greater demand for shipments to rather than from such areas. As McElhiney has observed, "Regional experts state that 38 percent more (general commodity common carrier) equipment is required for the inbound than the outbound movement."[4]

Economic regulation of the for-hire trucking industry has increased rates by an estimated \$5.5 billion per year, an amount equal to 25 percent of the operating revenues of Class I and II ICC-regulated trucking firms in 1976.[5] For rural shippers and receivers to be enjoying lower rates now than under an unregulated regime, users in high-traffic density areas would have to have been providing an annual subsidy in excess of \$5 billion per year! Since it is obvious that any internal subsidization is of far smaller magnitude, it follows that if rural areas have been the beneficiaries of *relatively* lower rates, they have shared with urban areas the *absolutely* higher rates induced by regulation.

Rural Areas as Objects of Discrimination: Hypothesis

Despite the contention of Glaskowsky, O'Neil, and Hudson that both the proponents and opponents of continued regulation agree on the dire consequences of deregulation for small communities, a respectable a priori case can be made that rural areas are more likely to be the victims than the beneficiaries of discrimination. This arises from the much more substantial amount of monopoly power that regulated carriers are able to wield in areas of lesser traffic density.

The number of regulated carriers operating in any particular market is heavily influenced by traffic density. As Snow has observed:

> For shipments between large cities, a number of carriers are usually available, perhaps a dozen or more. For smaller cities, especially if they are located in parts of the country which have experienced substantial growth in the years since motor carriers became regulated, the number of carriers available may be quite small, sometimes only one or two.[6]

The Motor Common Carrier Freight Rate Study, referred to earlier, provides data permitting a test of the statistical relationship between community size and truck service availability. This study of nine Rocky Mountain states listed all cities and towns with populations of 500 or more, if incorporated, and 1,000 or more, if unincorporated, together with the number of interstate common carriers authorized to provide service to each of such communities. In Nebraska the number of carriers authorized to serve the 103 cities and towns varied from 1 in 14 communities, all with populations of less than 2,500, to 23 in Grand Island, 39 in Lincoln, and 59 in Omaha, the third, second, and first cities in size, respectively, in the state.[7]

The Spearman coefficient of rank correlation between the population of each of these Nebraska communities and the number of interstate carriers authorized to serve them was 0.4712, significant at the 0.001 level. The Kendall coefficient of rank correlation, apparently a superior measure of association when there are a number of ties in rank,[8] was a somewhat lower 0.3531, but still significant at the 0.001 level.

The number of interstate carriers authorized to serve a particular community may not, however, be a good index of the number of carriers actually serving that community. Thus a Wyoming study revealed that, of 66 authorizations to serve 11 communities, only 33 were being exercised.[9] Furthermore, there was a tendency for the ratio of actual to authorized service to vary directly with population. The Pearsonian coefficient of correlation, 0.228, was not, however, statistically significant.

While the operation of rate bureaus, the requirement for publication of rates and advance notice of changes therein, and the prohibition of departures from published rates may limit severely competition among regulated carriers, whatever rivalry remains is likely to be greater with a dozen than with one or two carriers. As a consequence, the much greater seller concentration that typically occurs in areas of smaller traffic density is one ground for hypothesizing that rural communities are more likely to be subject to discrimination than to benefit from subsidization.[10]

The number of regulated carriers *actually* serving a particular area may still not be a satisfactory indication of the state of competition in that market. Thus even if there are several regulated carriers serving a rural area, the commodity, point, and route restrictions may transform each of them into a monopolist.

These regulated trucking monopolies may be offset to some extent by the presence of private carriage and by the intermodal competition provided by railroads. Both these sources of competition are less effective for small, isolated shippers than for large shippers in populous areas.

Small shippers characteristically ship products in quantities too small, to destinations too scattered, and pursuant to schedules too infrequent to make private carriage economically feasible. Table 8.1 reveals the obvious tendency for private carriage to vary directly with firm size.[11] If private carriage is, indeed, a less viable alternative for small than large shippers, the monopoly position of regulated carriers serving smaller communities is further entrenched.[12]

Table 8.1. *Percentage of Manufacturing Firms Reporting Private Truck Fleets and Private Trailer Fleets by Firm Size*

Firm Size (Employment)	Percentage of all Manufacturing Firms	
	With Private Truck Fleets	With Private Trailer Fleets
1–9	16.3	0.5
10–49	35.3	3.4
50–99	45.6	7.7
100–499	57.6	10.5
500 and over	72.9	18.8

Source: W. Y. Oi and A. P. Hurter, Jr., *Economics of Private Truck Transportation* (Dubuque, Iowa: Brown, 1965), 83, 135.

Insofar as railroad competition is concerned, small communities, rather than large ones, are more likely to suffer from limited rail service. The study prepared for the Federation of Rocky Mountain States revealed that of the 1,032 incorporated communities of 500 or more population or unincorporated communities of 1,000 or more, 218, or more than 20 percent, were not located on a rail line.[13] The places without rail transportation tended to be the smaller, isolated communities.

The a priori case for the proposition that economic regulation of trucking has had differentially adverse impacts upon small shippers and receivers and remote locations would appear to be at least as convincing as the much more widely held contention that regulation had conferred substantial benefits on such persons and areas. It remains to be seen which hypothesis the evidence will support.

Cross-Subsidization: Evidence

One possibility for testing the hypothesis that rural areas are the victims, rather than the beneficiaries, of discrimination is an adaptation of the method employed by Boyer to determine the relative extent of commodity rate discrimination in rail and highway carrier rate structures.[14] After excluding rail shipments of less than 10 tons and truck shipments of less than 10,000 pounds, he obtained a random sample of rail and truck freight bills involving the transportation of some thirty-seven commodities by rail and fifty-two by truck. He then developed a value per ton for each commodity so that he could correlate commodity value with commodity freight revenue separately for rail and truck shipments. The Spearman coefficient of rank correlation between commodity values and rail revenues was a statistically insignificant +0.25, while between commodity values and truck revenues it was a highly significant +0.43. Boyer notes that when the effect of commodity density is taken into consideration, there is a good deal more upward bias in the estimate of truck than rail commodity rate discrimination. Thus he concludes that this consideration supports "the hypothesis that there is no difference in the value of service component of rail and road structures."[15]

An analogous procedure to test the rural discrimination hypothesis would be to compare the truck commodity value and revenue correlations for urban and rural destinations. Should the correlation between commodity values and associated rates be higher for rural than nonrural destinations, this would tend to support the hypothesis. The reason is that if highway carriers can and do engage in *commodity* rate discrimination vis-a-vis rural communities, the likelihood that they combine this with place rate discrimination favorable to such communities would appear somewhat remote.

Unfortunately, the continuing Traffic Studies data file compiled by ten motor carrier freight rate bureaus is unavailable.[16] A roughly equivalent test, however, would be to compare the National Motor Freight Classification (NMFC) class rates applicable to less-than-truckload (LTL) traffic with the rates applicable to truckload (TL) traffic. Inasmuch as a larger percentage of traffic to rural locations is the LTL variety, the existence of a greater value-of-service element in LTL shipments means that rural locations tend to be the victims of commodity rate discrimination.[17]

Olson's study of the structure of motor carrier class rates reveals that adding commodity value to carrier transport costs increases the coefficient of determination by about 10 to 15 percentage points.[18] Furthermore, as the value of the commodity increases by $1.00 per cwt, the class rate increases by 2 to 3 mills per cwt.[19]

Before the work of Olson can be accepted as reliable evidence of discrimination in the NMFC class rates, it is necessary to consider the objections of DeVany and Saving. It is their contention that because of uncertainty of transport demands, the trucking industry must achieve some trade-off between capacity and shipper waiting time. Inasmuch as excess capacity imposes a cost on the shipper (with this cost directly related to the value of the commodity), "value of service pricing in truck transport (becomes) understandable as the result of normal competitive profit-maximizing behavior."[20]

Boyer has leveled extensive criticism against the DeVany-Saving model, noting that truck capacity is not generally dedicated to the transportation of single commodities and that high-value goods do not appear to enjoy faster transit times than do low-value goods.[21] Furthermore, even under somewhat extreme assumptions, the effect of additional waiting time on the inventory cost of high-value goods is likely to be far less than the kind of variation found in class rates. Thus if all commodities transported are worth $5,000 a ton, if the costs of holding these commodities is 25 percent per annum, if 100 tons per day on the average are transported 800 miles in trucks with a capacity of 24 tons each, and if an additional truckload results in the imposition of a 24-hour delay in the estimated time of commodity delivery, the "congestion toll" for such shipment would add only $0.018 (19.1 percent) to the average truck charge of $0.096 per ton mile. Since the highest NMFC class rate is more than 30 times as great as the lowest, Boyer would appear to be on sound ground in declaring, ". . . even were D-S' model correct, it could not explain the price variation that has traditionally been attributed to value-of-service pricing."[22]

By way of contrast with class rates, the commodity rates applicable to much of the truckload traffic appear to be competitively determined.[23] As Snow has commented:

> Almost all LTL shipments move under rates determined collectively by associations of carriers called rate bureaus and sanctioned by the ICC. . . . Thus . . . price competition on LTL traffic is almost completely stifled. Private carriage and railroads place a competitive discipline on truckload rates. Many TL rates are negotiated individually between carrier and shipper, and they are essentially competitive prices.[24]

If far more rural than nonrural regulated truck shipments are subject to class rates, if class rates are discriminatory, and the commodity rates applicable to truckload shipments are competitive in nature, then nonrural shipments cannot be a substantial source for the subsidization of rural traffic. On the contrary, the presence of commodity rate discrimination for rural traffic presupposes some monopoly power and provides the opportunity for enhanced carrier revenues from value-of-service pricing. While the evidence is not compelling, it is consistent with a hypothesis founded on conventional maximizing principles and observed market structure characteristics.

CHAPTER 9

Rural Impacts of Economic Regulation: A Case Study

The provisions of the Motor Carrier Act of 1935[1] and those of the more or less parallel statutes of most states[2] are regarded by many observers as having critical implications for shippers in small rural communities and for the carriers serving these communities. Rural areas are heavily dependent on motor carriers for their transportation needs. Many rural communities are without rail connections but, with or without rail service, most small communities rely on motor carriers for meeting virtually all of their nonbulk transport requirements.

Although unprocessed agricultural products are generally exempt from regulation, as are goods moved by private carriage, these exemptions do not render rural traffic free from regulatory restraints. Private carriage may be a relatively poor alternative since the transport requirements of most rural shippers are too modest to justify private vehicle ownership. Moreover, uncertified carriers of exempt products are not permitted to carry regulated products, even as backhauls. Most carriers of agricultural products outbound from rural areas thus have few oppor-

Elmo T. Falcon is Senior Manager, Corporate Planning Division, Far East Bank, Manila, Philippines. He received his M.S. in Agricultural Economics from the University of Nebraska-Lincoln in 1981.

Reprinted with permission from Dale G. Anderson and Elmo Falcon, "Implications of Motor Carrier Deregulation for a Case-Study Rural Community," *Proceedings, Twenty-second Annual Meeting, Transportation Research Forum* 22, no. 1(1981):33–40.

tunities for return hauls while at the same time regulated carriers have a preponderance of inbound traffic.

Proponents of continued regulation contend that shippers in small, relatively isolated areas would suffer reductions in services and increases in rates in a deregulated environment. They maintain that such areas are presently cross-subsidized from revenues received from more remunerative intercity and interregional hauls.[3]

Opponents of motor carrier regulation contend that the common carrier trucking industry would, in the absence of regulation, be highly competitive and far more efficient than at present. They maintain that the greater flexibility deregulation would afford carriers would yield reduced transport costs and the result would be lower rates and improved service to rural communities.[4]

The relative merits of these conflicting viewpoints were evaluated in an empirical investigation of the cost and service implications of motor carrier deregulation for a small, rural, case-study community.[5] Estimated costs of current common carrier service to the community were compared with published rates and with estimated costs under deregulated conditions.

Case-Study Area

The focus of the study was a community in southeastern Nebraska. The community was selected for the likelihood that cross-subsidization of common carriage service would exist there if it exists anywhere. The economy of the surrounding mixed-farming area is largely agricultural. The community, population about 1200, has little manufacturing activity and exists largely as a commercial center.

The area is relatively remote from major centers of manufacturing and distribution. No rail lines or major highways serve the community. All freight service is provided by motor trucks. Although the volume of bulk agricultural products shipped from the area far exceeds the volume of inbound traffic, the outbound volume of regulated goods is inconsequential.

The community is served by an owner-operated motor common carrier of general freight that hauls approximately 87 percent of the total for-hire regulated traffic to the case-study area. Two small-package common carriers account for the remaining 13 percent of the traffic. The general freight hauler provides less-than-truckload (LTL) route-delivery service from Omaha and Lincoln origins, the consolidation points for most of the freight shipped to the community. Traffic coming from Kansas City, a major supply and interchange point, is hauled by a large interstate common carrier to Lincoln and then transhipped to the area by the owner-operated carrier. Kansas City–Lincoln traffic moves in tractor-trailer vans. Most traffic from Lincoln and Omaha is carried in straight trucks over prescribed routes to the study community, which is the final point served on each of the two routes.

Research Procedures

Temporal and geographic flows of commodities carried in ordinary vans to and from the community were estimated based on personal interviews with local shippers and carriers. Owners or managers of all local commercial establishments provided monthly estimates of their transportation requirements for the most recent twelve-month period.[6] Data collected included volume, weight, destination or origin, commodity type or class, seasonality of the traffic, and type of carrier (private or common).

Excluded from the survey were commodities carried in refrigerated vans, bulk tanks, or other specialized types of equipment, even though specialization may in some instances have been prompted by the regulatory environment. Grain and livestock shipments were excluded from the survey even though their outbound volume is known to exceed by far the inbound volume of regulated products. Analysis of technical feasibility and costs of operating dual-purpose vehicles designed to carry both bulk agricultural products and general freight was beyond the scope of the study. Each of these exclusions increases the conservatism of estimated benefits from deregulation.

Operating authorities were examined to establish the nature of regulatory limitations imposed on common carriers serving the area. Further information came from carriers and shippers. Published tariffs provided rate information.

Costs of service under existing simulated deregulated conditions were estimated from economic-engineering evidence.[7] Cost-volume relationships of model firms were estimated and the resulting long- and short-run average costs were used as a basis for determining expected trucking costs under alternative regulatory situations. Information on carrier size, costs, service characteristics, load factors, and general operating and management practices was obtained by telephone and personal interviews of carriers serving the area.

Scale relationships were estimated from cost data obtained from a survey of thirteen Nebraska common carriers of various sizes. Intercity firms of four different sizes were modeled: 20-, 30-, 50-, and 80-vehicle units, respectively. Three sizes of an owner-operated route delivery firm were modeled: 2-, 4-, and 6-vehicle units, each. Cost estimates summarized in Tables 9.1 through 9.4 were used in calculating unit costs for the scale analysis and in estimating costs for each of the segments of the common carrier routes by which the study area is served.

Two carrier firm types were modeled to represent the two basic types of service to the area: (1) An intercity LTL carrier operating tractor-trailer vans over a 700-mile (including pickup and delivery) round-trip route and (2) An owner-operated LTL, route-delivery carrier operating straight-truck vans over a 300-mile (including pickup and delivery) round-trip route. The former was representative of the firm providing the study area with connecting service from Kansas City to Lincoln. The latter firm was representative of the company providing the study area with route-delivery service from Omaha and Lincoln. The model intercity carrier had eighty vehicles, while the owner-operated firm had four.

Allowance was made for freight assembly costs at the point of origin and customer delivery costs at the destination of the intercity traffic;

Table 9.1. Annual Fixed Costs, Model Intercity Trucking Firms, Nebraska, 1980

Cost Item	Number of Units[a]			
	20	30	50	80
Depreciation & interest	$290,490	$436,601	$737,382	$1,187,283
Taxes	12,301	18,570	32,121	52,964
Insurance	87,780	132,170	221,850	355,780
License & fees	10,030	15,077	25,169	40,213
Salaries	445,075	518,953	717,769	989,076
Gen. office expense	79,200	96,300	116,100	138,600
Total fixed cost/year	$924,876	$1,217,671	$1,850,391	$2,763,916

[a]A "20-unit" firm has 10 tractors, 20 trailers, and 10 straight trucks; proportions are the same for other firm sizes. Trailer vans are 42-foot, double-axle units and are used for shorter hauls and for terminal assembly operations.

Table 9.2. Variable Costs Per Mile, Model Intercity Trucking Firms, Nebraska, 1980

Cost Item	Semitrailer	Straight Truck
Drivers' wages	$0.248	$0.319
Gas/fuel	0.245	0.178
Tires	0.047	0.016
Oil	0.015	0.008
Maintenance	0.036	0.020
Miscellaneous	0.089	0.081
Total variable cost/mile	$0.680	$0.622

Table 9.3. *Annual Fixed Costs, Model Owner-operated Trucking Firms, Nebraska, 1980*

Cost Item	Number of Units[a]		
	2	4	6
Depreciation & interest	$22,689	$45,346	$67,513
Taxes	1,075	2,053	3,043
Insurance	8,233	16,374	24,535
License & fees	1,001	2,001	3,002
Salaries	59,748	108,246	148,016
Gen. office expense	6,000	12,000	18,000
Total fixed cost/year	$98,746	$186,020	$264,109

[a]A "two-unit" firm has one tractor, one trailer, and one straight truck; proportions are the same for other firm sizes. Truck sizes are identical to those used by intercity firms (Table 9.1).

Table 9.4. *Variable Costs Per Mile, Model Owner-operated Trucking Firms, Nebraska, 1980*

Cost Item	Semitrailer	Straight Truck
Fuel	$0.260	$0.189
Tires	0.047	0.016
Oil	0.015	0.008
Maintenance	0.036	0.020
Miscellaneous	0.054	0.035
Total variable cost/mile	$0.412	$0.268

cost estimates thus reflect customer-to-customer rather than terminal-to-terminal costs. The owner-operated firm provided largely an assembly/delivery service, but it, too, had a terminal in the study area and in some instances transferred incoming goods to a smaller truck for customer delivery.

Estimated costs of service under the existing regulated system were compared with published rates to determine the profitability of each of the three traffic segments involved in service to the community. Average costs per cwt were compared with the weighted average of published rates for the mix of commodities carried over each traffic segment. The results provide an indication of profitability of existing traffic.

Results of the rate-cost analysis suggest that monopoly profits accrue to firms operating in the present regulated environment. Results of the economies-of-scale analysis support the view of numerous investigators[8] that deregulation would yield cost savings by permitting improved coordination of backhaul traffic by providing flexibility in traffic routing and in the long run would permit greater competition through the elimination of monopoly profits.

Assuming rates under deregulation would decline to the level of average costs, further analysis was performed to determine the expected level of costs (and rates) if traffic presently moving to and from the area by private carrier were consolidated with that presently moving by common carriers. Only private shipments undertaken by local business firms or their suppliers were considered; no attempt was made to include shipments carried privately by the 1200 citizens of the community or by its surrounding farm population. Small-package shipments (accounting for about 13 percent of the community's common carrier shipment volume) transported by two carriers providing this specialized service were also ignored. Inasmuch as the latter firms provide a door-to-door service available to all residents of the community, calculations beyond the scope of the study would have been required in the simulation of costs of the service. Finally, no attempt was made to estimate the volume of additional traffic that might be generated by rate reductions. Estimated savings from deregulation are therefore based conservatively on effects of joining only a portion of present private traffic with that moving via existing common carriers.

Each carrier serving the area was authorized to carry general freight; commodity restrictions were minimal. Nor were the routes specified in carrier operating authorities an obvious source of inefficiency; existing routes appeared to be reasonably well organized. No direct measure was attempted of potential savings from route enlargement or from ability to make permanent adjustments in the routes serviced. In the end, traffic consolidation was the source of cost savings modeled most rigorously. The implied frequency of service for least-cost operations was determined, as was the cost of continuing present service levels under a deregulated/consolidated-traffic setting.

Results

Inbound shipments of regulated goods to the study area were largely of four general classes: (1) general merchandise such as garments and textiles, (2) appliances and furniture, (3) building materials such as tile and carpeting, and (4) automobile, tractor, and farm implement parts.

Seasonality of traffic was route specific. Traffic from Lincoln, including transhipments from Kansas City, had only minor seasonal fluctuations. Traffic from Omaha was more variable, the volume ranging from 88 percent of mean volume during spring and fall months to 112 percent during the winter and summer.

Very modest economies of size, stemming entirely from savings in terminal costs, were found in both the intercity and route-delivery operations. The smallest size intercity carrier modeled (20 vehicle units) — with a round-trip load factor of 65 percent, and traveling a round-trip route of 700 miles, five days per week — had average costs of $1.94/cwt. The largest size modeled (80 vehicle units) had costs of $1.73 under otherwise identical conditions, a savings of $0.21/cwt, or 11 percent (Fig. 9.1).

Size economies for the owner-operated, route-delivery carriers were less significant owing to the inherently localized nature of their operations and to the relative unimportance of terminal activities. Costs for a 2-vehicle firm with a 42.5 percent load factor (85 percent forward haul and zero backhaul), round-trip of 300 miles, operating five days per week, were $1.78/cwt. An otherwise similar 6-vehicle firm had costs of $1.63 for a savings of $0.15/cwt, or 8 percent (Fig. 9.2).

Varying the load factor had a more pronounced effect on average costs. Reducing the load factor for the largest (80-unit) intercity carrier from 65 percent to 30 percent of capacity increased costs by 117 percent, from $1.94 to $4.21 per cwt (Fig. 9.1). The 6-vehicle, route-delivery

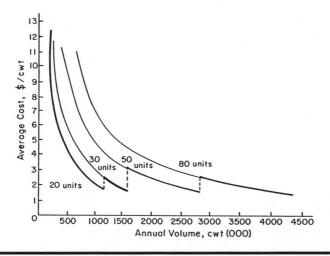

Fig. 9.1. Cost-volume relationships for alternative sizes (number of vehicle units) and volumes (load factors) of intercity trucking firms, average round-trip haul of 700 miles, Nebraska, 1980.

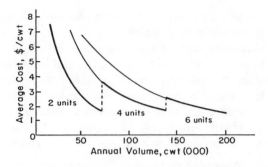

Fig. 9.2. Cost-volume relationships for alternative sizes (number of vehicle units) and volumes (load factors) of owner-operated trucking firms, average round-trip haul of 300 miles, Nebraska, 1980.

carrier had average costs of $1.78/cwt when load factor was 42.5 percent, $3.80 when the load factor was reduced to 20 percent, a 113 percent increase in costs (Fig. 9.2).

Estimated costs of common carrier service to the study area, including costs of freight assembly at the origin and delivery at destination over each of the traffic segments, are summarized in Table 9.5. Costs for the Kansas City to Lincoln segment were lowest ($2.29 per cwt), even

Table 9.5. Rates, Costs, and Service under Regulation Compared with Selected Alternatives, Case-study Area, Nebraska, 1980

| | Regulatory Model | | | |
Traffic Segment	Present Regulated System	Reduced Service	Consolidated Traffic	Intermarket Transfer
Omaha — study area				
Rate ($/cwt)	5.45			
Average cost ($/cwt)	3.06	2.85	2.49 (2.68[a])	1.85
Service (trips/week)	5	2–4	2–4	2.04
Lincoln — study area				
Rate ($/cwt)	5.19			
Average cost ($/cwt)	3.89	3.72	1.97	1.75
Service (trips/week)	3	1–2	3–5	3–5
Kansas City–Lincoln				
Rate ($/cwt)	8.74			
Average cost ($/cwt)	2.29	2.03	1.79	1.79
Service (trips/week)	5	3–4	5	5
Kansas City — study area				
Rate ($/cwt)	8.25			
Average cost ($/cwt)	6.18	5.75	3.76	3.54
Service (trips/week)	3–5	3–4	3–5	3–5

[a]Cost if existing level of service of 5 trips/week is maintained.

though the segment is the longest of the four, owing to the larger vehicles used for this haul and to the higher vehicle load factor, especially on the backhaul to Kansas City. Costs of moving goods to the study area ranged from $3.08/cwt from Lincoln to $6.18 from Kansas City (via Lincoln).

Published rates ranged from $5.19/cwt for Lincoln–study area to $8.74 for the Kansas City–study area haul—higher in every case than costs. The differential was widest for the Kansas City–Lincoln haul where rates were 382 percent of costs and lowest for the Lincoln–study area and the Kansas City–study area segments where rates were 133 percent of costs.

A modest reduction in average costs could be effected, assuming traffic flows were not adversely affected, by reducing the frequency of service over each of the segments (Table 9.5). A reduction in service from five days to three days per week over the Omaha to study area route would reduce costs by $0.21/cwt (7 percent), while cutting service from Kansas City to Lincoln from five days to three to four days per week would save $0.26/cwt (11 percent). Reducing service from Lincoln to the study area from five days per week to only two days would save $0.17 (4 percent).

Consolidation of private traffic with that moving by common carrier would increase traffic density sufficiently to restore minimum-cost service to levels existing under the present system except for the Omaha–study area where least-cost service would be effected by three rather than five trips per week (Table 11.1). Such consolidation of traffic reduced costs for the Omaha–study area haul by $0.57/cwt (19 percent) if service were also reduced, and by $0.38/cwt (12 percent), if existing service levels were maintained. Consolidation yielded relatively large benefits for the other segments: $0.50/cwt (22 percent) for Kansas City–Lincoln, $1.92 (49 percent) for Lincoln–study area and $2.42 (39 percent) for Kansas City–study area, all of the latter at original service levels.

Consolidation of private and common carrier traffic would improve carriers' load factors and yield significant cost savings, even at current service levels. There is potential, however, for further savings from a relaxation of regulatory restrictions. Temporal rate variability might reduce seasonal fluctuations in traffic. The ability to enlarge the geographic scope of carrier operating authorities might improve load factors and perhaps increase frequency of service as well. Finally, backhauls for general freight carriers might be increased substantially if shipments of agricultural products could be coordinated with inbound freight deliveries.

The potential for effecting such savings was not measured in the present study, although it was possible to calculate costs for conditions under which private and common carrier shipments were consolidated and where underutilized resources were assumed to shift to other markets. Such adjustments would yield cost savings, as compared with the present regulated system, ranging from $0.50/cwt (22 percent) for the Kansas City to Lincoln segment to $2.14 (55 percent) for the Lincoln to study area haul and $2.53 (41 percent) for Kansas City to Study Area.

Implications

Results of the case study suggest that costs of general freight transportation service to a small, rural, and geographically remote area in southeastern Nebraska might be reduced substantially if local commercial traffic now shipped privately were combined with common carrier traffic. Cost savings ranging from 12 to 49 percent, depending on the origin of the shipments, are possible without reductions in service. Additional savings of as much as 10 percent would result if carriers were able to shift seasonally underutilized resources to other markets. Further savings might accrue from coordinating backhauls of agricultural products with inshipments of general freight and from enlargement or rationalization of route territories. Neither of these latter possibilities was examined in the present study.

Although average load factors for carriers operating in the area generally ranged from 50 to 60 percent on forward hauls and from zero to 34 percent on backhauls, traffic over each of the routes by which the community was served was profitable. Accrual of monopoly profits to carriers serving this low-density area casts doubt on the contention that rural shippers are the beneficiaries of cross-subsidization. Rates exceeding full costs by 33 to 282 percent for service to an area chosen for its likelihood of not being able to provide remunerative traffic suggest that attracting carrier service to such areas in a deregulated market environment should be no problem.

CHAPTER 10

Entry Regulation: The Nebraska Experience

The constitutional basis of motor carrier regulation in Nebraska stems from a 1906 amendment creating an elective railway commission whose authority "shall include the regulation of rates, service, and general control of common carriers."[1] While the commission proceeded to establish a motor carrier freight classification system and a rate schedule for intrastate truck transportation as early as 1919,[2] it refrained from exercising control over entry into common carrier trucking until after the passage of the Nebraska Motor Carrier Act of 1937.[3]

Patterned after the federal Motor Carrier Act of 1935, the Nebraska legislation of 1937 made it unlawful for a common carrier to operate without a certificate of convenience and necessity and for a contract carrier to operate without a permit. The sole power to grant, amend, deny, and revoke was vested in the Nebraska Railway Commission, subsequently retitled the Nebraska Public Service Commission (NPSC).[4]

Applicants seeking authority to operate either as common or as contract carriers had to demonstrate that they were fit, willing, and able to perform properly the proposed services. Should the applications involve new or extended common carrier operations, the proponents had to demonstrate that such services were required by "present or future

By John Richard Felton and Ray C. Huttsell, Jr.

public convenience and necessity."[5] The Nebraska Supreme Court has ruled that such a demonstration includes the following two elements:

> In determining the issue of public convenience and necessity, the controlling questions are whether an operation will service a useful purpose responsive to a public demand or need; whether this purpose can or will be served by applicant in a specified operation without endangering or impairing the operations of existing carriers contrary to the public interest.[6]

Applications for contract carriage need not meet the exacting standards confronting proposals for common carriage. As set forth in the act, a permit will be issued if the proposed operations are "consistent with the public interest."[7]

Certificates and permits must contain specific descriptions of the services authorized. Each certificate must designate points of origin and destination, routes, types of commodities, nature of route (regular or irregular), terminals, and intermediate and off-route points. Permits must describe the nature and scope of the carriers' operations.

Once a certificate or permit has been issued, it may not be transferred without the approval of the NPSC. Such approval presupposes a commission finding that the transaction is consonant with the public interest and does not unduly restrict competition. If the operations subject to the proposed transfer have become "dormant," the transaction will become subject to the more rigorous standard of satisfying the public convenience and necessity.

Judicial and Administrative Interpretations

The NPSC has original jurisdiction and sole power over the award of certificates and permits. The Nebraska Supreme Court will not declare an order of the commission to be unreasonably arbitrary where there is evidence to sustain the commission's findings.[8] Despite the limited grounds for intervention, the court's decisions have played a major role in the development of the regulatory environment in Nebraska.

The environment the court has sought to foster in the trucking industry is best described as "regulated competition." The court has reasoned that too many motor carriers in a given market would inevitably lead to destructive competitive practices and the formation of monopoly. On the other hand, the court's logic has seemed to imply that too few competitors, even in a regulated market, would lead to many of the same abuses associated with unregulated monopoly.

Even prior to the passage of the Nebraska Motor Carrier Act of 1937, the court tended to identify the public interest with sufficient restraints on competition to protect the investment of established carriers. As the court declared in a case involving seven applicants for certificates to engage in taxicab operations in Omaha:

> The object in requiring such certificates is not only to protect those already occupying the field in their investment, but to protect the public as well. Unreasonable and unwarranted competition might be carried to the extent that it would not only injure and jeopardize the property of those operating the utilities, but it might even result in destroying them. Such a result might be disastrous to the interests of the public.[9]

The court's interpretation of the purpose of regulatory control, as expressed in the early cases involving taxicabs and buses,[10] was subsequently extended to trucks. In reviewing a decision of the commission in the *Canada* case, the court could not have made a more explicit identification of the interests of existing carriers with the interests of the public:

> The question of the adequacy of services of existing carriers is implicit in the issue of whether or not convenience and necessity demand the service of an additional carrier in the field. Obviously the existence of an adequate and satisfactory service by motor carriers already in the area is complete negation of a public need and demand for added service by another carrier.[11]

Some erosion of this equation of the interests of existing carriers and the public occurred in a case involving a commission grant of authority for an applicant to transport mobile homes over irregular routes throughout most of the state. In response to established carriers contending that the *Canada* rule would preclude entry as long as existing service was satisfactory, the court declared:

> Applying this evidentiary conclusion to applications for irregular route authority on a statewide basis would mean, once a certificate of public convenience and necessity had been issued granting such authority to a holder capable of and willing to satisfactorily serve the entire state, he would have an absolute right thereto and the commission would be without authority to grant such author-

ity to any other applicant. We do not think that was the intent
and purpose of the Motor Carrier Act.[12]

The court's rejection of the proposition that the protection of established carriers from competition was absolute, provided that service
was adequate, was an outgrowth of a realization that trucking was not a
"natural monopoly." In 1957 the court declared that the transportation
of drilling equipment over irregular routes did not exhibit "monopolistic
characteristics that are generally recognized in the regulation of . . .
public utilities."[13]

Rejection of the "natural monopoly" theory of trucking regulation
was by no means tantamount to the embracement of unlimited competition. Rather, emphasis shifted from an economic rationale to a legal one,
the protection of the property rights represented by operating authorities. While at one time the court maintained that a certificate of convenience and necessity "is not property in any legal or constitutional
sense,"[14] it subsequently held that it did not follow from this "that the
certificate holder does not have property rights flowing from the certificate while it is in force and effect."[15] A fair interpretation of the court's
change of heart on the nature of operating authorities is that regulation
had continued sufficiently long pursuant to an erroneous economic
theory to transform a mere privilege into a substantial right!

The court did, however, circumscribe its concern for the rights of
existing carriers with an equally important concern for the public
welfare. Black Hills Stage Lines sought to conduct service along a route
a portion of which, according to the court, was adequately served by
existing carriers. Despite its conclusion that the entry of Black Hills
would impair operations of existing carriers, the court upheld the grant
because it was convinced that Black Hills could not operate profitably
unless it served the proposed route in its entirety. As the court saw it, the
Motor Carrier Act "contemplates that the railway commission shall
weigh the need for the new service and the detriment accruing to existing
carriers, and determine which is more consistent with the public interest."[16]

With its decision in the *Black Hills* case, the Nebraska Supreme
Court ceased erecting virtually insurmountable barriers to the entry of
potential competitors. The court's interpretation of public convenience
and necessity had come to mean striking a balance between the opposing
interests of established carriers and potential entrants and the interests
of the public in the provision of transportation services believed to be
essential.[17] Nevertheless, the high court has never abandoned the notion

that established carriers are entitled to some considerable protection from potential entrants.

Lest the court's decision in the *Black Hills* case be interpreted as embodying a greater relaxation of entry controls than has occurred, it must be emphasized that absent any "inadequacy" in existing service, no balancing of the interests of existing carriers with those of the public is required. Thus minor complaints and even strong preferences for the service to be rendered by an applicant do not render existing service inadequate.[18] Even if the existing carrier has a monopoly with respect to the service available to a customer, a demonstrable deficiency in the present service is the sine qua non of certification.[19]

Perhaps the most frequent type of application made to the NPSC is for the transfer of existing operating rights rather than the approval of new or extended ones. The parties involved in a transfer of operating rights must merely demonstrate that the proposed transaction is consistent with the public interest and will not unduly restrict competition. If the present holder of the rights has discontinued any of the authorized service involved in the proposed transfer, the applicant must then meet the more rigorous standard of present or future public convenience and necessity. Unauthorized discontinuance is referred to as "dormancy" and may occur either as a result of willful abandonment or an absence of demand for the existing operator's services.

Since nearly all transfers are aimed at revitalization of unused or underutilized operating rights, the question of dormancy arises in almost every transfer proceeding. A favorite technique of the commission has been to forestall the entry of an aggressive competitor into a lucrative market by revoking the transferor's certificate. Revocations in these cases have usually been based on findings of willful dormancy.[20]

Whereas public convenience and necessity is the principal legal entry barrier confronting common carrier aspirants, an applicant for a permit to operate as a contract carrier is essentially confronted with two principal barriers. First, proposed contract operations must be consistent with the public interest, and the applicant must assume the burden of proof. Second, the permits must be designed to meet the distinct needs of each individual shipper or class of shipper, and the commission is not bound to accept the applicant's characterization of its proposal.

While the court has declared that the public interest standard is a less rigorous one than public convenience and necessity, in practice it has promulgated a nearly identical set of criteria for the two grants. Thus the public interest standard involves "weighing" the needs of shippers for specialized service against the adequacy of existing service and "balancing" the impact of a grant on established common carriers against the effect on shippers occasioned by a denial of the proposal.

Contract carriers are also required to demonstrate that their operations are somehow more specialized than those provided by common carriers. Whatever else may be comprehended by the term "specialization," a limited *number* of shippers, rather than merely a limited *class* of shippers, has been held to be an essential feature of contract carriage. Thus the Nebraska Supreme Court overturned an NPSC decision awarding a permit to Midwest Mail to transport documents among financial institutions, in part at least, on the ground that Midwest had failed to limit the scope of its proposal to a specific number of designated shippers.[21]

The major consequence of the foregoing interpretation of the public interest standard and the specialization requirement has been the protection of established common carriers and the suppression of contract carriage. As the court declared in the *Samardick* case, if the operations in an application for a permit can be performed by a common carrier, the need for contract carriage has not been established.[22]

There is little evidence that the passage of the federal Motor Carrier Act of 1980 has exerted any influence upon the NPSC or the Nebraska Supreme Court insofar as entry into the trucking industry is concerned. In a recent application, Petroleum Transport Service, Incorporated, sought to expand its authority for the transportation of fertilizer and ingredients thereof.[23] At the time of the application it already had common carrier authority to transport these products from a single origin in Nebraska over irregular routes to any destination within the state. Petroleum Transport Service proposed an extension to its existing authority to permit it to transport fertilizer products from and to any point in Nebraska.

Shippers testifying before the NPSC declared that the service provided by existing carriers was inadequate during the spring months when the peak demand occurred. At such time equipment was in short supply and shippers experienced refusals of service. The applicant indicated his intent to acquire whatever equipment might be necessary to serve shippers both during peak and off-peak periods.

Ruan and other protestants contended that the entry of Petroleum Transport Service would have an adverse impact on existing carriers' revenues during the remaining three-fourths of the year in which less than half of the annual fertilizer shipments occurred. While the shippers conceded that off-peak demand for equipment was slight, they maintained that future growth in fertilizer use would preclude any diversion of business from existing carriers.

While the NPSC acknowledged that the existing carriers could not meet shipper transport needs during peak periods, it nonetheless held that the proposed service did not meet the standard of public convenience and necessity. Their reason was that the protestants would suffer a loss of business during the slack season and this revenue was necessary to enable them to cover their costs.

The decision of the NPSC was upheld by a unanimous court. In words reminiscent of decisions rendered over the course of several decades, the court declared:

> . . . in determining the issue of public convenience and necessity, controlling questions are whether or not the operation will serve a useful purpose responsive to a public demand or need; whether or not this purpose can or will be served as well by existing carriers; and whether or not it can be served by the applicant in a specified manner without endangering or impairing the operations of existing carriers, contrary to the public interest.[24]

This decision indicates not only that the NPSC and the Nebraska Supreme Court were unaffected by the Motor Carrier Act of 1980, but also that their views had not changed in any fundamental way from the earliest days of truck regulation. If the interests of established trucking companies are paramount, then only the grossest mismanagement and cavalier disregard for public relations on their part are likely to render them vulnerable to authorized new entry. Since effective competition destroys monopoly rents, a policy oriented toward their preservation can, at best, pay only lip service to competition and to the right of the public to "adequate, economical and efficient service by motor carriers," as provided by the Motor Carrier Act of 1937. Thus entry will be permitted only in the interstices of the market where it poses no competitive threat to the entrenched positions of existing firms.

Economic Consequences of Entry Controls

All things considered, Nebraska's attempt to improve the performance of the intrastate trucking industry has proved to be both unnecessary and counterproductive. There is every indication that the industry's performance would be exemplary in the absence of regulation. On the other hand, there is a strong argument to be made that entry controls have actually worsened performance.

Entry regulation has probably elevated both the costs and rates of highway transportation. For example, given the commission's proclivity to remove authorization to haul cement and petroleum products in bulk whenever a certificate is transferred, seller concentration in the transportation of these goods is higher than would exist in an unregulated market. While there is no reason to believe that this policy has impaired technical efficiency, the elimination of intramodal rate competition seems clearly to have had an adverse impact on allocative efficiency in the transportation of these products.

Because of the commission's readiness to limit the origins and destinations of even a successful applicant's operations, the problem of idle truck time in such markets as the distribution of anhydrous ammonia and other liquid and dry fertilizers has probably been intensified. The same argument applies to the movement of mobile homes.

With respect to the transportation of general commodities, concrete conclusions concerning the impact of the state's entry controls are more difficult to make. It is almost certain that the entry barriers erected by the regulators have enhanced concentration, but reliable information pertaining to the number and size distribution of firms in particular markets within Nebraska is not generally available. Although commodity restrictions are not as extensive in Nebraska as have historically prevailed in interstate commerce, route and point restrictions are inherent in the classification of regular route carriers, and area restrictions are explicit in the authorities held by most irregular route carriers. Measures of the extent to which these restrictions have decreased average loads and contributed to circuitous travel have not been attempted, but it is unlikely that the impact upon capacity utilization has been marginal. Despite the scarcity of detailed information relating to Nebraska, it is fairly certain that the total effect of regulation has been to increase highway carrier rates. Comparisons between regulated and exempt carriage in interstate commerce and among regulating and nonregulating provinces in Canada suggest that the rate-increasing effect is not negligible.

The passage of the federal Motor Carrier Act of 1980 may create some additional allocative inefficiencies within the state and generate additional pressures for regulatory reform. If regulation of interstate trucking prior to 1980 did increase the level of interstate rates to the extent suggested in Chapter 4, and if the Motor Carrier Act of 1980 has increased efficiency in interstate truck transport as will be indicated in

Chapter 11, shippers located outside the borders of Nebraska but making sales within the state will be the recipients of a regulation-induced advantage over their in-state Nebraska competitors. It will be increasingly difficult for the Nebraska legislature and the NPSC to reconcile the public interest with a truck entry policy that burdens Nebraska shippers with higher transport costs than their out-of-state competitors and impedes the growth of the Nebraska economy.

While a continuation of present Nebraska policy on the approval of applications for new or extended operating authority may divert traffic from existing intrastate to interstate carriers, a competitively oriented entry policy may somewhat paradoxically occasion no such effect on established carriers. The high price and income elasticity of demand for for-hire trucking as discussed in Chapter 3, makes the entry of new firms entirely consistent with stable or even increased traffic volume for existing carriers.

A major reason for the high price elasticity of demand for common and contract carriage is that shippers will tend to abandon private carriage when for-hire transport is efficient and of high quality. Thus an efficiency-induced reduction in truck rates tends to result in a more than proportional increase in truck volume.

A major reason for the high income elasticity of demand is that economic growth is typically associated with an increase in the ratio of high-value to low-value commodities. Such a tendency is beneficial to the trucking industry relative to the railroad industry since the higher the value of the commodity transported the more important are the lower inventory costs associated with truck transport.

Potential for Relaxation of Entry Controls

As noted previously, applicants for new or extended operations as a common carrier must demonstrate that the proposal is required by the "present or future public convenience and necessity," while similar applications for contract carriage presuppose that operations will be "consistent with the public interest."[25] The proposition that the public convenience, necessity, and interest are inextricably associated with the financial viability of existing carriers is based not upon statute, however, but on case law and administrative decisions. Nothing but their own precedents would appear to prevent the NPSC and the Nebraska Supreme Court from reinterpreting the Nebraska statute so as to establish the presumption that competition is consonant with the public welfare.

The adoption of such a presumption would render any gains to shippers in the form of reduced rates or improvements in the frequency, reliability, and flexibility of service compelling evidence of public advantage, while testimony on diversion of business from established firms, without more, would be irrelevant. In the process, the burden of proof would shift to protestants, who would have to demonstrate that competition, in the particular circumstances, would somehow lessen public welfare. In view of the inherently competitive character of the trucking industry and the beneficial performance characteristics associated therewith, protestants' task would not be easy. Nevertheless, some regulation of entry could be justified in at least two circumstances: (1) to protect shippers from misrepresentation and discrimination and (2) to safeguard the public at large from bearing the burden of unsafe truck operations and accelerated highway wear.

When shippers are very small, numerous, and unsophisticated and make infrequent use of truck service, they are susceptible to misrepresentation and discrimination. The shippers most likely to exhibit these characteristics are persons utilizing household goods carriers. It is not surprising, therefore, that Beilock and Freeman, in their survey of Florida shippers and carriers, found household goods carriers to be far more favorable to deregulation than were the carriers of other goods (55 percent to 30 percent).[26] Moreover, a smaller percentage of household goods carriers reported increased competition (71 percent to 84 percent), and a larger percentage charged higher rates (65 percent to 24 percent) and enjoyed increased profits (39 percent to 25 percent) after deregulation.[27] Protestants might legitimately object to the award of operating authority to a firm that had acquired a well-deserved reputation for chicanery in its dealings with its customers.

A second acceptable ground for protest against the granting of operating authority would be that the applicant had a history of violating safety and/or weight regulations. The prevention of such negative externalities is in the public interest, and a protestant who abides by the law can appropriately maintain that the public welfare will be furthered by competition based on the social costs of rendering the service.

Inasmuch as the Nebraska Supreme Court has in the past identified so closely the interest of the public with the private interest of existing carriers, some question may arise as to the willingness of the court to embrace the presumption that competition will enhance the welfare of the public. It might well depend upon the care with which the commission compiled evidence to support such a "revolutionary" doctrine that in a private enterprise economy competition is generally deemed conducive to the public welfare. As the court has itself recently reaffirmed:

> The issue of public convenience and necessity is ordinarily one of fact, and where there is evidence in the record to sustain the Public Service Commission's order, this court cannot say that it is unreasonable and arbitrary. The determination of what is consistent with the public interest, or public convenience and necessity, is one that is peculiarly for the determination of the Public Service Commission. If there is evidence to sustain the finding of the commission, this court cannot intervene.[28]

Admittedly, should the court persist in its historic interpretation of the public interest, despite the best efforts of the commission to effect an administrative change, then statutory redefinition of the appropriate criteria for the award of new or extended operating authority would be in order. Experience in other states would suggest that any transformation in regulatory policy on entry into the trucking industry is much more likely to come from the courts or the legislature than the state commission.

A recent example of state judicial support for identification of the public interest with competition was expressed by the Missouri Court of Appeals for the Western District in its reversal of a Missouri Public Service Commission rejection of an application by the Gulf Transport Company:

> . . . the motor carrier industry is characterized by comparatively low fixed costs and capital investment requirements which serve as high entry barriers to new competition in natural monopoly industries (such as electrical power, communications, water and natural gas). The absence of these barriers to entry in the motor carrier industry reduces significantly the possibility of monopoly pricing because attempts to engage in such pricing attract new competition. Competition benefits the carrier-using public, because it forces prices closer to cost, and creates incentives to provide the service desired by consumers. The decisional law of our state and other jurisdictions makes competition an integral part of evaluating the need for additional service in the motor carrier context. The overriding consideration has been and remains the convenience of the public and not any individual or group of individuals.[29]

State legislatures, however, are more likely to be the agents of regulatory reform than are either courts or commissions. Three states, Arizona, Maine, and Florida, have deregulated the trucking industry completely in the wake of the Motor Carrier Act of 1980 and the legislatures of Idaho, Kansas, New Mexico, and South Dakota have all relaxed truck regulation to some greater or lesser extent since 1980.[30] Only in California does it appear that the commission took the initiative to ease regulation, an initiative subsequently validated by the California legislature.[31]

Inasmuch as the NPSC is a constitutionally authorized agency, the issue arises as to the limits of administrative and legislative discretion in the relaxation of entry barriers. As noted previously, the Nebraska constitution confers no specific control over entry upon the NPSC; prior to the passage of the Motor Carrier Act of 1937, the commission explicitly rejected the proposition that the constitution, as supplemented by the Motor Bus Law of 1927, conferred authority upon it to restrict entry through the issuance of certificates of convenience and necessity.[32] Should the legislature wish to curtail the power of the commission to deny entrance to for-hire carriage because of possible injury to existing carriers, the constitution should constitute no bar to such action.

Conclusions

While Nebraska law has never been interpreted to constitute so extensive a protection to the property rights of existing carriers as to forestall entry altogether, the expressed willingness of an applicant to provide more varied or frequent service or to provide the same service at lower rates has not generally been deemed to be in the public interest. Stability in certificate values and in traffic allocation has been regarded by both the court and the commission to be preferable to aggressive competition in rates and dynamic innovation in service.

Despite this preference for a quiescent trucking industry, it is possible that the changes taking place in interstate trucking will in due course exert sufficient impact upon the Nebraska economy to induce change at the legislative and administrative level. The court, on the other hand, may give weight to decisions rendered in other jurisdictions. The legislature and the commission, more responsive to the interests of their constituents, may react to complaints of domestic shippers that they are losing business to out-of-state shippers being served by lower-cost carriers. At that point, the public policy recommendations of academic economists may provide a convenient rationale for a far more relaxed policy of entry into the trucking industry in Nebraska.

CHAPTER 11

Motor Carrier Act of 1980: An Assessment

While the Motor Carrier Act of 1980[1] may not have deregulated the trucking industry, it certainly validated the relaxation of controls that had been pursued administratively in 1978 and 1979, and it provided a statutory foundation for the continuation of that trend. Specifically, it eased the criteria for common carrier certification; imposed a "fitness only" criterion for certain kinds of transportation; curtailed the ability of existing carriers to protest entry; required broadening of existing certificates containing overly restrictive provisions on commodities transported, points served, or routes traversed; extended the agricultural commodity exemption to include feed, seeds, and plants used in agricultural production; defined private carriage to include intercorporate for-hire transportation among wholly owned subsidiaries; permitted a motor carrier to operate both as a common and contract carrier; established a "zone of reasonableness" within which carriers were empowered to adjust rates free from commission investigation or suspension on grounds of unreasonableness; narrowed the scope of the exemption from antitrust laws enjoyed by rate bureaus; permitted the concurrent transportation of regulated and exempt commodities; increased the amount of regulated commodities a cooperative association might transport as a backhaul; and instructed the commission to simplify proce-

---

By John Richard Felton.

dures and comply with deadlines for accomplishing various regulatory tasks.

This chapter seeks both to assess the extent to which the Motor Carrier Act (MCA) of 1980 deregulated the trucking industry and to identify the areas in which the act has fallen short of deregulation. While it may not be possible to measure precisely the residue of regulation in the industry, some indication of the present position of trucking in the regulated-deregulated spectrum may be feasible.

Regulatory Reform

The major areas in which the MCA of 1980 has reduced the stringency of trucking regulation were noted above. A review of the principal changes initiated by law and commission rule making or decision in individual cases is appropriate.

ENTRY CRITERIA. For more than forty years the ICC held that even though an applicant for new or additional operating authority could demonstrate a public "need" for such operations, if this need could be fulfilled by carriers currently holding such authority, or if the entrant would divert revenue from the existing carriers to any appreciable extent, public convenience and necessity would not be promoted by such an award.[2] As Siegel[3] has noted, however, the commission eased these requirements in the years immediately preceding the MCA of 1980 by holding that the existence of "adequate" service was not a conclusive bar to new entry[4] and that the harm to existing carriers had to be balanced against the prospective public benefits of increased competition.[5]

The 1980 act provided a firmer statutory foundation for the commission's more liberal entry policy.[6] While an applicant must demonstrate his fitness to provide the proposed service and submit evidence as to its usefulness, "diversion of revenue or traffic from an existing carrier [was not] in and of itself inconsistent with the public convenience and necessity."[7] No longer need the commission balance carrier injury with public benefit. As the commission declared in an early case after the passage of the MCA of 1980:

> Confronting the protestant with more vigorous competition—indeed even competition which forces an existing carrier out of business—does not automatically cause harm to any as-

pect of the public interest. Congress, after all, requires us to foster efficiency in motor carrier transportation and there may well be situations in which, considering the transportation industry as a whole, it is preferable to replace an inefficient operator with a more efficient one and promote the introduction of innovative services and prices.[8]

In December 1980 the commission promulgated its policies that henceforth were to guide its grants of authority to for-hire carriers:

Under the new entry procedures, the applicant must still come forward with some information demonstrating the utility of its proposed service. Once that is established, however minimal applicant's case may be, the statute creates a presumption in favor of entry and competition, and we can deny the application (in whole or in part) only where the opponents can persuasively demonstrate that a grant would be inconsistent with the public convenience and necessity. To arrive at that conclusion, we must find that there is a demonstrated public harm which outweighs the benefits which are presumed to flow from a grant of authority.[9]

Despite the generally depressed economy in the period immediately following the passage of the MCA of 1980, there was an unprecedented outpouring of applications. In 1976, prior to the initial easing of entry constraints, there were 6,746 requests for new and expanded permanent operating rights, of which the commission approved 70 percent; in 1981 there were 28,414, of which the commission approved 97 percent.[10]

In the first twenty-three months after the act was adopted, the commission approved more than 43,000 requests for operating authority. While, as Breen has noted, most of these requests involved existing carriers, almost 8,000 covered carriers not previously certificated by the ICC.[11]

The combination of more applications and higher approval rates has increased greatly the number of carriers subject to ICC jurisdiction. After hovering in the 15,000 to 17,000 range for many years, the number of ICC-regulated carriers increased very rapidly in the last few years (see Table 11.1). The expansion has occurred primarily in the smallest size class, with negligible changes in the number of Class I carriers. With scale economies so inconsequential in the industry, this is not an unanticipated consequence of easier entry.

Table 11.1. Motor Carriers of Freight Reporting to the ICC, FY 1978–FY 1983

Carrier Class	Number of Carriers, Year Ending September 30					
	1978	1979	1980	1981	1982	1983
Class I, subject to uniform accounts	1,045	992	947	1,031	1,144	1,139
Class II, subject to uniform accounts	2,929	2,754	2,164	2,293	2,139	1,631
Class I and II, not subject to uniform accounts	None	1,129	324	383	380	336
Class III	12,900	13,337	14,610	18,563	22,059	24,111
Total	16,874	18,212	18,045	22,270	25,722	27,517

Source: *Annual Report of the Interstate Commerce Commission* (various years).

SCOPE OF OPERATING AUTHORITY. Relaxation of entry barriers relates not merely to the admission of new firms into the industry but also to the scope of the authority granted both new and existing firms. Thus the MCA of 1980 required the commission to eliminate gateway restrictions and other limitations that would impose circuitous routes upon carriers. It also charged the commission with the obligation of broadening commodity, intermediate point, backhaul, and territorial restrictions.[12] The commission then proceeded to promulgate rules to effectuate these congressional mandates.[13]

The greatly enhanced authority with respect to commodities, routes, service points, and directions tended to transform highly segmented transport markets into ones in which the inherent ability of carriers to transfer their principal assets, that is, trucks, among different commodities and locations could be much more readily realized. Thus the carriers currently engaged in transporting a particular commodity between points A and B at any given time are no longer synonymous with supply in view of the ease with which carriers can shift trucks from one product or location to another in response to seasonal and secular trends in demand.

Breen has contended that entry restrictions have been mitigated to such an extent since 1980 that the market for intercity highway freight transport should be regarded as national in scope:

> With regulatory reform . . . the city-pair approach to market definition is no longer useful. . . . It seems most useful to think in terms of a national market for trucking, and given that definition, one must conclude that individual carriers lack market power. . . . The four-firm and eight-firm ratios, for ex-

ample, are estimated to be 13.89 percent and 20.8 percent, respectively, for 1980, and the market share of the largest firm, Roadway Express, was only 4.7 percent[14]

In view of the ease with which both entry and exit can be effected in the trucking industry—"contestability," as Baumol, Panzar, and Willig have termed it,[15]—an even greater concentration of the national market would appear to be consistent with a competitive outcome. Bailey and Baumol in a recent article declare that "with the possible exception of barge transportation, trucking should be perhaps the most contestable of the economy's industries" and that recent studies "illustrate an important feature of contestable markets: if left alone, contestable markets will tend to move toward the most efficient organization of productive forces."[16]

OWNER-OPERATORS. In addition to the general relaxation of entry barriers, the MCA of 1980 contained a provision specifically designed to assist owner-operators. Food products and agricultural soil conditioners and fertilizers could henceforth be transported by such carriers without a demonstration of public convenience and necessity, provided that the operator meets the "fitness" test and that the carrier's annual tonnage of such commodities not exceed the tonnage transported pursuant to the agricultural exemption.

In a 1982 hearing before the Senate Subcommittee on Surface Transportation, ICC chairman Reese H. Taylor, Jr., expressed some disappointment that owner-operators had not responded in greater number to the opportunities provided by the act to obtain certificates. While there were some 300,000 owner-operators in the industry at the time the MCA of 1980 went into effect,[17] the commission had issued certificates to only 14,000 new carriers in the two and one-half years following its passage.[18] He attributed the limited response of owner-operators to their lack of information on application procedures, misperceptions as to the cost of acquiring a certificate, and difficulty in obtaining insurance because of the small size of operations.[19]

Another possible explanation of the failure of owner-operators to seek their own authority is that the terms of the agreement whereby owner-operators transport commodities pursuant to the authority of certificated carriers may well have become more favorable to the former. In early 1978 owner-operators were generally offered between 65 percent and 70 percent of gross revenues if the owner-operator provided only the tractor and 75 percent to 80 percent if he provided a tractor-trailer combination.[20] A review of *Transport Topics* advertisements by certificated carriers for owner-operators during the period May 16, 1983, through May 14, 1984, revealed only four in which the percentage of gross revenues to be paid the operator was announced: two paid the more-or-less standard 75 percent to operators who provided their own tractor-trailer combinations, one offered 85 percent to 89 percent under the same circumstances, and the fourth paid 69 percent without trailer plus reimbursement for fuel.[21] More important, perhaps, is the tendency for certificated carriers to attract operators by other benefits such as payment for empty mileage and group insurance.

Despite some apparent improvement in the terms in the agreements owner-operators are negotiating with certificated carriers, there appears to have been a precipitous decline in the number of such operators, from approximately 300,000 at the time of the passage of the MCA of 1980 to perhaps 100,000 today.[22] There is some obvious discrepancy between the exodus from the owner-operator ranks, on the one hand, and new certifications by the ICC, on the other. Whether this difference is to be explained by the exit of owner-operators from the industry or an increase in illegal for-hire transport is not known. ICC Chairman Taylor, however, declared that the MCA of 1980 "did not, as some have been erroneously led to believe, totally deregulate the industry" and that "we will certainly do our best to cope with the current high level of unlawful transportation activities."[23]

A potentially more beneficial change in regulatory policy insofar as owner-operators are concerned occurred when the ICC decided to reverse the policy theretofore precluding "owner-operators and others not holding operating authority from the Commission from leasing their equipment with drivers directly to private carriers."[24] To qualify as "private" transportation, notwithstanding the payment of compensation by the private carrier to the owner-operator, the lease agreement needed to establish that "the lessor holds out only the use of the instrumentalities of transportation, i.e., truck and driver [rather than] what is in substance a complete transportation service for compensation."[25] To meet this requirement, the owner-operator had to commit the equipment exclusively to a particular private carrier for at least thirty days, and the latter had to secure public liability insurance, assume the costs of complying with safety regulations, accept the risk of loss or damage to cargo, and in general exercise control over the transportation operation.[26]

Until very recently the ICC's "single-source" leasing policy, as it came to be known, had little practical impact because of an injunction against its implementation, pending judicial resolution. That came on

April 2, 1984, when the Supreme Court declined to hear an appeal from the Eleventh Circuit Court of Appeals, which had ruled in favor of the ICC.[27]

PRIVATE CARRIERS. In addition to the efficiencies that might be associated with the leasing of equipment and drivers by private carriers, better utilization of private carrier equipment was furthered through a provision of the MCA of 1980 to exempt intercorporate transportation for compensation where the participants were members of a corporate system in which "the parent corporation owns directly or indirectly a 100 percent interest in each of the subsidiaries."[28] This exemption was subsequently interpreted to exclude subsidiaries that were themselves for-hire trucking companies: *"No corporation engaged primarily in operations as a for-hire carrier may use an affiliate operating under the* [private carrier] *exemption. . . . for movement of freight tendered to it in its capacity as a carrier."*[29]

The exemption associated with intercorporate hauling seems to have been applied to a large number of corporations maintaining their own fleet of trucks. A survey conducted jointly by A. T. Kearney and the Private Truck Council found that approximately "45 percent [of the respondents] were . . . participating in intercorporate hauling last year [1983], matching the year earlier survey."[30]

A decision of the ICC, which promises ultimately to be of more far reaching importance in the enhancement of efficient truck utilization by private carriers, declared its willingness to entertain applications from such carriers to engage in for-hire transportation as an adjunct to private carriage. The rule adopted by the commission included the following proviso:

> The Commission's present policy is that motor carrier operating authority will be granted to an applicant who intends to use it primarily in an incident to the carriage of its own goods and its own transportation-business, provided (1) that the standard criteria for motor common or contract carrier applications, as the case may be, are met, and (2) that the applicant is agreeable to the imposition of conditions requiring it to conduct its for-hire motor carrier activities and its other activities independently and to maintain separate records for each."[31]

The survey of private carriers, alluded to previously in this section, also included a response to whether the carrier had received a grant of operating authority from the ICC: "Nineteen percent . . . stated that they had received authority, up 11 percent from 1982."[32] It may, of course, be some time before private carriers will be able to exploit fully the opportunities for combining self and for-hire transport.

CONTRACT CARRIERS. Historically, contract carriers have been less extensively regulated than have common carriers.[33] While a contract carrier was subject to the same fitness requirements as a common carrier, it had merely to establish that its proposed operation was consonant with public interest rather than required by public convenience and necessity. This meant that the presence of adequate service by existing carriers did not preclude the issuance of a permit to an applicant for contract carriage.

Perhaps the most important change in contract carriage wrought by the MCA of 1980 was that "the Commission may not require such carrier to limit its operations to carriage for a particular industry or within a particular geographic area."[34] A provision of almost equal significance was the elimination of the prohibition against a carrier's holding common and contract authority simultaneously. Finally, the act deleted the requirement, which had been a part of the Interstate Commerce Act since 1957, that in deciding whether to issue a permit, "the Commission shall consider the number of shippers to be served by the applicant."[35]

ZONE OF RATE FREEDOM. The MCA of 1980 sought to relax rate regulation by creating a zone within which the commission could "not investigate, suspend, revise, or revoke any rate proposed by a motor common carrier . . . on the grounds that such rate is unreasonable."[36] Initially, the zone of rate freedom was to be 10 percent above or below the rate in effect one year prior to any change. After two years, however, the magnitude of the allowed increase or decrease was to be determined by the percentage change in the Producers Price Index. Finally, the commission might, if it found competition to be sufficiently effective, add as much as an additional 5 percent to the foregoing percentages.

ICC Chairman Taylor has offered the following assessment of the consequences of greater carrier rate-making freedom:

> Since passage of the Motor Carrier Act, there has been greater pricing innovation . . . total motor carrier filings have increased substantially: from 427,043 in fiscal year 1980 [just prior to the passage of the Act]; to 512,184 in fiscal year 1981; to

725,864 in fiscal year 1982. This represents a 42 percent increase in the number of tariff filings over the last fiscal year.

The vast majority of the filings are rate reductions. Volume discounts, multiple shipment discounts, shipper allowances, and aggregate tender discounts are among the new price options being offered by carriers . . . while some of the rate reductions may be due to economic conditions, it is clear that the Act has had a substantial pre-competitive [sic] effect.[37]

The record of common and contract carrier freight tariffs and schedules received, criticized, and rejected during fiscal years 1978 through 1983 is set forth in Table 11.2. Clearly the total number of filings has increased in the three fiscal years since the passage of the act while the percentage of criticized or rejected tariff changes has remained small. The number of investigations and suspensions, on the other hand, has fallen drastically, from 320 in FY 1978 to 11 in FY 1983[38] The zone of rate freedom established by the MCA of 1980 is, presumably, a major factor in this decline.

RATE BUREAUS. In one respect, regulatory reform cannot be equated with relaxation of federal control. The price for increased carrier freedom in ratemaking was some curtailment of rate bureau activity. Henceforth, such organizations were foreclosed from discussing or voting on rates falling within the zone of rate freedom. Bureau consideration of single-line rates was prohibited after 1984, but, subject to certain restrictions, general rate increases or decreases might still be agreed upon by the concerted action of bureau members.[39]

This section also established an ad hoc Motor Carrier Ratemaking Study Commission to assess the desirability of perpetuating the antitrust immunity rate bureaus had enjoyed since the passage of the Reed-Bulwinkle Act of 1948. In the performance of this task, the study commission was to ascertain the probable effect of the loss of such immunity on rate levels and rate structures, with special attention to the impact on small communities and isolated areas.

The study commission's report declared that collective ratemaking tended to raise rates for several reasons: (1) it reduced carrier incentives to resist wage increases because of the greater ease of passing them on to shippers through general rate increases, and (2) it provided an umbrella for high-cost carriers through reliance on historical costs as the basis for rate increases.[40] The commission also maintained that it was both feasi-

Table 11.2. *Freight Tariff and Schedule Filings and Dispositions, FY 1978–1983*

Year	Filings and Dispositions	Common		Kind of Carrier Contract		All	
		Number	Percent of Receipts	Number	Percent of Receipts	Number	Percent of Receipts
1978	Received	255,790	100.0	23,039	100.0	278,829	100.0
	Criticized	4,355	1.7	774	3.4	5,129	1.8
	Rejected	1,851	0.7	330	1.4	2,181	0.8
1979	Received	403,146	100.0	44,420	100.0	447,566	100.0
	Criticized	4,250	1.1	788	1.8	5,038	1.1
	Rejected	2,152	0.5	292	0.7	2,444	0.5
1980	Received	393,149	100.0	5,468	100.0	398,617	100.0
	Criticized	3,172	0.8	54	1.0	3,266	0.8
	Rejected	2,488	0.6	36	0.7	2,524	0.6
1981	Received	467,373	100.0	44,816	100.0	512,189	100.0
	Criticized	2,307	0.5	401	0.9	2,708	0.5
	Rejected	3,938	0.8	745	1.7	4,683	0.9
1982	Received	673,156	100.0	6,262	100.0	679,418	100.0
	Criticized	3,912	0.6	41	0.7	3,953	0.6
	Rejected	7,619	1.1	68	1.1	7,687	1.1
1983	Received	980,098	100.0	76,000	100.0	1,056,108	100.0
	Criticized	2,402	0.3	48	0.1	2,510	0.2
	Rejected	4,418	0.5	71	0.1	4,489	0.4

Source: *Annual Report of the Interstate Commerce Commission* (various years).

ble and desirable to continue collective commodity classification procedures while eliminating collective rate making:

> Classification can facilitate competition by helping carriers establish cost-related rates and by easing the task of rate comparison by shippers. Classification can also reduce transactions costs involved in the pricing of motor common carrier services. Subjecting the current classification process to the antitrust laws would separate the collective behavior which facilitates competition (pure classification) from that which restrains competitive market behavior (ratemaking through classification).[41]

With these considerations in mind, the commission recommended the withdrawal of the antitrust immunity exemption for the trucking industry.[42]

The study commission also endeavored to allay apprehensions that an end to antitrust immunity would jeopardize rate agreements involving interline shipments. As the commission noted: "There is nothing in the Sherman Act which forbids direct competitors from selling to or buying from each other."[43]

While greater ratemaking freedom constituted the rationale for increased restrictions on rate bureau activity, it is the relaxation of entry barriers that has been most important in undermining the monopolistic potential which they previously enjoyed. Prior to the MCA of 1980 the combination of strict control over entry, publication of rates, advance notice of any changes therein, and prohibition against departure from published rates provided a set of circumstances in which even an industry as inherently competitive as trucking could achieve successful cartelization.

While the post-1980 environment may make collective ratemaking largely ineffective in raising rates, there may still be circumstances in which rate bureau activities are not innocuous,[44] and there seems to be no good grounds in principle for immunizing this industry from the application of the antitrust laws. Breen contends that "the welfare gains from successful prosecution of horizontal-restraint cases are likely to be slight, since the costs of reaching and maintaining an effective agreement in the less regulated environment are substantially higher, and therefore the probability of success is substantially lower."[45] This, however, is an argument for the employment of cost-benefit analysis in the administration of the antitrust laws, not the exemption of an industry from their application.

AGRICULTURAL CARRIERS. Several provisions of the MCA of 1980 were designed to reduce restrictions on agricultural carriers. These included broadening the agricultural exemption, permitting mixed loads, and increasing the amount of for-hire traffic in which agricultural cooperatives might engage.

The act added animal feeds and agricultural seeds and plants transported to farms or farm supply businesses to the list of commodities exempt from regulation.[46] While the original agricultural exemption applied to agricultural outputs, the 1980 exemption extended the exemption to some agricultural inputs, as well. As noted above, the act also eased barriers to the transportation of other farm inputs, agricultural soil conditioners and fertilizers, when carried by owner-operators. Henceforth, they need pass only a "fitness" test.

Prior to 1980 the transportation of agricultural and nonagricultural commodities in the same vehicle at the same time nullified the agricultural exemption. The MCA of 1980 permitted trucks to transport both agricultural and nonagricultural commodities in the same load without affecting "the unregulated status of such exempt property or the regulated status of the property which the carrier is authorized to transport."[47]

Pursuant to Public Law 90-433 (1968) agricultural cooperatives might transport agricultural commodities for nonmembers, provided that such carriage was incidental to transportation for members and necessary for the efficient conduct of the latter and provided, further, that the tonnage transported for nonmembers not exceed 15 percent of the total annual tonnage. The MCA of 1980 increased the percentage to 25.[48]

It would not appear that the combined impact of these provisions would be substantial. A USDA study reported that only 6 percent of agricultural feed shipments were interstate and that private carriage accounted for more than three-fourths of such movement. It is not surprising, therefore, that "regulated motor carriers and independent truckers alike indicated that there is no hard evidence that the expanded exemption has had a significant impact."[49]

The ability to transport agricultural and nonagricultural commodities in the same load would seem to be of even lesser consequence. While the possibility of such mixing may provide some "loading flexibility," as Johnson has noted,[50] the circumstances under which the advantageous exercise of this opportunity was feasible might be rare indeed. Such mixing would presuppose not only a common origin and destination, but also the movement of both exempt and regulated commodities in less-than-truckload lots and compatibility of equipment and loads. It is much easier to visualize situations in which one or more of these prerequisites would not be met than situations in which all would be fulfilled.

Hutchinson has commented on the marginal importance of permitting the annual tonnage of commodities for nonmembers of cooperatives to rise from 15 percent to 25 percent of the total:

> In 1975, only 106 of 1,265 farmer cooperative associations surveyed indicated that they were hauling non-member goods under the pre-1980 cooperative exemption. Less than 4 percent of all trips made by these associations involved non-member goods. While certain cooperatives can be expected to use the increased tonnage limitation to expand their market and/or improve operating efficiency, the overall impact does not promise to be large.[51]

If a cooperative found that a backhaul of nonmember commodities was essential to efficient operation, it might be preferable to seek operating authority directly rather than to operate within the limits of the exemption.

Quantitative Assessment of Regulatory Change

If entry regulation restricts the kinds of commodities a carrier may transport and rate regulation its ability to respond to seasonal variations in transport demand, then relaxation of regulation should increase the average load. By the same token, if entry regulation restricts the geographic scope of carrier service, the easing of such limitations should reduce interlining and increase the average length of haul.

Table 11.3 compares the average load and average length of haul in 1976 and 1982 for general and specialized common carriers and contract carriers. Trucking operations during 1976 were unaffected by the administrative deregulation that began to occur in the latter part of the Carter administration. Operations in 1982, on the other hand, were influenced by the two and one-half years under the MCA of 1980, as well as the administrative relaxation of regulation in the years immediately preceding the 1980 legislation.

All carrier types experienced a substantial reduction in interlining and achieved a significant increase in average length of haul. The contribution of reduced interlining to this result can be inferred from Table

Table 11.3. *Average Load and Average Haul of General, Specialized Common, and Contract Carriers, 1976 and 1982*

	Average Load (tons)			Average Haul (miles)		
Kind of Carrier	1976	1982	Percent Change	1976	1982	Percent Change
General freight, common	13.0	12.9	(0.8)	387.9	484.8	25.0
Specialized freight, common	12.7	13.8	8.7	201.6	232.0	15.1
Contract	10.8	11.9	10.2	164.2	220.8	34.5

Sources: *Trinc's Blue Book of the Trucking Industry* (Washington, D.C.: Trinc's Transportation Consultants, 1977) and *1982 Motor Carrier Annual Report* (Washington, D.C.: American Trucking Associations, 1983).

11.4. The percentage reduction in interlining is very substantial for all types of carriers, but the absolute reduction was more important for common carriers of general freight because interlining is far more prevalent for these carriers. It should be emphasized, finally, that, to the extent that regulatory relaxation tended to reduce circuity, the reported increase in average length of haul may understate the improvement in efficiency occasioned by the broadened geographic scope of operating authorities.

The improvement in average load was less marked, and the carriers of general freight experienced a negligible decline. The more meager gains here are probably attributable primarily to 1982 being a period of recession in which total truck ton-miles were actually below those of 1976.[52] In view of the substantial number of new trucking firms entering the industry during this interval, together with the decline in the overall volume of truck traffic, the average loads achieved in 1982 seem impressive, indeed.

Another factor inhibiting improvement in average loads was rate inflexibility, produced by a combination of collective ratemaking, rate publication requirements, and the notice required to effect rate increases and decreases. If the power of rate bureaus is further curtailed, especially among carriers of general freight where it has been most pronounced, this source of inflexibility may diminish. It should also be noted that the ICC has recently decided to shorten drastically the previously required thirty-day notice for rate increases and decreases. As of June 25, 1984, rate increases can be effected on seven workdays' notice and rate decreases after only one.[53]

Another change in the trucking industry that might be predicted as a consequence of the MCA of 1980 is the more rapid growth of contract

Table 11.4. Extent of Interlining by General, Specialized Common, and Contract Carriers, 1976 and 1982

	Interlining						
	1976			1982			
Kind of Carrier	Ave. Tons (thousands)		Multi as a % of Single	Ave. Tons (thousands)		Multi as a % of Single	1982 as a Percent of 1976
	Single	Multi		Single	Multi		
General freight, common	188.4	66.7	35.4	211.2	30.7	14.5	43.8
Specialized freight, common	360.5	10.8	3.0	321.2	4.2	1.3	43.3
Contract	96.5	2.8	2.9	109.6	1.4	1.3	44.8

Sources: *Trinc's Blue Book of the Trucking Industry* (Washington, D.C.: Trinc's Transportation Consultants, 1977) and *Trinc's Blue Book of the Trucking Industry* (McLean, Virginia: Trinc's Transportation Consultants, 1983).

carriers vis à vis their common carrier counterparts. As noted previously, prior to 1980 the ICC tended to restrict rather severely the number of shippers a specialized carrier might serve. Inasmuch as the act deleted the number of shippers served as a criterion of ICC approval of contract carrier permits, a comparison of the change in the average operating revenues of specialized common and contract carriers between 1976 and 1982 should provide some evidence on the validity of this conjecture.

Table 11.5 sets forth the average size of specialized common carriers and contract carriers, as measured by operating revenue, for the years 1976 and 1982. In 1976, with the exception of carriers of motor vehicles, the contract carriers tended to be a good deal smaller than the specialized common carriers. Motor-vehicle carriers were presumably an exception because, owing to the large size and small number of shippers of motor vehicles, a restriction on the number of shippers which a contract carrier of motor vehicles might serve was not a serious impediment to the growth of such a carrier.

With the exception of motor vehicles, the contract carriers also tended to grow more rapidly than specialized common carriers. Actually, the refrigerated and agricultural products contract carriers experienced a growth rate double or more that of their common carrier counterparts.

Perhaps the most important indicator of the impact of the MCA of 1980 on the trucking industry is the loss in the value of operating rights. Pustay[54] has endeavored to measure the pre-1980 value of such rights by extrapolating the value of operating rights transferred by a sample of 296 firms between 1971 and 1979. He describes the process as follows:

> The extrapolation was performed by first calculating the average ratio of the price at which an operating right sold [defined as the present value of the stream of payments made by the purchasing carrier] to the annual revenues the right was expected to generate [as estimated by the acquiring carrier] for each of the four kinds of operating rights [regular route general commodity, irregular route general commodity, specialized common, and contract] for the cases in our sample. Multiplying this ratio by the total revenues generated in the regulated motor carrier industry by that kind of operating right yielded the estimate of the pre-reform market value of all ICC-issued operating rights of that type.[55]

On the basis of the foregoing calculation, Pustay estimates the pre-1980 value of operating rights at approximately $5.1 billion, presumably the present value of expected future monopoly profits attributable to

Table 11.5. Average Operating Revenue, Specialized Common and Contract Carriers, 1976 and 1982

| Kind of Carrier | Average Operating Revenues (thousands) | | | | | |
| | Specialized Common | | | Contract | | |
	1976	1982	Percent Change	1976	1982	Percent Change
Petroleum products	$ 8,106	$12,962	59.9	$ 1,681	$ 2,838	68.8
Refrigerated products	9,676	11,073	14.4	2,667	7,639	186.6
Agricultural products	2,996	5,129	71.2	2,288	5,917	158.6
Motor vehicles	15,370	30,649	99.4	37,648	68,279	81.4
Building materials	4,304	8,596	99.7	2,755	6,236	126.4

Sources: *Trinc's Blue Book of the Trucking Industry* (Washington, D.C.: Trinc's Transportation Consultants, 1977) and *1982 Motor Carrier Annual Report* (Washington, D.C.: American Trucking Associations, 1983).

entry constraints. While Pustay offers several reasons for believing that this is a conservative estimate of the aggregate value of these authorities, there are also several reasons, not mentioned by Pustay, for believing that it is an overstatement. Thus there may have been some incentive for the purchasing carrier to inflate the estimate of the additional revenues the right was expected to generate, so as to enhance chances for approval. Furthermore, to the extent that the transfer of rights included a ready-made clientele of shippers, the transaction may have involved the acquisition of an intangible other than operating authority, namely, "good will" or "going-concern value" in the form of reduced prospective search costs.[56]

Whatever the ultimate balance between the sources of under- and overestimation of pre-1980 operating rights values, it is clear that they were substantial indeed. It is also clear that the MCA of 1980 had a drastic impact on the value of these rights. In recognition of this loss in value, the Internal Revenue Service permitted carriers to write off operating rights over a five-year period, beginning July 1, 1980.[57] It is Pustay's contention that the write-off of operating rights and the disappearance of a market for operating rights immediately after the passage of the act indicate that regulatory reform was responsible for transferring at least $5.1 billion in wealth from trucking companies to their customers.[58]

The amortization of operating rights is a matter of tax policy, however, and does not prove that operating rights had become valueless.[59] Furthermore, there is at least some market for operating rights as current issues of *Transport Topics* reveal. A review of the "Rights Wanted" and "Rights for Sale" classified advertisements in that publication for the nineteen weeks from January 2, 1984, through May 7, 1984, disclosed thirteen offers to buy and ninety-seven offers to sell interstate operating rights. The disparity between the number advertising to buy and sell rights says something about the state of the market, however, especially since, during this same time period, there were fifty-one prospective purchasers of intrastate rights, as compared with thirty-seven prospective sellers.

As to the asking price, the offers to sell forty-eight-state general commodity authority seemed to range between $15,000 and $20,000, a meager amount, indeed, compared to the asking price of $250,000 to $1,000,000 for more limited authorities in the pre-1980 years.[60] Nevertheless, in early 1984 transportation attorneys were advertising that they would prepare applications for operating rights for as little as $600 for "fitness only" requests and as much as $2,500 for nationwide general commodity authority. To what extent the disparity between the price of existing rights and attorney's fees to apply for them is attributable to well-founded apprehensions of ICC rejection,[61] to a reduction in time required to obtain operating authority, to the acquisition of goodwill, or to lack of information on the part of potential entrants is unknown.

Conclusions

There are many respects in which the MCA of 1980 falls short of the kind of deregulation accomplished by the Airline Deregulation Act of 1978 or even the Staggers Rail Act of 1980. Former ICC member Trantrum, for example, has noted that the Staggers Act "directs the ICC to exempt all competitive railroad services from regulation"[62] while the MCA of 1980 contains no comparable provision.

Among the continuing restrictions are the following: a nontrivial showing of the useful public purpose served by the applicant's entry; the requirement that the ICC establish public convenience and necessity on a case-by-case procedure rather than on the basis of general findings; commodity, route, and place specifications that are still to appear in certificates of convenience and necessity; mandatory filing of tariffs and strict adherence to such published rates; and the latent power the commission possesses to investigate and to determine the reasonableness of rates falling outside the zone of rate freedom established by the act.

The importance of the residual regulation in the MCA of 1980 is dependent to a great extent upon the composition of the commission and philosophy of the commissioners. Not only has commission policy been affected by its changing membership, but also by the changing views of members. Chairman Taylor, who earlier in his tenure on the commission could be counted on to resist overly broad grants of authority, has modified his position rather substantially. After two years experience on the ICC, he responded to a question from the chairman of the House of Representatives' Subcommittee on Surface Transportation on the desirability of removing the antitrust immunity of rate bureaus by declaring: "I think we should also get rid of regulation for freight carriers."[63] A commissioner's perception of the merits of regulation can clearly affect his interpretation of the statute, for, as Moore has observed, "the difficulty with the 1980 act is that you can interpret it in a proregulation way as well as a procompetitive way."[64]

Several conclusions emerge from the foregoing considerations. The first is that even a pronounced proregulation commission in the future might not be able to reverse the deregulatory tide. The reason is that there has been such an influx of new firms and such an expansion of the scope of operating authorities that the reinstitution of stringent controls would only be effective over a long period of time.

In view of the virtual irreversibility of motor carrier deregulation and the erosion of the bulk of the monopoly profits attributable to entry restrictions, the regulated carriers themselves may ultimately come to question whether the meager protection afforded by operating authorities is worth the associated constraints on carrier initiatives. In the absence of industry support for some continued regulation, it is unlikely that it would long survive.

Notes

CHAPTER 1

1. 267 U.S. 307 (1925).
2. 118 U.S. 557 (1886).
3. 53 U.S. (12 How.) 299 (1851).
4. To a far greater extent than rail transportation, truck traffic, particularly during the early years, was geographically circumscribed. As of 1929 the Interstate Commerce Commission reported that 80 percent of truck ton-miles was of an intrastate nature and that only one-fourth of truck interstate ton-miles was effected by common carriers. *Coordination of Motor Transportation,* 182 I.C.C. 263, 275 (1932).
5. James C. Nelson, "The Motor Carrier Act of 1935," *Journal of Political Economy* 44, no.4(Aug. 1936):465.
6. *Motor Bus and Truck Operation,* 140 I.C.C. 685, 742 (1928).
7. Brice Edwards and J. W. Park, *The Marketing and Distribution of Fruits and Vegetables by Motor Truck,* Technical Bulletin No. 272 (Washington: USDA, Oct. 1931), 13.
8. *Coordination of Motor Transportation,* 182 I.C.C. 263, 382 (1932).
9. Ibid., 280.
10. Ibid., 362–63.
11. Ibid., 383.
12. *Regulation of Transport Agencies: A Report of the Federal Coordinator of Transportation,* Senate Document No. 152, 73d Cong., 2d sess. (Washington: GPO, 1934), 14.
13. Ibid., 15–16.
14. Ibid., 45.
15. See John Richard Felton, "Commodity Rate Discrimination in Railroad Transport," in *Transportation Problems and Policies in the Trans-Missouri West,* ed. Jack R. Davidson and Howard W. Ottoson, (Lincoln: Univ. of Nebraska Press, 1967), 55–60.
16. *Regulation of Transport Agencies,* 23, 45.
17. Ibid., 16, 23.
18. William M. Duffus, "Commercial Motor Transportation — Discussion," *American Economic Review, Supplement* 19, no. 1(Mar. 1929):249.
19. Henry R. Trumbower, "The Regulation of the Common Carrier Motor Vehicle with Respect to Its Competitive Aspects," *American Economic Review, Supplement* 19, no. 1 (Mar. 1929):235.
20. M. H. Hunter, "The Commercial Motor Vehicle and the Public," *American Economic Review, Supplement* 19, no. 1 (Mar. 1929):245. John L. George, on the other hand, deemed the regulation of contract carriers to be necessary since otherwise the operational and legal advantages of such carriers would prove to be "such a handicap over both

common carrier motor and railroad freight service as to constitute the contract carrier a devastating competitor." "Public Control of Contract Motor Carriers," *Journal of Land and Public Utility Economics* 9, no.3(Aug. 1933):233.

21. Emory R. Johnson, Grover B. Huebner, and G. Lloyd Wilson, *Principles of Transportation* (New York: Appleton, 1928), 455.

22. Shan Szto, "Federal and State Regulation of Motor Carrier Rates and Services" (Philadelphia: Ph.D. diss., University of Pennsylvania, 1934), 13.

23. Ibid., 24.

24. Ibid., 235.

25. Harold G. Moulton and Associates, *The American Transportation Problem* (Washington, D.C.: Brookings, 1933), 889–90.

26. Sidney L. Miller, *Inland Transportation: Principles and Policies* (New York: McGraw-Hill, 1933), 626–29.

27. D. Philip Locklin, *Economics of Transportation*, 7th ed. (Homewood, Ill.: Irwin, 1972), 670.

28. G. Shorey Peterson, "Motor Carrier Regulation and its Economic Bases," *Quarterly Journal of Economics* 43, no.4(Aug. 1929):611.

29. Ibid., 619.

30. Ibid., 639.

31. W. T. Jackman, *Economics of Transportation* (Chicago: Shaw, 1926), 807.

32. "Statement of Fred Brenckman," *Regulation of Interstate Motor Carriers,* Hearing before a Subcommittee on Interstate and Foreign Commerce, House of Representatives, 74th Cong., 1st sess., Feb. 19–Mar. 5, 1935 (Washington: GPO, 1935), 294–95.

33. "Statement of W. S. Campfield," *Regulation of Interstate Motor Carriers,* Hearing, 299.

34. "Statement of Charles E. Blaine," *Regulation of Interstate Motor Carriers,* Hearing, 334–35.

35. "Statement of E. H. Everson," *Regulation of Interstate Motor Carriers,* Hearing, 291.

36. "Statement of Donald Kane," *Regulation of Interstate Motor Carriers,* Hearing, 396–97.

37. R. A. Cooke, representing the American Newspaper Publishers Association, stated that the ANPA "takes a position in opposition to the enactment of this bill . . . because it is of the belief that the proposed law . . . would . . . generally burden the public with an increased cost of transportation . . . and eventually destroy the usefulness and flexibility which transportation by motor vehicles . . . affords the general shipping public." "Statement of R. A. Cooke," *Regulation of Interstate Motor Carriers,* Hearing, 314–15. The response of Congress was to exempt the transportation of newspapers, as well as agricultural commodities, from the Motor Carrier Act.

38. *Schechter Poultry Corp.* v. *U.S., 295* U.S. 495 (1935).

39. Harold S. Shertz, who represented the ATA at the 1935 House subcommittee hearing on transportation regulation, stated: "We believe the NRA code comes closer to providing a constructive, effective, and enforceable means of coordination and regulation than does this type of bill." "Statement of Harold S. Shertz," *Regulation of Interstate Motor Carriers,* Hearing, 216.

40. Nelson, "Motor Carrier," 470.

41. 49 Stat. 543, Public Act 255, 74th Cong., 1st sess., Aug. 9, 1935, incorporated as Part II of the Interstate Commerce Act.

42. A proposal of Representative Fred C. Gilcrist of Iowa to amend this provision so

as to substitute "primarily" for "exclusively" was defeated. See Warren H. Wagner, *A Legislative History of the Motor Carrier Act, 1935* (Denton, Md.: Rue, 1935), 24. An amendment of June 29, 1938, changed the wording of the exemption to read "motor vehicles used in carrying property consisting of livestock, fish (including shell fish), or agricultural commodities (not including manufactured products thereof), if such motor vehicles were not used in carrying any other property, or passengers for compensation." As originally worded, the law would not have exempted from regulation a for-hire agricultural carrier if it also, at any time, operated as a private carrier of nonexempt commodities. There was, however, still an ambiguity in the phraseology, for it was not clear whether a regulated common or contract carrier might transport agricultural commodities pursuant to the exemption, provided that the regulated and agricultural commodities did not form part of the same load. The ICC's more restrictive interpretation that the exemption was inapplicable if the motor vehicle had ever been used to transport regulated commodities, the "poisoned vehicle" doctrine as it came to be known, was rejected by the federal courts in *I.C.C.* v. *Dunn,* 166 F. 2d 116 (1948), and *I.C.C.* v. *Service Trucking Co.,* 91 Fed. Supp. 533 (1950), 186 F. 2d 400 (1951).

 43. Nelson, "Motor Carrier," 498–504.

 44. Ibid., 504.

CHAPTER 2

 1. 49 Stat. 543 (1935).

 2. Public Law 96-296 (1980).

 3. 49 U.S.C.A. Sec. 10101 (1987).

 4. Public Law 85-625 (1958).

 5. 49 U.S.C.A. Sec. 10922, n. 30 (1978).

 6. *Pan-American Bus Lines Operation,* 1 M.C.C. 190, 202–3 (1936).

 7. *C&D Oil Co. Contract Carrier Application,* 1 M.C.C. 329, 332 (1936); see also *Walter C. Benson Co., Inc., Extension, New York, New Jersey, and Pennsylvania,* 61 M.C.C. 128, 130 (1952); *New York Central Railroad Co. Extension, Congers, N.Y.– Jersey City, N.J.,* 61 M.C.C. 457, 462 (1953); *L.C. Jones Trucking Co., Extension–Utah,* 69 M.C.C. 273, 276 (1956); *Lawrence G. Willman Contract Carrier Application,* 77 M.C.C. 535 (1958).

 8. *Zephan Odell Clark Common Carrier Application,* 1 M.C.C. 445, 448 (1937).

 9. *Nashua Motor Express, Inc.* v. *United States,* 230 F. Supp. 646, 652–53 (1964).

 10. *Petroleum Carrier Corporation* v. *United States,* 258 F. Supp. 611 (1966); *Morgan Drive-Away, Inc.* v. *United States,* 268 F. Supp. 886 (1967); *Younger Brothers, Inc.* v. *United States,* 289 Supp. 545 (1968).

 11. *Dixie Highway Express, Inc.* v. *United States,* 268 F. Supp. 239, 241 (1967).

 12. Ibid.

 13. 389 U.S. 409 (1967).

 14. Ibid., 411. See also *Interstate Commerce Commission* v. *Parker,* 326 U.S. 60, 70 (1945); *Schaffer Transportation Co.* v. *United States,* 355 U.S. 83, 90–91 (1957).

 15. Thomas Gale Moore, *Freight Transportation Regulation: Surface Freight and the Interstate Commerce Commission* (Washington: American Enterprise Institute, 1972), 42.

 16. John H. Shenefield, "Prepared Statement," U.S. Senate, Committee on the Judiciary, Subcommittee on Antitrust and Monopoly, 95th Congress, 1st and 2d sess., *Over-*

sight of Freight Rate Competition in the Motor Carrier Industry, Hearings (Washington: GPO, 1978), 23.

17. *Michigan Public Utilities Commission* v. *Duke,* 266 U.S. 570 (1925).

18. *Frost and Frost Trucking Co.* v. *Railroad Commission of California,* 271 U.S. 583 (1926); *Smith* v. *Calhoon, Sheriff,* 283 U.S. 553 (1931).

19. *Stephenson* v. *Binford,* 287 U.S. 251 (1932).

20. *Interstate Commerce Commission* v. *J-T Transport Co., Inc.,* 368 U.S. 81, 89– 90 (1961).

21. Public Law 85-163 (1957).

22. *Keystone Transportation Co. Contract Carrier Application,* 19 M.C.C. 475 (1939).

23. Ibid., 498.

24. *N. S. Craig Contract Carrier Application,* 31 M.C.C. 705, 712 (1941). See also *Transportation Activities of Midwest Transfer Co. of Illinois, et al.,* 49 M.C.C. 383, 390 (1949).

25. *Motor Ways Tariff Bureau* v. *Steel Transportation Co., Inc.,* 62 M.C.C. 413 (1954).

26. *United States* v. *Contract Steel Carriers, Inc.,* 350 U.S. 409, 412 (1956).

27. 49 U.S.C.A. Sec. 10102 (1978).

28. Ibid.

29. *Connell Transport Co. Extension—New York, N.Y.,* 91 M.C.C. 113 (1962).

30. *Umthun Trucking Co., Extension—Phosphatic Feed Supplements,* 91 M.C.C. 691, 697 (1962).

31. *Contractors Cargo Co. —Extension of Operations,* 96 M.C.C. 306 (1964); *E. A. Gallagher & Sons, et al.* v. *Cleveland General Transport,* 98 M.C.C. 356 (1965).

32. *Bass Transportation Co., Inc., Extension—St. Louis, Mo.,* 125 M.C.C. 233 (1976).

33. *Policy Statement Regarding the "Rule of Eight" in Contract Carrier Application,* Ex Parte No. MC-119, 43 Fed. Reg. 38756 (1978).

34. Public Law 85-163 (1957).

35. *T. T. Brooks Trucking Co., Inc., Conversion Application,* 81 M.C.C. 561, 576 (1959).

36. James C. Nelson, "The Effects of Entry Control in Surface Transport," in *Transportation Economics: A Conference of the University—National Bureau Committee for Economic Research* (New York: National Bureau of Economic Research, 1965), 392, citing the *Wall Street Journal,* Mar. 26, 1963, 2.

37. *P. E. Gallot, Jr. —Purchase—Max Emil Holst,* 45 M.C.C. 1, 4 (1946); *James La Casse Extension—Dairy Products,* 79 M.C.C. 222 (1959); *Telishak Trucking, Inc., Extension—Precast Concrete Slabs and Beams,* 92 M.C.C. 553 (1963).

38. *McCormick's Express, Inc., Common Carrier Application,* 12 M.C.C. 532 (1938); *John Klann Moving & Trucking Co., Contract Carrier Application,* 29 M.C.C. 409 (1941); *Oil Carriers Co. Extension—Colorado,* 79 M.C.C. 169 (1959).

39. *Dual Operations,* Ex Parte No. 55, Sub 27, 43 Fed. Reg. 14664 (1978).

40. *American Bus Association* v. *United States,* 627 F. 2d 525 (1980).

41. *Woitishek Contract Carrier Application,* 42 M.C.C. 193 (1943).

42. *H. B. Church Truck Service Co. Common Carrier Application,* 27 M.C.C. 191 (1940); and *United States* v. *Drum,* 368 U.S., 370 (1962).

43. *Lenoir Chair Co. Contract Carrier Application,* 51 M.C.C. 65, 75 (1949).

44. *Brooks Transportation Co.* v. *United States,* 93 F. Supp. 517 (1950), 340 U.S. 925 (1951).

45. Public Law 85-625, Sec. 8 (1958); 49 U.S.C.A. Sec. 10524 (1978).

46. *Charles F. Geraci, Contract Carrier Application,* 7 M.C.C. 369 (1938), and *Ralph A. Veon, Inc., Contract Carrier Application,* 92 M.C.C. 248 (1963).

47. *Toto Purchasing & Supply Co. Inc., Common Carrier Application,* 128 M.C.C. 873 (1978); and *Grant of Operating Authority to an Applicant Who Intends to Use It Primarily as an Incident to the Carriage of Its Own Goods and Its Own Nontransportation Business,* Ex Parte No. MC-118, 43 Fed. Reg. 55051 (1978).

48. *Mercury Motor Express, Inc.* v. *United States,* 648 F. 2d 315 (1981).

49. *Schenley Distillers Corp.* v. *United States,* 61 F. Supp. 981 (1945); 326 U.S. 432 (1946).

50. *Lukens Steel Co., Contract Carrier Application,* 42 M.C.C. 672 (1943).

51. *Intercorporate Hauling: Proposed Policy Statement,* Ex Parte No. MC-122, 44 Fed. Reg. 42838 (1979).

52. John E. Lansing, *Transportation and Economic Policy* (New York: Free Press, 1966), 256.

53. Alexander Volotta, *The Impact of Federal Entry Controls on Motor Carrier Operations* (University Park: Center for Research of the College of Business Administration, Pennsylvania State Univ., 1967), 102.

54. Nelson, "Effects of Entry Control," 390–91.

55. Ibid., 391.

56. Ibid.

57. *Regulations Governing the Transportation in Interstate or Foreign Commerce of Hazardous Materials by Motor Vehicle over Direct Routes,* 111 M.C.C. 575 (1970).

58. Ibid., 598.

59. Public Law 82-472 (1952).

60. *Interstate Commerce Commission* v. *Dunn,* 166 F. 2d 116 (1948); *Interstate Commerce Commission* v. *Service Trucking Co., Inc.,* 91 F. Supp. 533 (1950), 186 F. 2d 400 (1951).

61. Dudly F. Pegrum, *Transportation Economics and Public Policy,* rev. ed. (Homewood, Ill.: Irwin, 1968), 354.

62. *East Texas Lines, Inc.,* v. *Frozen Food Express,* 351 U.S. 49, 54 (1956).

63. Public Law 85-625, Section 7, Subsection (a) (1958).

64. *Rail General Exemption Authority—Fresh Fruits and Vegetables,* Ex Parte No. 346, 361 I.C.C. (1979).

65. 12 U.S.C.S. Sect. 1141j (a) (1978).

66. *Northwest Agricultural Cooperative Association, Inc.* v. *I.C.C.* 350 F. 2d 252 (1965).

67. Ibid., 255.

68. Public Law 90-433 (1968).

69. *Implementation of Public Law 90-433—Agricultural Cooperative Transportation Exemption,* 108 M.C.C. 799, 827 (1969).

70. *Interstate Commerce Commission* v. *Milk Producers Marketing Co.,* 405 F. 2d 639, 641–42, 649 (1969).

71. *Middle Atlantic States Motor Carrier Rates,* 4 M.C.C. 68 (1937); *Central Territory Motor Carrier Rates,* 8 M.C.C. 233 (1938); *New England Motor Carrier Rates,* 8 M.C.C. 287 (1938); *Trunk Line Territory Motor Carrier Rates,* 24 M.C.C. 501 (1940); *Midwestern Motor Carrier Rates,* 27 M.C.C. 297 (1941).

72. Larry Dobesh, "Earnings Control Standards for Regulated Motor Carriers" (Pullman: Ph.D. diss., Washington State University, 1973).

73. Ibid., 40–49.

74. 49 U.S.C.S. Sec. 15a (2) (1982).

75. *Increased Common Carrier Rates in the East,* 42 M.C.C. 633 (1943); *Increased Common Carrier Truck Rates in New England,* 43 M.C.C. 13 (1943); *Increases, Middle Atlantic and New England, 1948,* 49 M.C.C. 357 (1949); *Increased Motor Carrier Rates in New England, 1949,* 49 M.C.C. 477 (1949).

76. *Union Bus Lines, Inc. — Purchase — Joe Amberson,* 5 M.C.C. 201, (1937); *Increases, Transcontinental-Intermountain Coast,* 304 I.C.C. 15, 23 (1958).

77. Dobesh, "Earnings Control," 59–62.

78. *General Increases — Eastern Central Territory,* 316 I.C.C. 467 (1962); *General Increase — Middle Atlantic and New England Territories,* 319 168 (1963).

79. Dobesh, "Earnings Control," 62–3.

80. Edward S. Hymson, "An Evaluation of the Accuracy of the Interstate Commerce Commission Measures of Profitability of Motor Carriers Applying for General Rate Increases" (Washington: National Science Foundation), mimeo, n.d., 8.

81. *D.C. Transit System, Inc.,* v. *Washington Metropolitan Area Transit Commission,* 350 F. 2d 753 (1965).

82. Ibid., 777–79.

83. Hymson, *Evaluation,* 8–9.

84. *General Increase, Middle Atlantic and New England Territories,* 332 I.C.C. 820, 838 (1969).

85. *Increased Rates and Minimum Charges within, from, and to the South,* 335 I.C.C. 77, 98 (1969).

86. *Increased Rates and Charges, from, to, and between Middlewest Territory,* 335 I.C.C. 142, 149, and 155 (1969).

87. *Increased LTL, AQ, and TL Rates, to, from, and between New England Territory,* 335 I.C.C. 185, 189-90 (1969).

88. *Rate Increases and Charges, Southwestern States,* 335 I.C.C. 361, 373 (1969).

89. *Increased Rates and Charges, Central and Southern Territories,* 335 I.C.C. 676 (1969); for further discussion of the issue see Harvey A. Levine, "A Historical Analysis of the Criteria to Determine the Revenue Need of Motor Common Carriers," *ICC Practitioners' Journal,* 40, no. 2(Jan.–Feb., 1973):158–76.

90. Ibid., 690–91.

91. *General Increase — Southern Motor Carriers Rate Conference* I. and S. Doc. No. M-29772 43 Fed. Reg. 15550 (1978).

92. Merton J. Peck, "Competitive Policy for Transportation?" in *Perspectives on Antitrust Policy,* ed. Almarin Phillips, (Princeton, N.J.: Princeton Univ. Press, 1965), 257.

93. Merrill J. Roberts, "Transport Costs, Pricing, and Regulation," in *Transportation Economics: A Conference of the Universities* (New York: National Bureau of Economic Research, 1965), 3–40.

94. Ibid., 19.

95. *United States* v. *Trans-Missouri Freight Association,* 166 U.S. 290 (1897); *United States* v. *Joint Traffic Association,* 171 U.S. 505 (1898).

96. *Georgia* v. *Pennsylvania Railroad Co.,* 324 U.S. 439, 456 (1945).

97. 62 Stat. 472 (1948).

98. Edward M. Kennedy, "Opening Statement," U.S. Senate, Committee on the Judiciary, Subcommittee on Antitrust and Monopoly, 95th Congress, 1st and 2d sess., *Oversight of Freight Rate Competition in the Motor Carrier Industry,* Hearings (Washington: GPO, 1978), 2.

99. Gloria J. Hurdle, "Statement before the California Public Utilities Commission," Case No. 10368, July 13, 1978, 13.

100. Nelson, "Effects of Entry," 406.

101. *Rate Bureau Investigation,* Ex Parte No. 297, 349 I.C.C. 811 (1975).

102. *Rate Bureau Investigation,* Ex Parte No. 297, 351 I.C.C. 437, 460 (1976).

103. 49 U.S.C.A. Sec. 11707 (1978).

104. 49 U.S.C.A. Sec. 10730 (1978).

105. *Dry Goods, Piece Goods, Dependent on Value,* 53 M.C.C. 157 (1951).

106. *Released Rate Rules—National Motor Freight Classification,* 316 I.C.C. 499, (1962).

107. Gloria J. Hurdle, "Statement," 16.

108. Ann F. Friedlaender, *The Dilemma of Freight Transport Regulation* (Washington: Brookings Institution, 1969), 38–42.

109. Alfred E. Kahn, *The Economics of Regulation: Principles and Institutions,* vol. 2 (New York: Wiley, 1971), 309–10.

110. *Substituted Service-Charges and Practices of For-Hire Carriers and Freight Forwarders (Piggyback Service),* Ex Parte No. 230, 322 I.C.C. 301, 336–37 (1964); *American Trucking Associations, Inc.* v. *Atchison, Topeka and Santa Fe Railway Co.,* 387 U.S. 397 (1967).

111. *Substituted Service,* 301, 355.

112. Interstate Commerce Commission, *54th Annual Report* (Washington: GPO, 1940), 107–8; *69th Annual Report,* 1955, 100; *86th Annual Report,* 1972, 131.

113. Interstate Commerce Commission, Bureau of Transport Economics and Statistics, *Intercity Ton-miles 1939-1959,* Statement No. 6103, Apr. 1969, 17; *ibid.,* Statement No. 531, Jan. 1953, 4; and *Transport Economics,* Jan. 1963, 2; cited in John W. Fuller, ed., *Regulation and Competition in Transportation: Selected Works of James C. Nelson* (Vancouver: Centre for Transportation Studies, 1983), 269; *Transport Economics* 5, no. 1(1978):2, 13; I.C.C. *90th Annual Report,* 141; and I.C.C., *94th Annual Report,* 122.

114. Robert C. Lieb, *Transportation: The Domestic System,* 2d ed. (Reston, Va.: Reston, 1981), 299.

115. Fuller, *Regulation and Competition,* 270.

116. Ibid.

117. Lieb, *Transportation,* 299.

118. Fuller, *Regulation and Competition,* 264.

119. Colin Barrett, "The 'Big-Company' Era in the Trucking Industry," *Traffic World* 137, no. 8(Feb. 22, 1969):81–82, cited in James C. Johnson, *Trucking Mergers* (Lexington, Mass.: Lexington Books, 1973), 55.

120. Johnson, *Trucking Mergers,* 65.

121. Ibid., 65–75.

122. Ibid., 81–84.

123. Ibid., 87–88, 96.

124. *Associated Transport, Inc.—Control and Consolidation—Arrow Carrier Corp., et al.,* 38 M.C.C. 137 (1942); see also, Johnson, *Trucking Mergers,* 88–91.

125. *McLean Trucking Co.* v. *U.S. 321 U.S. 67* (1944); see also, Johnson, *Trucking Mergers,* 91–92.

126. Johnson, *Trucking Mergers,* 98–99.

127. Ibid., 105–11.

128. Fuller, *Regulation and Competition,* 264.

129. Interstate Commerce Commission, Bureau of Transport Economics and Statistics, *Statement No. 6010,* 81; U.S. Senate, *Control of Illegal Interstate Motor Carrier Transportation,* Hearings before the Surface Transportation Subcommittee, Senate Committee on Commerce, in S. 2560 and S. 2764, 87th Cong., 2d sess. (Washington: GPO, Feb. and Apr. 1962), 99 and 108.

130. U.S. Senate, *National Transportation Policy,* 87th Cong., 1st sess. (Washington: GPO, 1961), 49–85, 507–46.

131. C. P. Schumaier, "Characteristics of Agriculturally Exempt Motor Carriers," *Conference on Private and Unregulated Transportation* (Evanston, Ill.: Transportation Center, Northwestern University, Oct. 29–30, 1962), 2–4, 8–11; U.S. Department of Agriculture, *The Role of Truck Brokers in the Movement of Exempt Agricultural Commodities,* Marketing Research Report No. 525 (Washington: USDA, Feb. 1962), 8, 13, 20–27; and U.S. Department of Agriculture, *For-Hire Carriers Hauling Exempt Agricultural Commodities,* Marketing Research Report No. 585 (Washington: USDA, Jan. 1963), 2–3, 6–10, 13.

132. U.S. Senate, *Trucking Mergers and Concentration,* Hearings before the Senate Select Committee on Small Business, 85th Cong., 1st sess. (Washington: GPO, July 1957), 240, 242, 250, 252, 255, 320.

133. James C. Nelson, "Coming Organizational Changes in Transportation," in *Transportation Problems and Policies in the Trans-Missouri West,* ed. Jack R. Davidson and Howard W. Ottoson (Lincoln: Univ. of Nebraska Press, 1967), 320–21.

134. Thomas Gale Moore, *Trucking Regulation: Lessons From Europe* (Washington: American Enterprise Institute, 1976), 121–33.

135. Fuller, *Regulation and Competition,* 302–10.

136. Roy J. Sampson and Martin T. Farris, *Domestic Transportation: Practice, Theory, and Policy,* 4th ed. (Boston: Houghton Mifflin, 1979), 486–87.

137. Lieb, *Transportation,* 231.

138. For a discussion of several of these reports, see Karen Borlaug Phillips, "The Role of Research in Transportation Policy: The Case of Motor Carrier Regulatory Reform," *Proceedings—Twenty-fourth Annual Meeting, Transportation Research Forum,* 24, No. 1(1983):399–409.

139. Robert C. Fellmeth, *The Interstate Commerce Omission: The Public Interest and the ICC,* Ralph Nader Study Group Report on the Interstate Commerce Commission and Transportation (New York: Grossman, 1970), 324.

140. Lieb, *Transportation,* 241.

141. *Sunkist Growers, Inc., Petition for Declaratory Order—Member Transportation,* 121 M.C.C. 448 (1975).

142. *Petition for Enlargement of the Amount of Operational Circuity Reduction Permitted under Certain Provisions of the Property Motor Carrier Superhighway and Deviation Rules,* 121 M.C.C. 685 (1975).

143. Interstate Commerce Commission, *Annual Report,* years 1975–1980 (Washington: GPO, 1975–1980).

144. Lieb, *Transportation,* 240.

145. *Central Transport, Inc.—Purchase (Portion)—Piedmont Petroleum Products, Inc..,* 127 M.C.C. 284 (1978).

146. *Appleyard's Motor Transportation Co., Inc.* v. *United States,* 592 F. 2d 8 (1st Cir. 1979).

147. *May Trucking Co.* v. *United States and Interstate Commerce Commission* 593 F. 2d 1349 (D.C. Cir. 1979).

148. *J. V. McNicholas Transfer Co. — Control — Tom's Express, Inc.*, 127 M.C.C. 309 (1978).

149. *Dual Operations*, Ex Parte No. 55, Sub. No. 27, 43 Fed. Reg. 14664 (1978).

150. *Southwest Equipment Rental, Inc. — Purchase (Portion) — Interstate Contract Carrier Corp.*, 127 M.C.C. 223, (1978).

151. *Association of American Railroads v. United States, 603 F. 2d 953 (1979).*

152. *Notification of Rate Proposals Following Prior Independent Action*, Ex Parte No. 297, Sub. No. 2, 358 I.C.C. 487 (1978).

153. Interstate Commerce Commission, *93rd Annual Report* (Washington: GPO, 1980) 50.

154. *Toto Purchasing & Supply Co., Inc. Common Carrier Application.*, 128 M.C.C. 873 (1978).

155. *Change of Policy Consideration of Rates in Operating Rights Application Proceedings*, 359 I.C.C. 613 (1979).

156. *Applications to Substitute Single-Line for Joint-Line Operations*, Ex Parte No. MC-109 (1969).

157. *Grant of Motor Carrier Operating Authority to an Applicant Who Intends to Use It Primarily as an Incident to the Carriage of Its Own Goods and Its Own Non-Transportation Business*, Ex Parte No. MC-118, 43 Fed. Reg. 55051 (1978).

158. *Protest Standards in Motor Carrier Application Proceedings*, Ex Parte No. MC-55, Sub. No. 26, 43 Fed. Reg. 17008 (1978).

159. *American Trucking Associations, Inc. v. United States, 627 F. 2d 1313 (1980).*

160. *Liberty Trucking Co., Extension — General Commodities*, 131 M.C.C. 573 (1979).

161. *Ex-Water Traffic*, Ex Parte No. MC-105, 44 Fed. Reg. 3723 (1979).

162. *Substituted Service (Fishyback Service) — Water For Motor Service — Alaskan Trade*, 361 I.C.C. 359 (1979).

163. *Motor Transportation of Property Incidental to Transportation by Aircraft*, 131 M.C.C. 87 (1978).

164. *Railroad-Freight Forwarder Contract Rates*, Ex Parte No. 364 (1979).

165. *Clipper Express Co. Petition for a Declaratory Order: Exempt Agricultural Commodities*, 361 I.C.C. 301 (1979).

166. *Special Tariff Authority*, Decision No. 79-3070-M, decided July 31, 1979.

167. *Special Procedures Governing Applications for Motor Carrier Authority Complementary to Movements of Exempt Agricultural Commodities*, Ex Parte No. MC-127, 45 Fed. Reg. 61648 (1980).

168. *Special Limited Authority: Proposed Procedures*, Ex Parte No. MC-131, 45 Fed. Reg. 2871 (1980).

169. *Intermediate Point Restrictions*, Ex Parte No. MC-132 (not printed), decided Aug. 8, 1980.

170. *Direct Routes for Regular Route Movements*, Ex Parte No. MC-136 (not printed), decided Aug. 8, 1980.

CHAPTER 3

1. Cf. Joe S. Bain, *Industrial Organization*, 2d ed. (New York: Wiley, 1968), Chap. 6.

2. Ibid., 5.

3. It is possible for potential entrants to enjoy an advantage over established firms. Technological change might render the costs of newcomers lower than the average total costs, or even the average variable costs, of existing enterprises.

4. Bain, *Industrial Organization,* 253.

5. U.S. Bureau of the Census, *1972 Census of Transportation: Truck Inventory and Use Survey,* vol. 2 (Washington: GPO, 1974), Table 2, p. 2, United States.

6. Joe S. Bain, "Economies of Scale, Concentration, and the Condition of Entry in Twenty Manufacturing Industries," *American Economic Review* 44, no. 2(Mar. 1954), Table 7, p. 36.

7. Merrill J. Roberts, "Some Aspects of Motor Carrier Costs: Firm Size, Efficiency and Financial Health," *Land Economics* 32, no. 3(Aug. 1956):228–38.

8. Cf. Bain, *Industrial Organization,* 238.

9. Bruce H. Wright, *For-Hire Trucking of Exempt Farm Products,* Marketing Research Report No. 649 (Washington: USDA, Mar. 1964), 7–9.

10. D. Philip Locklin, *Economics of Transportation,* 7th ed. (Homewood, Ill.: Irwin, 1972), 653, 670.

11. *Yearbook of Railroad Facts, 1977 Edition* (Washington: Association of American Railroads, 1977), 36.

12. Haskel Benishay and Gilbert R. Whitaker, Jr., "Demand and Supply in Freight Transportation," *Journal of Industrial Economics* 14. no. 3(July 1966):251.

13. Eugene D. Perle, *The Demand for Transportation: Regional and Commodity Studies in the United States* (Chicago: Univ. of Chicago Press, 1964), 43.

14. Alexander L. Morton, "A Statistical Sketch of Intercity Freight Demand," *Highway Research Record,* No. 296, Transportation Pricing (Washington: Highway Research Board, 1969), 53.

15. U.S. Department of Labor, Bureau of Labor Statistics, *Indexes of Output Per Man Hour: Selected Industries, 1939 and 1947–65* (Washington: GPO, 1966), Table 1, p. 6, Table 22, p. 27; *American Trucking Trends, 1965* (Washington: GPO, 1966), 207; and *Economic Report of the President* (Washington: GPO, 1966), Table C-20, p. 232, Table C-31, p. 245.

16. Department of Labor, Bureau of Labor Statistics, *Indexes of Output Per Man-Hour, Selected Industries, 1939 and 1947-65,* 6–26; *Transport Statistics in the United States for 1957,* Part V, 222–23; and *Transport Statistics in the United States for 1957,* Part V, 7, 12.

17. Patrick P. Boles, *Cost of Operating Trucks for Livestock Transportation,* Marketing Research Report No. 982 (Washington: USDA, Jan. 1972), 6.

18. Alfred E. Kahn, *The Economics of Regulation,* vol. 2 (New York: Wiley, 1971), 178, is quite emphatic on this point: " . . . does trucking have the economic attributes of an industry subject to destructive competition? It would be difficult to find one less qualified."

CHAPTER 4

1. *American Trucking Trends, 1976 Statistical Supplement* (Washington: American Trucking Associations, 1976), 16.

2. See, for example, George St. George and Charles Rust, *Grain Trucking Costs for Montana,* Bulletin 636 (Bozeman: Montana Agricultural Experiment Station, Montana State University, Mar. 1970); E. W. Tyrchniewicz, A. H. Butler, and O. P. Tangri, *The Cost*

of Transporting Grain by Farm Truck, Research Report No. 8 (Winnipeg: Center for Transportation Studies, University of Manitoba, July 1971); Merrill J. Roberts, "Some Aspects of Motor Carrier Costs: Firm Size, Efficiency and Financial Health," *Land Economics* 32, no. 3(Aug. 1956): 228–38; Robert A. Nelson, *Motor Carrier Freight Transportation in New England, A Report to the New England Governors' Council* (Boston: New England Governors' Committee on Public Transportation, 1956); Michael Chisholm, "Economies of Scale in Road Goods Transport? Off-Farm Milk Collection in England and Wales," *Oxford Economic Papers* 11, no. 3(Oct. 1959): 282–90; Dale G. Anderson and Wayne W. Budt, *A Rate/Cost Analysis of Nebraska Meat Trucking Activities with Livestock Trucking Cost Comparisons* (Lincoln: Nebraska Agricultural Experiment Station, Mar. 1975); and Thomas Gale Moore, *Trucking Regulation: Lessons from Europe* (Washington, D.C.: American Enterprise Institute, 1976).

3. Edward Miller, "Effects of Regulation on Truck Utilization," *Transportation Journal* 13, no. 1(Fall 1973):10.

4. J. R. Snitzler and R. J. Byrne, *Interstate Trucking of Fresh and Frozen Poultry Under Agricultural Exemption,* Marketing Research Report No. 224 (Washington: USDA 1958), and *Interstate Trucking of Frozen Fruits and Vegetables under Agricultural Exemption,* Marketing Research Report No. 316 (Washington: USDA, 1959).

5. Walter Miklius, *Economic Performance of Motor Carriers Operating under the Agricultural Exemption,* Marketing Research Report No. 838 (Washington: USDA, 1969), 4–5.

6. Richard N. Farmer, "The Case for Unregulated Truck Transportation," *Journal of Farm Economics* 46, no. 2(May 1964):389–409.

7. James Sloss, "Regulation of Motor Freight Transportation: A Quantitative Evaluation of Policy," *Bell Journal of Economics and Management Science* 1, no. 2(Autumn 1970): 327–66.

8. Ibid., 351.

9. Thomas Gale Moore, *Trucking Regulation: Lessons from Europe* (Washington: American Enterprise Institute, 1976).

10. Ibid., 10.

11. *Transportation Facts and Trends,* 13th ed. (Washington: Transportation Association of America, July 1977), S8.

12. Ibid., S3.

13. Stephen Hannahs and Joseph Tune, *1977 Financial Analysis of the Motor Carrier Industry* (Union Oil, Union 76 Division, n.d.), 11, 28.

14. Thomas Gale Moore, "Deregulating Surface Transportation," in *Promoting Competition in Regulated Markets,* ed. Almarin Phillips (Washington, D.C.: Brookings, 1976), 60–61.

15. James E. Annable, Jr., "The ICC, the IBT, and the Cartelization of the American Trucking Industry," *Quarterly Review of Economics and Business* 13, no. 3(Summer 1973):44.

16. David Schwartzman, "Monopoly and Wages," *Canadian Journal of Economics and Political Science* 35, no. 3(Aug. 1969):428.

17. Ibid., 438.

18. Annable, "The ICC," 41.

19. Moore, "Deregulating Surface Transportation," 62.

20. Haskel G. Benishay and Gilbert R. Whitaker, Jr., "Demand and Supply in Freight Transportation," *Journal of Industrial Economics* 14, no. 3(July 1966):251.

21. Other studies have suggested substantially higher values for the price elasticity of

demand for truck transportation. Eugene D. Perle, *The Demand for Transportation* (Chicago: Univ. of Chicago, Department of Geography, 1964), 43, placed the overall elasticity coefficient at −2.0223 and Alexander Morton, "A Statistical Sketch of Intercity Freight Demand," *Highway Research Record*, no. 296, Highway Pricing (Washington: Highway Research Board, 1969), 53, at −1.841. Not only does the Benishay and Whitaker estimate produce the most conservative welfare loss, but also, more important, their methodology seems clearly to be superior. They employ a longer span of years, and they include population, urbanization, industrial production, and time trend in their regression equation.

22. This implies that in the absence of regulation the rates of common carriers of general freight would have been reduced to a competitive level, namely, long-run average costs. Some question has arisen as to the applicability of the competitive model to all phases of the trucking industry. J. C. Spychalski, "Criticisms of Regulated Transport: Do Economists' Perceptions Conform with Institutional Realities?" *Transportation Journal* 14, no. 3(Spring 1975):18, has pointed out that "the supply characteristics of LTL-oriented truckers, coupled with the fact that aggregate amounts of LTL traffic moving and potentially movable between many if not a majority of origin-destination point pairs can be accommodated by relatively few carriers, suggest that tendencies toward concentration would exist in this sector of trucking even in the absence of institutionally imposed constraints." While such concentration might render the competitive *model* less applicable to the LTL segment of the common carriage of general freight, it does not negate a competitive *outcome*. E. S. Mason, *Economic Concentration and the Monopoly Problem* (Cambridge: Harvard Univ. Press, 1959), 34, observed long ago that while a "substantial degree of concentration is a necessary condition to the exercise of monopoly power . . . it is not a sufficient condition." In the trucking industry, as noted in the preceding chapter, the potential competition of firms not currently transporting commodities between particular origin-destination pairs is the primary reason that concentration is not a sufficient condition for the exercise of monopoly power.

23. The welfare gain can be calculated as [($0.143 − $0.107) × 113 billion ton-miles − 98 billion ton-miles] ÷ 2 = ($0.036 × 15 billion ton-miles) ÷ 2 = $270 million.

24. Miller, "Effects of Regulation," 11.

25. *Trinc's Blue Book of the Trucking Industry* (Trinc Transportation Consultants, Sept. 1977), Table 2, p. 2; Table 11, p. 16; and Table 29, p. 4.

26. This "private capacity shortfall," as Moore, "Deregulating Surface Transportation," 63, has called it, is calculated as (0.81 regulated van utilization − 0.688 private van utilization) ÷ 0.688 private van utilization = 0.1773 × 8.095 million private van-miles = 1,435 million van-miles of private capacity shortfall. This is a conservative estimate of the effect of regulation on private truck utilization, since regulated carriers themselves would probably be able to reduce their empty backhauls were it not for limitations on their routes, commodities, and intermediate points served.

27. *American Trucking Trends, 1976*, 8.

28. Interstate Commerce Commission, *89th Annual Report* (Washington: 1975), 100–101.

29. Ibid., 92.

30. While the inclusion of other regulated carriers and other vehicle types would have increased somewhat the estimate of social costs, common carriers of general freight are the most important single constituent of the regulated trucking industry. Furthermore, the ordinary van—the truck type providing the greatest opportunity for backhauls because of its unspecialized nature—tends to overshadow in numerical importance all other truck types engaged in intercity freight transport.

31. *A Cost and Benefit Evaluation of Surface Transport Regulation* (Washington: ICC, Bureau of Economics, 1976), 23–24.

32. Ibid., 7. Since Wyckoff's findings were the subject of an oral presentation rather than published writings, the evidence on which he based them is unknown. At any rate, the findings are in direct conflict with those of Moore. He notes, first of all, that "historical data on industry revenues, profits, and the return on investment [in Great Britain] do not exist." Moore, *Trucking Regulation: Lessons from Europe*, 35. Furthermore, he cites several instances in which real rates fell in 1972 and 1973, that is, subsequent to deregulation (ibid., 37–38). Finally, Moore points out that "in the small-consignment market several companies offer premium service at premium prices, but the largest firms do not" (ibid., 38). It may well be that Wyckoff had reference to this little used service when he noted a 40 percent increase in LTL rates following deregulation.

33. *A Cost and Benefit Evaluation*, 16–20.

34. *The Case Against Deregulation* (Washington: American Trucking Associations, n.d.), 50.

35. Gilbert L. Gifford, "The Small Shipments Problem," *Transportation Journal* 10, no.1(Fall 1970):19.

36. *Economic Analysis and Regulatory Implications of Motor Carrier Service to Predominantly Small Communities, A Final Report to the U.S. Department of Agriculture* (Washington: R. L. Banks and Associates, June 24, 1976), 5.

37. A more extended discussion of the alleged internal subsidization of rural areas can be found in Chapter 8.

CHAPTER 5

1. See Thomas Gale Moore, "Deregulating Surface Freight Transportation," in *Promoting Competition in Regulated Markets*, ed. Almarin Phillips (Washington: Brookings, 1975), 57–58.

2. *Foodstuffs from Jacksonville to Georgia and Alabama*, 62 M.C.C. 689 (1954), 693.

3. *Rules to Govern the Assembling and Presenting of Cost Evidence*, 337 I.C.C. 298 (1970), 402.

4. *Refrigeration Material from Memphis, Tenn., to Dayton, Ohio*, 4 M.C.C. 187 (1938), 189.

5. D. Philip Locklin, *Economics of Transportation*, 7th ed. (Homewood, Ill.: Irwin, 1972), 516.

6. See, for example, *Animal Feed—Kansas City Mo., to Chicago*, 325 I.C.C. 147 (1965); and *Carbon Black, Southwest to Ind., Ohio and Mo.*, 325 I.C.C. 138 (1965).

7. *Aluminum Extrusions from Miami to Chicago*, 325 I.C.C. 188 (1965).

8. See, for example, *Rates over Carpet City*, 4 M.C.C. 589 (1938); *Paper Articles—Twin Cities—Chicago and Milwaukee*, 12 M.C.C. 453 (1939); *Coffee, Roasted, from Omaha, Nebr., to Twin Cities*, 22 M.C.C. 529 (1940); *Onions and Potatoes from North Dakota to Twin Cities*, 26 M.C.C. (1940); *Gypsumboard, Paper, from Kansas City, Mo., to Chicago*, 304 I.C.C. 125 (1958); *Milk from Iola to Kansas City*, 304 I.C.C. 13 (1958); and *Composition Roofing, Stroud, Okla., to St. Louis, Mo.*, 329 I.C.C. 612 (1967).

9. *Atchison, Topeka and Santa Fe Railway Company* v. *Morris*, 329 I.C.C. 326 (1967), 334.

10. The production of cotton and cotton seed, beef and hides, and wheat and straw

are oft-mentioned examples of joint products. Herbert Mohring, *Transportation Economics* (Cambridge, Mass.: Ballinger, 1976), 60–61, uses wool and mutton as an illustration of joint production, but this is clearly in error, since the production of wool does not presuppose the production of mutton in fixed or any other proportions.

11. It is reasonable to assume that terminal costs would increase proportionally with the volume of backhaul traffic. On the other hand, line-haul costs would be much less affected, except for the additional driving that might be involved in picking up and delivering commodities in a truck that otherwise would return empty. Some increase in fuel consumption might also occur with a loaded truck, especially in hilly terrain. Trucking firm representatives in the Lincoln, Nebraska, area indicated that fuel consumption might increase about 11 percent, from 4.5 miles per gallon unloaded to 4.0 miles per gallon loaded. Transit time might also increase somewhat, though the 55 mile-per-hour national speed limit has probably tended to reduce any loaded-empty transit-time disparities.

12. Cf. Alfred E. Kahn, *The Economics of Regulation* (New York: Wiley, 1970), 1:80–81.

13. The demands are also assumed to be certain. A. A. Walters, "The Allocation of Joint Costs with Demands as Probability Distributions," *American Economic Review* 50, no. 3(June 1960):429, has observed that if the demands for forward and backhauls are uncertain, they need to be represented as probability distributions, and "the allocation of joint cost is both rational and necessary in order to find profit-maximizing price and output." If the probability is negligible that backhaul traffic would exceed the capacity employed on the forward haul, the marginal expected cost is merely the additional cost of a loaded (or partially loaded) vehicle over an empty one, and there are no joint costs to "allocate." On the other hand, if the joint costs are sufficiently large and/or the difference between the demands for forward and backhauls is sufficiently small, some of the joint costs will be borne by the backhaul whether demands are certain or uncertain. See Figure 5.2.

14. The oft-quoted study by Stanley L. Warner, "Cost Models, Measurement Errors and Economies of Scale in Trucking," in *The Cost of Trucking: An Econometric Analysis,* ed. M. L. Burstein (Dubuque, Iowa: Brown, 1965), 1–46, estimates that a 10 percent increase in size occasions about a 9.7 percent increase in costs. A more recent study by Richard Klem, "Market Structure and Conduct," in *Regulation of Entry and Pricing in Truck Transportation,* ed. Paul W. MacAvoy and John W. Snow, (Washington: American Enterprise Institute, 1977), 119–38, after partitioning the sample into two different size groups, concludes that only the smaller Class I carriers were operating under conditions of increasing returns and that carriers with operating revenues of $10 million or more per year faced diseconomies of scale. Richard Koenker, "Optimal Scale and the Size Distribution of American Trucking Firms," *Journal of Transport Economics and Policy* 11, no. 1(Jan. 1977):54–76, who attempted to replicate Warner's results with more recent data, found that a 10 percent increase in size yielded a 10.022 percent increase in costs. Furthermore, his own model revealed that trucking firms whose output exceeded a relatively modest 6.7 million ton-miles per year (some 85 to 90 percent of the industry in terms of revenue generated) encountered increasing costs.

15. Bruce H. Wright, *For-Hire Trucking of Exempt Farm Products,* Marketing Research Report No. 649 (Washington: USDA, 1964), 7–9.

16. Conrad J. Oort, "The Theory of Economic Efficiency as Applied to the Road Transport Industry," in *Criteria for Transport Pricing,* ed. James R. Nelson (Washington: Transportation and Logistics Center, American University, 1969), 269.

17. Thomas Gale Moore, *Trucking Regulation: Lessons from Europe* (Washington: American Enterprise Institute, 1976), 12.

18. A. W. J. Thompson and L. C. Hunter, *The Nationalized Transport Industries* (London: Heinemann Educational Books, 1973), 241.

19. A. A. Walters, *Integration in Freight Transport* (London: Institute of Economic Affairs, 1968), 23–24.

20. Ibid., 24.

21. Michael Chisholm and Patrick O'Sullivan, *Freight Flows and Spatial Aspects of the British Economy* (Cambridge: Cambridge Univ. Press, 1973).

22. Ibid., 63.

23. B. T. Bayliss and S. L. Edwards, *Industrial Demand for Transport* (London: Her Majesty's Stationery Office, 1970), App. 3.

24. Ibid., 160.

25. It may also be that regional exports in Great Britain do not vary as widely in value-weight ratios as in the United States.

26. H. M. Kolsen, *The Economics and Control of Road-Rail Competition* (Sydney: Sydney Univ. Press, 1968), 137–38.

27. Stewart Joy, "Unregulated Road Haulage: The Australian Experience," *Oxford Economic Papers* 16, no. 2(July 1964):85.

28. Kolsen, *Economics,* 137.

29. James C. Nelson, "Performance of Unregulated Trucking in Australia," *Proceedings of the National Symposium on Transportation for Agriculture and Rural America* (Washington: U.S. Department of Transportation, 1977), 89–90.

30. Joy, *Unregulated,* 278.

31. Ibid., 281.

32. D. C. Ferguson, "Joint Products and Road Transport Rates in Transport Models," *Journal of Transport Economics and Policy* 6, no. 1(Jan. 1972):69–76.

33. Ibid., 72–73.

34. Ibid., 73.

35. *Trinc's Blue Book of the Trucking Industry* (Washington, D.C.: Trinc Transportation Consultants, 1977).

36. U.S. Bureau of the Census, *1972 Census of Transportation, Truck Inventory and Use Survey* (Washington: U.S. Department of Commerce, 1973), 1:16.

37. *Empty/Loaded Truck Miles on Interstate Highways during 1976* (Washington, D.C.: ICC, 1977), 46.

38. Ibid., 8.

39. *Trinc's Blue Book,* 1977, S8.

40. The words "as much as" are used advisedly, since not all nonempty trucks are fully loaded, and the saving in line-haul costs of an empty as compared with a loaded truck diminishes as the size of the load declines.

41. Haskel G. Benishay and Gilbert R. Whitaker, Jr., "Supply and Demand in Freight Transportation," *Journal of Industrial Economics* 14, no. 3(July 1966):243–62, estimated the elasticity of demand for motor carriers of freight by multiple-regression analysis in which the influences of income population concentration, the price charged by alternative modes, and the time trend as well as the price charged by trucking firms, are all incorporated into the estimating equation. Despite its relative obscurity, the Benishay and Whitaker study would appear to be methodologically superior to the better known studies of Eugene D. Perle, *The Demand for Transportation: Regional and Commodity Studies in the*

United States, Geography Research Paper no. 95 (Chicago: Univ. of Chicago, 1964), and Alexander L. Morton "A Statistical Sketch of Intercity Freight Demand," Highway Research Record Number 296, Highway Pricing (Washington: Highway Research Board, 1969).

42. The effect of rate reductions on backhauls is subject to two constraints: (1) the rate may not fall below the marginal cost of loaded backhaul trips, and (2) the number of additional loaded backhaul trips may not exceed the number of empty ones. A reduction in the average backhaul charge from $648 to MC_{bl}, viz., $513, would presumably occasion an increase in loaded backhauls from 6.1 million to 8.8 million and an expansion of revenue from $3,920.4 million ($648 × 6.1 million loaded backhaul trips) to $4,545.7 million ($3,920.4 million × 1.15, the assumed price elasticity of demand for truck transport). Some 2 million backhauls (10.8 million − 8.8 million) would remain empty with rates at the level of the additional costs of transporting goods in backhaul.

43. The welfare gain can be calculated:

$$\frac{91(\$648 - \$513) \times 2.7 \text{ million trips}}{2}$$
$$= \$182 \text{ million.}$$

44. *Empty/Loaded Truck Miles,* 6.
45. Ibid., 12.

CHAPTER 6

1. See Chap. 3.

2. Cf. Michael R. Bonavia, *The Economics of Transport,* 2d ed. (London: Pitman, 1947), 103–4.

3. Donald H. Wallace, "Joint and Overhead Cost and Railway Rate Policy," *Quarterly Journal of Economics* 48, no. 4(Aug. 1934):586. Bonavia, *Economics,* 104–5, maintains that "true" joint supply also presupposes "no interaction between the demand for two services," as well as fixed output coefficients. The rationale for Bonavia's assertion is unclear, and he provides no argument to support it. Cross-relationships in supply are dependent upon technical factors in the production process, while cross-relationships in demand are a function of consumer tastes. Supply complementarity is just as "true" whether the demands for joint products are substitutive, complementary, or independent. Cf. Kenneth E. Boulding, *Economic Analysis,* 3d ed. (New York: Harper, 1955), 226–31.

4. Cf. Herbert Mohring, *Transportation Economics* (Cambridge, Mass.: Ballinger, 1976), 62–65.

5. Marcel Boiteux, "Peak-Load Pricing," in *Marginal Cost Pricing in Practice,* ed. James R. Nelson (Englewood Cliffs, N.J.: Prentice-Hall, 1964), 79–80.

6. James C. Nelson, "The Motor Carrier Act of 1935," *Journal of Political Economy* 44, no. 4(Aug. 1936):479.

7. *Regulation of Transport Agencies: A Report of the Federal Coordinator of Transportation,* Senate Doc. No. 152, 73d Cong., 2d sess. (Washington: GPO, 1934), 33.

8. John H. Hunter, Jr., *The Role of Truck Brokers in the Movement of Exempt Agricultural Commodities,* Marketing Research Report No. 525. (Washington: USDA, Feb. 1962).

9. Ibid., 26–27. The "percentage variation" is computed by dividing the difference between the maximum and minimum of the range of rates by the midpoint of the range.

10. Walter Miklius, *Economic Performance of Motor Carriers Operating Under the Agricultural Exemption in Interstate Trucking,* Marketing Research Report No. 838 (Washington: USDA, Jan. 1969), 3.

11. Hunter, *Role of Truck Brokers,* 25–27.

12. H. M. Kolsen, *The Economics and Control of Road-Rail Competition.* (Sydney, Australia: Sydney Univ. Press, 1968), 132–33.

13. James C. Nelson, "Performance of Unregulated Trucking in Australia," *Proceedings of the National Symposium on Transportation for Agriculture and Rural America* (Washington: U.S. Department of Transportation, 1977), 88.

14. Stewart Joy, "Unregulated Road Haulage: The Australian Experience," *Oxford Economic Papers* 16, no. 2(July 1964):278–79.

15. Nelson, "Performance," 90. The other 40 per cent is accomplished by 60 to 80 trucking firms, owning their own trucks and numbering 21 or fewer vehicles each.

16. Ibid., 90.

17. Frederick J. Beier, "Off-Peak Freight Rates: Effect on Shippers and Carriers," *Traffic Quarterly* 33, no. 1(Jan. 1979):117.

18. Ibid., 121–22.

19. Ibid., 120.

20. Ibid., 134-35.

21. Ibid., 137.

22. Cf. George E. McCallum, *New Techniques in Railroad Ratemaking* (Pullman, Wash.: Bureau of Economics and Business Research, Washington State Univ., 1968), 4–7.

23. Robert C. Fellmeth, *The Interstate Commerce Omission* (New York: Grossman, 1970), 121–22. Almost two decades earlier, the Board of Investigation and Research, created by Congress pursuant to the Transportation Act of 1940, developed evidence as to the magnitude of these geographic restrictions. Over 7 per cent of regular rate general commodity carriers were without authority to provide *any* service to *any* intermediate points and almost one-third of them lacked off-route authority. As for the irregular route carriers of general freight, only about one-fourth were authorized to transport commodities freely among all points in the territories they served. *Federal Regulatory Restrictions upon Motor and Water Carriers,* Sen. Doc. No. 78, 79th Cong., 1st sess. (Washington: GPO, 1945), 78, 80, 88.

24. Fellmuth, *Interstate Commerce Omission,* 122. A number of years earlier the Board of Investigation and Research had noted that only slightly more than 2 percent of general freight carriers had *no* limitation on commodities they might transport. Since carriers of general freight have more latitude than specialized commodity carriers and contract carriers in the kinds of commodities they may transport, the potential impact of restrictive commodity licensing upon truck utilization is obvious. *Federal Regulatory Restrictions upon Motor and Water Carriers,* 33, 36, 43.

25. Fellmuth, *Interstate Commerce Omission,* 122–23.

26. U.S. Bureau of the Census, *1972 Census of Transportation,* Truck Inventory and Use Survey 2(1973): Table 2, p. 2.

27. Ibid., 2.

28. *Empty/Loaded Truck Miles on Interstate Highways during 1976* (Washington: ICC, Aug. 1977).

29. Since operating authorities tend to include both territorial and commodity restrictions, these adverse impacts tend to be additive.

CHAPTER 7

1. Janna L. Cowen, "The Operating Ratio and Alternative Earnings Control Standards for Regulated Highway Freight Carriers" (Lincoln: Ph.D. diss., University of Nebraska-Lincoln, 1979), 72–74.

2. James Freeman and Richard Beilock, "State Regulatory Responses to Federal Motor Carrier Deregulation," *University of Florida Law Review* 35, no. 1(Winter 1983):67.

3. Ibid., 65.

4. Harvey Averch and Leland R. Johnson, "Behavior of the Firm Under Regulatory Constraint," *American Economic Review* 52, no. 5(Dec. 1962):1052–69. Almost simultaneously and independently, the issue was explored by Stanislaw H. Wellisz, "Regulation of Natural Gas Pipeline Companies: An Economic Analysis," *Journal of Political Economy* 71, no. 1(Feb. 1963):30–43, whose work, however, dealt primarily with the effects of regulation on peak-load pricing.

5. Elizabeth E. Bailey, *Economic Theory of Regulatory Constraint* (Lexington, Mass.: Heath, 1973), 53.

6. Alfred E. Kahn, *The Economics of Regulation: Principles and Institutions* (New York: Wiley, 1971), 2:54.

7. Russell C. Cherry, "The Operating Ratio Effect and Regulated Motor Carriers," *Proceedings of a Workshop on Motor Carrier Economic Regulation* (Washington: National Academy of Sciences, 1978), 269–89.

8. The operating ratio and the rate of return on investment are related through the operating ratio: rate of return on investment + working capital = (1 − operating ratio) (capital turnover ratio). Therefore $(1 - 0.93)(4) = 0.28$.

9. ICC regulations provide such leases must be for a period of not less than thirty days, except in the case of agricultural carriers that lease their vehicles to an authorized carrier for a return haul. Leasing arrangements for periods of less than thirty days are known as "trip leasing."

10. A staff member of the Nebraska Public Service Commission notes that there are only two cement haulers operating in the state but over ninety general freight carriers.

11. Unfortunately, cases involving the investigation of specialized common carrier rate increases tend merely to be listed in the ICC's *Motor Carrier Cases* without any indication of the background, issues, or commission reasoning. One case, however, *Independent Movers—Rates on Household Goods,* I. & S. No. M-2640, 46 M.C.C. 878 (1946), which was disposed of without a printed report, was reproduced in Commerce Clearing House, *Federal Carrier Cases—ICC,* vol. 2, CCH Nos. 31, 218, pp. 516–17. In comparison with the hundreds of general freight carriers involved in regional rate bureau proceedings, only four household goods carriers were represented in this case by the Independent Movers' and Warehousemen's Association, a number sufficiently small to elicit tacit or overt collusion with respect to operating ratios. Despite the fact that the proposed rates were in no instance less and, for some distances, higher than those of any carrier in the comparison group, the ICC examiner declared them "to be within the zone of reasonableness." The fact that "the information presented by Atlas Van Lines [one of the respondents, was] typical" and that its "operating ratio for 1945 was 99.07" apparently counted for more than the rates for the comparison group.

12. A superior control group would be carriers operating in the exempt agricultural trucking market. Unfortunately, most trucking industry data are a by-product of regulation, and comparable information on exempt firms is not available. The ICC computer

tape indicates that of 858 trucks exempt from ICC regulation and carrying exempt agricultural commodities, 11.5 percent were leased with drivers. Since this leasing rate approximates that of contract carriers, it suggests that contract carriers probably constitute an acceptable control group.

13. The authors wish to thank an anonymous reviewer for pointing out the importance of business risk to leasing decisions.

14. Charles A. Taff, *Commercial Motor Transportation,* 5th ed. (Homewood, Ill.: Irwin, 1975), 209–10. While ownership of vehicles does not presuppose "in-house" maintenance, a carrier might well conclude that a lessor would have a greater incentive than would an independent truck repair facility both to make no unnecessary repairs and to engage in a program of preventive maintenance.

15. Andrew A. Arentz, Jr., "The Impact of Equipment Leasing on Innovation," *Papers, Sixth Annual Meeting,* Transportation Research Forum (Oxford, Ind.: Cross, 1965), 351–54.

16. *Empty/Loaded Truck Miles on Interstate Highways During 1976* (Washington: ICC, 1977).

17. Calculated from ICC computer tape.

18. *Trinc's Blue Book of the Trucking Industry* (Washington: Trinc Transportation Consultants, 1977).

19. No suitable proxies for seasonal and innovational incentives for leasing suggested themselves. Neither omission, however, is believed to be serious. The presumably minor role of seasonality was noted above, and equipment innovations can be effected about as readily through purchasing as through leasing because of a very active secondhand market in highway carrier equipment.

20. *Trinc's Blue Book of the Trucking Industry* (Washington: Trinc Transportation Consultants, 1965).

21. Freeman and Beilock, "State Regulatory Responses," 64.

CHAPTER 8

1. Some supporters of continued economic regulation, e.g., N. A. Glaskowsky, Jr., B. F. O'Neil, and D. R. Hudson, *Motor Carrier Regulation* (Washington: ATA Foundation, 1976), 15, go so far as to maintain that the adverse impact of deregulation on rural areas is no longer even a matter of debate:

> . . . both the proregulators and deregulators agree that service to thousands of small communities and locations will cease in many cases and be sharply curtailed in others. Where very limited service is maintained rates will be very much higher, particularly "minimums." We find no essential disagreement on this point, although the deregulators tend to "waffle" on the question.

2. Several expositions of this theme can be found in a series of statements favorable to continued regulation compiled by the American Trucking Association, *The Case Against Deregulation* (Washington: n.d.). See testimony of E. V. Kiley, 6; T. B. Alfriend, 50; C. J. McCormick, 100; and L. L. Waters, 108.

3. G. L. Gifford, "The Small Shipments Problem," *Transportation Journal* 10, no. 1(Fall 1970):19.

4. P. T. McElhiney, *Motor Carrier Common Carrier Freight Survey,* prepared for Federation of Rocky Mountain States (Washington: U.S. Department of Transportation, 1975), 238.

5. See Chap. 4.

6. J. W. Snow, "The Problem of Motor Carrier Regulation and the Ford Administration's Proposal for Reform," in *Regulation of Entry and Pricing in Truck Transportation,* ed. P. W. MacAvoy and J. W. Snow, (Washington: American Enterprise Institute, 1977), 3–4.

7. McElhiney, *Motor Carrier,* 23–27. The principal anomalies appeared to be small communities either contiguous to large population centers or located on major highways.

8. N. H. Nie, et al., *Statistical Package for the Social Sciences* (New York: McGraw-Hill, 1975), 289.

9. McElhiney, *Motor Carrier,* 50–51.

10. While small communities following deregulation would continue to be served by fewer carriers than large communities, meager scale economies, low entry barriers, and ease of intermarket transference would render futile any attempt on the part of a carrier serving isolated areas to exploit its nominal monopoly position.

11. "Small shipper" is not, of course, synonymous with "small employer," since the volume of shipments is a function of, among other things, the industry as well as the number of employees. Nevertheless, W. Y. Oi and A. P. Hurter, Sr., *Economics of Private Truck Transportation* (Dubuque, Iowa: Brown, 1965), 134–36, found that firm size, as measured by employment, explained more than three times as much variance in private truck and trailer fleet size than did the industry.

12. Somewhat ironically, while smallness is a deterrent to private carriage, rural location is an incentive for shippers to acquire their own fleets. A case study of the factors which led twenty-six industrial shippers of widely varying size, producing a great variety of products, and operating plants in many different locations to engage in private highway transport, revealed that fifteen of them identified unfavorable rural location as a motive. R. M. Sutton, R. S. Potter, and D. W. Weitz, *Private Carriage Motivation and Impact of Rural Location,* prepared for U.S. Department of Transportation (New York: Drake Sheehan/Stewart Dougall, Mar. 28, 1975), 2a.

13. McElhiney, *Motor Carrier,* 11. It should be added that the mere location on a rail line carries with it no guarantee of rail service.

14. K. D. Boyer, "How Similar are Motor Carrier and Rail Rate Structures?: The Value of Service Component," *Proceedings,* Nineteenth Annual Meeting, Transportation Research Forum (Oxford, Ind.: Cross, 1978), 523–31.

15. Ibid., 530.

16. While both the Senate Judiciary Committee and the ICC also have the CTS data on computer tapes, the conditions under which they secured the tapes preclude the release of information to persons outside these agencies.

17. R. L. Banks and Associates, "Service to Small Communities," in MacAvoy and Snow, *Regulation,* 138, found that one-half the tonnage transported by nine predominantly rural common carriers of general freight was of the LTL variety, while only about one-third of the tonnage of an industrywide sample of 614 general freight carriers was LTL in nature.

18. J. E. Olson, "Price Discrimination by Regulated Motor Carriers," *American Economic Review* 62, no. 3(June 1972), Table 1, p. 401, n. 14, p. 402.

19. Ibid., Table 1, p. 401.

20. A. S. DeVany and T. R. Saving, "Product Duality, Uncertainty and Regulation: The Trucking Industry," *American Economic Review* 67, no. 4(Sept. 1977):583.

21. Kenneth D. Boyer, "Queuing Analysis and Value of Service Pricing in the Trucking Industry: Comment," 70, no. 1 *American Economic Review* 70, no. 1(Mar. 1980):174–80.

22. Ibid., 179.

23. This does not imply that truckload rates are at the same level as if the industry were to be deregulated. Competition for the traffic moving in truckload lots under commodity rates may eliminate commodity rate discrimination and the monopoly profits of regulated trucking firms, but it does so on a foundation of regulatory-induced inflation of transport costs.

24. Snow, "The Problem," 5.

CHAPTER 9

1. 49 Stat. 543 (9 Aug. 1953), 49 Code Section 301 *et seq.,* as amended. Passage of the Motor Carrier Act of 1980 (Public Law 96-296), along with a relaxation of rule-making practices by the Interstate Commerce Commission, have made entry into interstate trucking activities substantially easier than previously. Other basic provisions of the Act of 1935 continue to apply, however.

2. Provisions of the Nebraska law were and remain similar to those of the original Federal Act. (The Nebraska legislature has not responded to the revisions in the federal statutes.) See Nebraska Revised Statutes, Sections 75-118 to 75-134 and 75-301 to 75-332.01 (Reissue 1976 and Cumulative Supplement 1980).

3. See, for example, Nicholas A. Glaskowsky, Jr., Brian F. O'Neil and Donald R. Hudson, *Motor Carrier Regulation: A Review and Evaluation of Three Major Current Regulatory Issues Relating to the Interstate Common Carrier Trucking Industry* (Washington: ATA Foundation, 1976), 12–15.

4. For a statement of this position see John W. Snow, "The Problem of Motor Carrier Regulation and the Ford Administration's Proposal for Reform," in *Regulation of Entry and Pricing in Truck Transportation,* ed. Paul W. MacAvoy and John W. Snow, (Washington: American Enterprise Institute, 1977), 27–33.

5. A more detailed account of the procedures and findings is found in Elmo Falcon, "Impact of Motor Carrier Deregulation on a Small Rural Community—A Case Study" (Lincoln: M.S. thesis, University of Nebraska-Lincoln, 1981).

6. The survey was conducted during the summer of 1980 and covered operations for a period which immediately preceded implementation of the Motor Carrier Act of 1980.

7. For discussions of the theoretical and procedural bases for economic-engineering cost-finding techniques, see Ben C. French, "The Analysis of Productive Efficiency in Agricultural Marketing: Models, Methods, and Progress," in *A Survey of Agricultural Economics Literature,* ed. Lee R. Martin (Minneapolis: Univ. of Minnesota Press, 1977) 1:97–120, 132–41; and Dale G. Anderson and Delmer L. Helgeson, "Problems and Techniques of Intra-Firm Cost Identification and Analysis: Multi-Product and Multi-Service Suppliers," in *Farm/Ranch Input Research—Yesterday, Today, and Tomorrow,* North Central Regional Research Publication 215 and Michigan State Agricultural Experiment Station Research Report 208, ed. Paul E. Nelson, Jr. (East Lansing: Michigan State Univ., 1973), 117–43.

8. See, for example, Thomas Gale Moore, *Trucking Regulation: Lessons from Europe* (Washington: American Enterprise Institute, 1976); Richard N. Farmer, "The Case for Unregulated Truck Transportation," *Journal of Farm Economics,* 46, no. 2(May 1964):398–409; and J.R. Snitzler and R.J. Byrne, *Interstate Trucking of Fresh and Frozen Poultry under Agricultural Exemption,* Marketing Research Report No. 224 (Washington: USDA, 1958).

CHAPTER 10

1. *Nebraska Constitution,* Art. 4, Sec. 20.

2. Nebraska State Railway Commission, *Fourteenth Annual Report* (1921), 529.

3. *Laws of Nebraska,* Chap. 142 (1937).

4. *Effenberger* v. *Marconnit,* 135 Neb. 558 (1939); *Moritz* v. *N.S.R.C.,* 147 Neb. 400 (1946); *Christensen* v. *Highway Motor Freight,* 158 Neb. 601 (1954); *Houk* v. *Peake,* 162 Neb. 717 (1956); and *Preisendorg Transp.* v. *Herman Bros.,* 169 Neb. 693 (1960).

5. *Nebraska R.R.S.,* 1943 Chap. 75, Sec. 311 (1976).

6. *Moritz* v. *Transcontinental Bus Lines,* 153 Neb. 206 (1950), 210.

7. *Nebraska R.R.S.,* 1943 Chap. 75, Sec. 311 (1976).

8. *Ace Gas* v. *Peake,* 184 Neb. 448 (1969), 453.

9. *Yellow Cab & Baggage* v. *Public Cars,* 126 Neb. 138 (1934), 146.

10. *Effenberger* v. *Omaha Y C.B. St. Ry. Col,* 150 Neb. 13 (1948), and *Moritz* v. *Transcontinental Bus Lines,* 153 Neb. 206 (1948).

11. *Application of Canada,* 154 Neb. 256 (1951), 261. See also *Edgar* v. *Wheeler Transport,* 157 Neb. 1 (1953).

12. *Young* v. *Morgan Drive Away,* 171 Neb. 784 (1961), 789.

13. *Ferguson Trucking Co.* v. *Rogers Truck Line,* 164 Neb. 85 (1957), 98. See also *Black Hills Stage Lines* v. *Greyhound,* 174 Neb. 425 (1962), 429, in which the court said flatly that intercity "bus and truck operations . . . are not natural monopolies."

14. *Effenberger* v. *Marconnit,* 135 Neb. 558 (1939), 563.

15. *R. B. "Dick" Wilson, Inc.* v. *Hargleroad,* 165 Neb. 468 (1957), 475.

16. *Black Hills Stage Lines* v. *Greyhound,* 174 Neb. 425 (1962), 430.

17. *Robinson* v. *National,* 188 Neb. 474 (1972), 475–76.

18. *Simmerman* v. *National,* 179 Neb. 400 (1965), 403–4.

19. *Ruan* v. *Herman Bros.,* 192 Neb. 343 (1974).

20. See, for example, *Union Transfer* v. *Bee Line,* 150 Neb. 280 (1948); *Application of Resler,* 154 Neb. 624 (1951); *Houk* v. *Peake,* 162 Neb. 717 (1956); *Schmunk* v. *West Nebraska Express,* 159 Neb. 134 (1959); *Ace Gas* v. *Peake,* 184 Neb. 448 (1969); and *Dahlsten* v. *Harris,* 191 Neb. 714 (1974).

21. *Midwest Mail* v. *B.D.C.,* 174 Neb. 809 (1963). See also *Wells Fargo* v. *B.D.C.,* 186 Neb. 261 (1971); and *Wells Fargo* v. *B.D.C.,* 188 Neb. 584 (1972).

22. *Samardick* v. *B.D.C.,* 183 Neb. 229 (1968), 237.

23. *Petroleum Transport Service, Inc.* v. *Ruan Transport Corporation, et al.,* 210 Neb. 411 (1982).

24. Ibid., 214.

25. Neb. R.R.S., 1943, Chap. 75, Sec. 311 (1976).

26. Richard Beilock and James Freeman, "Motor Carrier Deregulation in Florida," *Growth and Change* 14, no. 2(Apr. 1983):32.

27. Ibid., 32.

28. *Petroleum Transport Service, Inc.* v. *Ruan Transport Corporation, et al.,* 210 Neb. 411 (1982), 415.

29. *Gulf Transport Company* v. *Public Service Commission of Missouri,* 658 S.W. 2d 448 (Mo. App. 1983), 456.

30. James Freeman and Richard Beilock, "State Regulatory Responses to Federal Motor Carrier Reregulation," *University of Florida Law Review* 35, no. 1(Winter 1983):70–71.

31. Ibid., 72.

32. *S.Y.A. Bus Line,* 1928E P.U.R. 98 (1928), 101.

CHAPTER 11

1. Public Law 96-296, 94 Stat. 793 (July 1, 1980).

2. *Pan-American Bus Lines Operation,* 1 M.C.C. 190, 203 (1936).

3. Kenneth E. Siegel, ed., "Motor Carrier Transportation," *ICC Practitioners' Journal* 48, no. 4(May-June 1981):451–55.

4. *Superior Trucking Co. Extension-Agricultural Machinery,* 126 M.C.C. 292 (1977).

5. *Liberty Trucking Co., Extension-General Commodities,* 130 M.C.C. 243 (1978).

6. Donald V. Harper, "Entry Control and the Federal Motor Carrier Act of 1980," *Transportation Law Journal,* 12, no. 1(1981):57.

7. 94 Stat. 794 (1980).

8. *La-Bar's Inc., Extension-Mountaintop Insulation,* (Wilkes-Barre, Pa.); Sub. No. 14, 132 M.C.C. 263 (1980); Commerce Clearing House, *1980–82 Carrier Cases,* Section 36,941.04, p. 47,742.

9. *Rules Governing Applications for Operating Authority,* Ex Parte No. 55, Sub-No. 43, 364 I.C.C. 508 (1980).

10. Oliver W. Kreuger, "Statement," in *Oversight-Motor Carrier Act of 1980,* Hearings before the Subcommittee on Surface Transportation of the Committee on Public Works and Transportation, House of Representatives, 97th Cong., 2d sess., June 23, Nov. 30, Dec. 1, 1982, 37.

11. Denis A. Breen, "Antitrust and Price Competition in the Trucking Industry," *Antitrust Bulletin* 28, no. 1(Spring 1983):213–14.

12. 94 Stat. 796.

13. See, especially, *Elimination of Gateway Restrictions and Circuitous Route Limitations,* Ex Parte No. MC-142, 132 M.C.C. 174 (1980) and *Removal of Restrictions from Authorities of Motor Carriers of Property,* Ex Parte No. 142 (Sub-No. 1), 132 M.C.C. 374 (1980).

14. Breen, "Antitrust," 216–17.

15. William J. Baumol, John C. Panzar, and Robert D. Willig, *Contestable Markets and the Theory of Industry Structure* (San Diego: Harcourt Brace Jovanovich, 1982).

16. Elizabeth E. Bailey and William J. Baumol, "Deregulation and the Theory of Contestable Markets," *Yale Journal on Regulation,* 1, no. 2(1984):133–34.

17. "Good Owner-Operators Hard to Find, Costly When Lost," *Transport Topics* no. 2522(Dec. 12, 1983), 1, 6.

18. "Statement of Honorable Reese H. Taylor, Jr.," *Motor Carrier Act of 1980,* Hearing before the Subcommittee on Surface Transportation of the Committee on Commerce, Science, and Transportation, U.S. Senate, 97th Cong., 2d sess., Dec. 14, 1982 (Washington, D.C.: GPO, 1982), 26.

19. Ibid., 32.

20. The offers of certificated carriers for owner-operators in several issues of *Transport Topics* between Jan. 30 and June 5, 1978, were recorded wherever the percentage of gross revenue to be received by such operators was set forth. The mean offer for operators without trailers was 66.5 percent (n = 15) and with trailers, 78.7 percent (n = 12).

21. *Transport Topics,* Sept. 19, 1983, and Mar. 12, Apr. 23, and May 14, 1983.

22. "Good Owner-Operators Hard to Find, Costly When Lost," *Transport Topics* no. 2522 (Dec. 12, 1983):1, 6.

23. "Statement of Honorable Reese H. Taylor, Jr.," *Trucking Deregulation: Is it Happening?* Hearing before the Joint Economic Committee, Congress of the United States, 97th Cong., 1st sess., Nov. 17, 1981 (Washington, D.C.: GPO, 1982), 37–38.

24. *Lease of Equipment to Private Carriers,* Ex Parte No. MC-122 (Sub-No. 2), 132 M.C.C. 756 (1982).

25. Ibid., 758.

26. "Statement of Honorable Reese H. Taylor, Jr.," *Oversight-Motor Carrier Act of 1980,* Hearings before the Subcommittee on Surface Transportation of the Committee on Public Works and Transportation, House of Representatives, 97th Cong., 2nd sess., June 23, Nov. 30, Dec. 1, 1982 (Washington, D.C.: GPO, 1982), 336.

27. David J. Airozo, "Supreme Court Ruling Upholds ICC's 'Single-Source' Leasing Policy," *Traffic World* 198, no. 2(Apr. 9, 1984):23.

28. 94 Stat. 898 (1980).

29. *Interpretation-Incorporate Hauling,* Ex Parte No. M.C.C. 122, Sub-No. 3, 132 M.C.C. 736 (1981).

30. Private Truck Fleet Operation Cost Placed at $1.29 per Mile in 1982, *Traffic World* 198, no. 5(Apr. 30, 1984):27.

31. *Rules Governing Applications for Operating Authority,* Ex Parte No. 55, Sub-No. 43, 364 I.C.C. 508, 536 (1980).

32. "Private Truck Fleet Operation Cost," *Traffic World* 198, no. 5(Apr. 30, 1984):27.

33. Donald V. Harper, *Transportation in America: Users, Carriers, Government,* 2nd ed. (Englewood Cliffs, NJ: Prentice-Hall, 1982), p. 533.

34. 94 Stat. 800 (1980).

35. Public Law 85-163 (1957), 71 Stat. 411. The MCA of 1980 continued to define motor contract carrier as one that provided transportation for "a person or limited number of persons," but the ICC, itself, had held this to mean a very substantial number of persons if the service was sufficiently specialized. In *Armored Motor Service, Inc., Conversion Proceeding,* the commission found that "respondents' operations . . . conform to the . . . definition of a contract carrier" even though one of the respondents, Brinks, served some 314 shippers. 77 M.C.C. 433, 436, and 439 (1958). On the other hand, the commission denied an extension to an applicant already serving seven shippers on the ground that "contract carriers whose services do not possess . . . a high degree of specialization [and who seek to provide] service to more than six or eight separate shippers will be scrutinized with great care." *Umthun Trucking Co. Extension—Phosphatic Feed Supplements,* 91 M.C.C. 691 (1962). This subsequently became known as the "rule of eight." See Robert C. Lieb, *Transportation: The Domestic System,* 2d ed. (Reston, Va.: Reston, 1981), 240.

36. 94 Stat. 801 (1980).

37. *Motor Carrier Act of 1980,* Hearing before the Senate Subcommittee on Surface Transportation, 29–30.

38. ICC, *Annual Report* (1978), 102, and ICC, *Annual Report* (1983), 103.

39. 94 Stat. 803–4.

40. *Collective Ratemaking in the Trucking Industry,* A Report of the President and the Congress of the United States, submitted by the Motor Carrier Ratemaking Study Commission, June 1, 1983, 257.

41. Ibid., 455.

42. Ibid., 534.

43. Ibid, 508.

44. James P. Rakowski, "Deregulation Route for Truckers Remains Rough in Several Places," *Traffic World* (Dec. 12, 1983):15–17, notes that there are "major barriers to entry for a potential less-than-truckload operator" and that concentration in the LTL market has increased perceptibly within recent years. He then proceeds to defend rate bureaus, the mechanism presumably by which the concentrated LTL sector can translate entry barriers and market power into monopoly profits! A representative of the Small Shipments Traffic Conference, by way of contrast, has maintained that rate bureaus still exert too much control over the rates for LTL shipments: "While Congress thought that it was creating a better world for shippers by the Motor Carrier Act of 1980, the practical result, due to Commission inaction, has been the worst of all world[s] for the less-than-truckload shipper: the carriers can collectively set rate increases and the Commission disclaims responsibility for examining their reasonableness." Larry Smith, "Critics of Deregulation and ICC Predominate at House MCA Hearing," *Traffic World* 196, no. 5(Oct. 31, 1983):76.

45. Breen, "Antitrust," 224.

46. 94 Stat. 797.

47. 94 Stat. 812.

48. 94 Stat. 814.

49. *An Assessment of the Impacts on Agriculture of the Staggers Rail Act and Motor Carrier Act of 1980* (Washington, D.C.: Office of Transportation, USDA, Aug. 1982), 9.

50. Marc A. Johnson, "Impacts on Agriculture of Deregulating the Transportation System," *American Journal of Agricultural Economics* 63, no. 5(Dec. 1981):917.

51. T. Q. Hutchinson, *Implications of the Motor Carrier Act of 1980* (Washington, D.C.: USDA, Nov. 1982), 10.

52. *Yearbook of Railroad Facts* (1978), 34; (1983), 32.

53. "ICC Will Allow Short-Notice Data Changes June 25," *Transport Topics* no. 2546(May 28, 1984):1.

54. Michael W. Pustay, "Regulatory Reform and the Allocation of Wealth: An Empirical Analysis," *Quarterly Review of Economics and Business* 23, no. 1(Spring 1983): 19–28.

55. Ibid., 21.

56. If the rights were dormant, their market value would presumably be reflective of monopoly profits alone. According to Pustay, prior to 1977 the ICC generally rejected transfers of dormant operating rights on the ground that it would foster increased competition. Ibid., 25.

57. "IRS Posts Final Rules on Deduction for Carriers Rights," *Transport Topics* no. 2537(Mar. 26, 1984).

58. Pustay, "Regulatory Reform," 25.

59. Pustay, himself, notes that some carriers had recorded operating rights, particularly grandfather rights, at zero prior to the passage of the MCA of 1980. Ibid., 19.

60. See *Transport Topics,* various issues prior to 1980.

61. In *Pre-Fab Transit Company Extension-Nationwide General Commodities,* 132 M.C.C. 409, 410 and 415 (1981), for example, the ICC concluded that Pre-Fab had "not established a threshold case (specifically on the issue of useful public purpose) for author-

ity to transport general commodities between points in the United States," despite the fact "evidence shows that Pre-Fab [already] has 48-state authority to transport multifold specified commodities primarily used in the building and construction industry." Similarly, in *Greenfield Transport Company, Inc., Extension-General Commodities, United States,* 132 M.C.C. 485, 489 (1981), the commission declared: "An applicant cannot simply leap from a showing of its existing service to a single major industry, or a few such industries, plus perhaps scattered additional authority, to the full breadth of nationwide general-commodity authority, without showing shipper needs, marketing studies, studies of potential operating efficiencies or other cogent evidence which makes it appear that a grant of such broad authority will indeed serve a useful public purpose, responsive to public demand or need."

 62. "Statement of Thomas A. Trantrum," *Trucking Deregulation: Is it Happening?* 6.

 63. "Statement of Honorable Reese M. Taylor, Jr.," *Motor Carrier Act of 1980,* 22.

 64. "Statement of Thomas Gale Moore," *Trucking Deregulation: Is it Happening?,* 26.

References

ARTICLES

Airozo, David J. "Supreme Court Ruling Upholds ICC's 'Single Source' Leasing Policy." *Traffic World* 198, no. 2(Apr. 9, 1984):23–24.

Annable, James E., Jr. "The ICC, the IBT, and the Cartelization of the American Trucking Industry." *Quarterly Review of Economics and Business* 13, no. 3(Summer 1973):33–47.

Arentz, Andrew A., Jr. "The Impact of Equipment Leasing on Innovation." *Papers, Sixth Annual Meeting,* Transportation Research Forum. Oxford, Ind.: Cross, 1965, 361–54.

Averch, Harvey, and Leland R. Johnson. "Behavior of the Firm Under Regulatory Constraint." *American Economic Review* 52, no. 5(Dec. 1962):1052–69.

Bailey, Elizabeth E., and William J. Baumol. "Deregulation and the Theory of Contestable Markets." *Yale Journal on Regulation* 1, no. 2(1984):111–37.

Bain, Joe S., "Economies of Scale, Concentration, and the Condition of Entry in Twenty Manufacturing Industries." *American Economic Review* 44, no. 1(Mar. 1954):15–39.

Barrett, Colin. "The 'Big-Company' Era in the Trucking Industry." *Traffic World* 137, no. 8(Feb. 22, 1969):81–85.

Beier, Frederick J. "Off-Peak Freight Rates: Effect on Shippers and Carriers." *Traffic Quarterly* 31, no. 1(Jan. 1979):117-38.

Beilock, Richard, and James Freeman. "Motor Carrier Deregulation in Florida." *Growth and Change* 14, no. 2(Apr. 1983):30–42.

Benishay, Hoskel, and Gilbert R. Whitaker, Jr. "Demand and Supply in Freight Transportation." *Journal of Industrial Economics* 14, no. 3(July 1966):243–62.

Boyer, Kenneth D. "How Similar are Motor Carrier and Rail Rate Structures? The Value of Service Component." *Proceedings, Nineteenth Annual Meeting, Transportation Research Forum.* Oxford, Ind.: Cross, 1978, 523–31.

———. "Queuing Analysis and Value of Service Pricing in the Trucking Industry: Comment." *American Economic Review* 70, no. 1(Mar. 1980):174–80.

Breen, Denis A. "Antitrust and Price Competition in the Trucking Industry." *Antitrust Bulletin* 28, no. 1(Spring 1983):201–25.

Cherry, Russell C. "The Operating Ratio Effect and Regulated Motor Carriers." *Proceedings of a Workshop on Motor Carrier Economic Regulation.* Washington, D.C.: National Academy of Sciences, 1978, 269–89.

Chisholm, Michael. "Economies of Scale in Road Goods Transport? Off-Farm Milk Collection in England and Wales." *Oxford Economic Papers* (Oct. 1959):282–90.

Cowen, Janna L., and John Richard Felton. "Operating-Ratio Regulation and Truck Leasing Practices." *Logistics and Transportation Review* 21, no. 2(June 1985):145–60.

Devany, A. S., and T. R. Saving. "Product Quality, Uncertainty, and Regulation: The Trucking Industry." *American Economic Review* 67, no. 4(Sept. 1977):583–94.

Duffus, William H. "Commercial Motor Transportation — Discussion." *American Economic Review, Supplement* 19, no. 1(Mar. 1929):246–51.

Farmer, Richard N. "The Case for Unregulated Truck Transportation." *Journal of Farm Economics* 46, no. 2(May 1964):389–409.

Ferguson, D. C. "Joint Products and Road Transport Rates in Transport Models." *Journal of Transport Economics and Policy* 6, no. 1(Jan. 1972):69–76.

Freeman, James, and Richard Beilock. "State Regulatory Responses to Federal Motor Carrier Deregulation." *University of Florida Law Review* 35, no. 1(Winter 1983):56–79.

George, John J. "Public Control of Contract Motor Carriers." *Journal of Land and Public Utility Economics* 9, no. 3(Aug. 1933):233–46.

Gifford, Gilbert L. "The Small Shipments Problem." *Transportation Journal* 10, no. 1(Fall 1970):17–27.

"Good Owner-Operators Hard to Find, Costly When Lost." *Transport Topics* no. 2522(Dec. 12, 1983):1, 6.

Harper, Donald V. "Entry Control and the Federal Motor Carrier Act of 1980." *Transportation Law Journal* 12, no. 1(1981):51–73.

Hunter, Merlin H. "The Commercial Motor Vehicle and the Public." *American Economic Review, Supplement* 19, no. 1(Mar. 1929):236–45.

"ICC Will Allow Short-Notice Data Changes June 25." *Transport Topics* no. 2546(May 28, 1984):1.

"IRS Posts Final Rules on Deduction for Carrier Rights." *Transport Topics* no. 2537(Mar. 26, 1984):1, 5.

Johnson, Marc A. "Impacts on Agriculture of Deregulating the Transportation System." *American Journal of Agricultural Economics* 63, no. 5(Dec. 1981):913–20.

Joy, Stewart. "Unregulated Road Haulage: The Australian Experience." *Oxford Economic Papers* 16, no. 2(July 1964):275–85.

Koenker, Richard. "Optimal Scale and the Size Distribution of American Trucking Firms." *Journal of Transport Economics and Policy* 11, no. 1(Jan. 1977):54–67.

Levine, Harvey A. "A Historical Analysis of the Criteria to Determine the Revenue Need of Motor Common Carriers." *ICC Practitioners Journal* 40, no. 2(Jan.–Feb. 1973):158–76.

Miller, Edward. "Effects of Regulation on Truck Utilization." *Transportation Journal* 13, no. 1(Fall 1973):5–14.

Morton, Alexander L. "A Statistical Sketch of Intercity Freight Demand." *Highway Research Record,* no. 296, Transportation Pricing. Washington: Highway Research Board, 1969, 47–65.

Nelson, James C. "The Motor Carrier Act of 1935." *Journal of Political Economy* 44, no. 4(Aug. 1936):464–504.

_____. "The Effects of Entry Control in Surface Transport." In *Transportation Economics: A Conference of the Universities-National Bureau Committee for Economic Research.* New York: Nation Bureau of Economic Research, 1965.

_____. "Performance of Unregulated Trucking in Australia." *Proceedings of the National Symposium on Transportation for Agriculture and Rural America.* Washington, D.C.: U.S. Department of Transportation, 1977, 87–94.

Olson, Josephine E. "Price Discrimination by Regulated Motor Carriers." *American Economic Review* 62, no. 3(June 1972):395–402.

Peterson, G. Shorey. "Motor Carrier Regulation and Its Economic Bases." *Quarterly Journal of Economics* 43, no. 4(Aug. 1929):604–47.

Phillips, Karen Borlaug. "The Role of Research in Transportation Policy: The Case of Motor Carrier Regulatory Reform." *Proceedings—Twenty-fourth Annual Meeting, Transportation Research Forum* 24, no. 1(1983):399–409.

"Private Truck Fleet Operation Cost Placed at $1.29 per Mile in 1982." *Traffic World* 198, no. 5(Apr. 30, 1984):27–28.

Pustay, Michael W. "Regulatory Reform and the Allocation of Wealth: An Empirical Analysis." *Quarterly Review of Economics and Business* 23, no. 1(Spring 1983):19–28.

Rakowski, James P. "Deregulation Route for Truckers Remains Rough in Several Places." *Traffic World* 196, no. 11(Dec. 12, 1983):15–17.

Roberts, Merrill J. "Some Aspects of Motor Carrier Costs: Firm Size, Efficiency and Financial Health." *Land Economics* 32, no. 3(Aug. 1956):228–38.

Schumaier, C. P. "Characteristics of Agriculturally Exempt Motor Carriers." *Conference on Private and Unregulated Transportation.* Evanston, Ill.: Transportation Center, Northwestern University, October 29–30, 1962.

Schwartzman, David. "Monopoly and Wages." *Canadian Journal of Economics and Political Science* 26, no. 3(Aug. 1960):428–38.

Siegel, Kenneth E., ed. "Motor Carrier Transportation." *ICC Practitioners' Journal* 48, no. 4(May–June 1981):451–55.

Sloss, James. "Regulation of Motor Freight Transportation: A Quantitative Evaluation of Policy." *Bell Journal of Economics and Management Science* 1, no. 2(Autumn 1970):327–66.

Smith, Larry. "Critics of Deregulation and ICC Predominate at House MCA Hearing." *Traffic World* 196, no. 5(Oct. 31, 1983):39–40.

Spychalski, J. C. "Criticisms of Regulated Transport: Do Economists' Perceptions Conform with Institutional Realities?" *Transportation Journal* 14, no. 3(Spring 1975):5–17.

Trumbower, Henry R. "The Regulation of the Common Carrier Vehicle with Respect to Its Competitive Aspects." *American Economic Review, Supplement* 19, no. 1(Mar. 1929):226–35.

Wallace, Donald H. "Joint and Overhead Cost and Railway Rate Policy." *Quarterly Journal of Economics* 48, no. 4(Aug. 1934):583–619.

Walters, A. A. "The Allocation of Joint Costs with Demands as Probability Distributions." *American Economic Review* 50, no. 3(June 1960):419–32.

Wellisz, Stanislaw H. "Regulation of Natural Gas Pipeline Companies: An Economic Analysis." *Journal of Political Economy* 71, no. 1(Feb. 1963):30–43.

BOOKS AND MONOGRAPHS

American Trucking Trends, 1976 Statistical Supplement. Washington, D.C.: American Trucking Associations, 1976.

Anderson, Dale G., and Wayne W. Budt. *A Rate/Cost Analysis of Nebraska Meat Trucking Activities with Livestock Trucking Cost Comparisons.* Research Bulletin 269. Lincoln: Nebraska Agricultural Experiment Station, Mar. 1975.

Bailey, Elizabeth E. *Economic Theory of Regulatory Constraint.* Lexington, Mass.: Heath, 1973.

Bain, J. S. *Industrial Organization.* 2d ed. New York: Wiley, 1968.

Baumol, William J., John C. Panzar, and Robert D. Willig. *Contestable Markets and the*

Theory of Industry Structure. San Diego: Harcourt Brace Jovanovich, 1982.

Bayliss, Brian T., and S. L. Edwards. *Industrial Demand for Transport.* London: Her Majesty's Stationery Office, 1970.

Bonavia, Michael R. *The Economics of Transport.* 2d ed. London: Pitman, 1947.

Boulding, Kenneth E. *Economic Analysis.* 3d ed. New York: Harper, 1955.

Burstein, M. L., ed. *The Cost of Trucking: An Econometric Analysis.* Dubuque, Iowa: Brown, 1965.

The Case Against Deregulation. Washington, D.C.: American Trucking Associations, n.d.

Chisholm, Michael, and Patrick O'Sullivan. *Freight Flows and Spatial Aspects of the British Economy.* Cambridge: Cambridge Univ. Press, 1973.

Davidson, Jack R., and Howard W. Ottoson, eds. *Transportation Problems and Policies and Policies in the Trans-Missouri West.* Lincoln: Univ. of Nebraska Press, 1967.

Fellmeth, Robert C. *The Interstate Commerce Omission.* New York: Grossman, 1970.

Friedlaender, Ann F. *The Dilemma of Freight Transport Regulation.* Washington, D.C.: Brookings Institution, 1969.

Fuller, John W., ed. *Regulation and Competition in Transportation: Selected Works of James C. Nelson.* Vancouver: Centre for Transportation Studies, 1983.

Glaskowsky, N. A., Jr., B. F. O'Neil, and D. R. Hudson. *Motor Carrier Regulation.* Washington, D.C.: ATA Foundation, 1976.

Hannahs, Stephen, and Joseph Tune. *1977 Financial Analysis of the Motor Carrier Industry.* Union Oil, Union 76 Division, n.d.

Harper, Donald V. *Transportation in America: Users, Carriers, Government.* 2d ed. Englewood Cliffs, N.J.: Prentice-Hall, 1982.

Jackman, W. T. *Economics of Transportation.* Chicago: Shaw, 1926.

Johnson, E. R., G. B. Huebner, and G. L. Wilson. *Principles of Transportation.* New York: Appleton, 1928.

Johnson, James C. *Trucking Mergers.* Lexington, Mass.: Lexington Books, 1973.

Kahn, Alfred E. *The Economics of Regulation.* 2 vols. New York: Wiley, 1971.

Kolsen, H. M. *The Economics and Control of Road-Rail Competition.* Sydney: Sydney Univ. Press, 1968.

Lansing, John E. *Transportation and Economic Policy.* New York: Free Press, 1966.

Lieb, Robert C. *Transportation: The Domestic System.* 2d ed. Reston, Va.: Reston, 1981.

Locklin, D. P. *Economics of Transportation.* 7th ed. Homewood, Ill.: Irwin, 1972.

MacAvoy, Paul W., and John W. Snow, eds. *Regulation of Entry and Pricing in Truck Transportation.* Washington, D.C.: American Enterprise Institute, 1977.

McCallum, George E. *New Techniques in Railroad Ratemaking.* Pullman, Wash.: Bureau of Economic and Business Research, Washington State Univ., 1968.

Martin, Lee R., ed. *A Survey of Agricultural Economics Literature.* Minneapolis: Univ. of Minnesota Press, 1977.

Mason, Edward S. *Economic Concentration and the Monopoly Problem.* Cambridge: Harvard Univ. Press, 1959.

Miller, S. L. *Inland Transportation: Principles and Policies.* New York: McGraw-Hill, 1933.

Mohring, Herbert. *Transportation Economics.* Cambridge, Mass.: Ballinger, 1976.

Moore, Thomas Gale. *Freight Transportation Regulation: Surface Freight and the Interstate Commerce Commission.* Washington, D.C.: American Enterprise Institute, 1972.

_____. *Trucking Regulation: Lessons from Europe.* Washington, D.C.: American Enterprise Institute, 1976.

Moulton, H. G., and Associates. *The American Transportation Problem.* Washington, D.C.: Brookings, 1933.

Nelson, James R. *Marginal Cost Pricing in Practice.* Englewood Cliffs, N.J.: Prentice-Hall, 1964.

Nelson, James R., ed. *Criteria for Transport Pricing.* Washington, D.C.: Transportation and Logistics Center, American Univ., 1969.

Nelson, Paul E., Jr., ed. *Farm/Ranch Input Research: Yesterday, Today, and Tomorrow.* North Central Regional Research Publication 215 and Michigan State Agricultural Experiment Station Research Report 208. East Lansing: Michigan State Univ., 1973.

Nelson, Robert A. *Motor Carrier Freight Transportation in New England, A Report to the New England Governors' Council.* Boston: New England Governors' Committee on Public Transportation, 1956.

Nie, N. H., et al. *Statistical Package for the Social Sciences.* New York: McGraw-Hill, 1975.

Oi, W. Y., and A. P. Hurter, Sr. *Economics of Private Truck Transportation.* Dubuque, Iowa: Brown, 1965.

Pegrum, Dudley F. *Transportation Economics and Public Policy.* Rev. ed. Homewood, Ill.: Irwin, 1968.

Perle, Eugene D. *The Demand for Transportation: Regional and Commodity Studies in the United States,* Department of Geography Research Paper no. 95. Chicago: Univ. of Chicago Press, 1964.

Phillips, Almarin, ed. *Perspectives on Antitrust Policy.* Princeton, N.J.: Princeton Univ. Press, 1965.

_____. *Promoting Competition in Regulated Markets.* Washington, D.C.: Brookings, 1975.

St. George, George, and Charles Rust. *Grain Trucking Costs for Montana.* Bulletin 636. Bozeman: Montana Agricultural Experiment Station, 1970.

Sampson, Roy J., and Martin T. Farris. *Domestic Transportation: Practice, Theory, and Policy.* 4th ed. Boston: Houghton Mifflin, 1979.

Taff, Charles A. *Commercial Motor Transportation.* 5th ed. Homewood, Ill.: Irwin, 1975.

Thompson, A. W. J., and L. C. Hunter. *The Nationalized Transport Industries.* London: Heinemann Educational Books, 1973.

Transportation Economics: A Conference of the Universities — National Bureau Committee for Economic Research. New York: National Bureau of Economic Research, 1965.

Transportation Facts and Trends, 13th ed. Washington, D.C.: Transportation Association of America, July 1877.

Tyrchniewicz, E. W., A. H. Butler, and O. P. Tangri. *The Cost of Transporting Grain by Farm Truck.* Research Report No. 8. Winnipeg: Center for Transportation Studies, Univ. of Manitoba, July 1971.

Volotta, Alexander. *The Impact of Federal Entry Controls on Motor Carrier Operations.* University Park, Pa.: Center for Research of the College of Business Administration, Pennsylvania State Univ., 1967.

Wagner, W. H. *A Legislative History of the Motor Carrier Act, 1935.* Denton, Md.: Rue, 1935.

Walters, A. A. *Integration in Freight Transport.* London: Institute of Economic Affairs, 1968.

GOVERNMENT PUBLICATIONS

American Trucking Trends, 1965. Washington, D.C.: GPO, 1966.

An Assessment of the Impacts on Agriculture of the Staggers Rail Act and the Motor Carrier Act of 1980. Washington, D.C.: Office of Transportation, USDA, Nov., 1982.

Banks, R. L., and Associates. *Economic Analysis and Regulatory Implications of Motor Carrier Service to Predominantly Small Communities, A Final Report to the U.S. Department of Agriculture.* Washington, D.C., June 24, 1976.

Boles, P. P. *Cost of Operating Trucks for Livestock Transportation.* Marketing Research Report No. 982. Washington, D.C.: USDA, Jan., 1972.

Collective Ratemaking in the Trucking Industry. A Report of the President and the Congress of the United States, Submitted by the Motor Carrier Ratemaking Study Commission, June 1, 1983. Washington, D.C.: GPO, 1983.

A Cost Benefit Evaluation of Surface Transport Regulation. Washington, D.C.: ICC, Bureau of Economics, 1976.

Economic Report of the President. Washington, D.C.: GPO, 1966.

Edwards, B., and J. W. Park. *The Marketing and Distribution of Fruits and Vegetables by Motor Truck.* Technical Bulletin No. 272. Washington, D.C.: USDA, Oct., 1931.

Empty/Loaded Truck Miles on Interstate Highways During 1976. Washington, D.C.: ICC, 1977.

Federal Regulatory Restrictions upon Motor and Water Carriers. Sen. Doc. No. 78, 79th Cong., 1st sess. Washington, D.C.: GPO, 1945.

Hunter, John H., Jr. *The Role of Truck Brokers in the Movement of Exempt Agricultural Commodities.* Marketing Research Report No. 525. Washington, D.C.: USDA, Feb., 1962.

Hurdle, Gloria J. "Statement before the California Public Utilities Commission." Case No. 10368, July 13, 1978.

Hutchinson, T. Q. *Implications of the Motor Carrier Act of 1980.* Washington, D.C.: USDA, Nov., 1983.

Hymson, Edward S. "An Evaluation of the Accuracy of the Interstate Commerce Commission Measures of Profitability of Motor Carriers Applying for General Rate Increases." Washington, D.C.: National Science Foundation. Mimeo, n.d.

Interstate Commerce Commission. Annual Report. Washington, D.C.: GPO, various issues.

––––––. *Statement No. 531.* Washington, D.C.: GPO, Jan. 1953.

––––––. *Transport Economics.* Washington, D.C.: GPO, Jan., 1963.

Interstate Commerce Commission, Bureau of Transport Economics and Statistics. *Statement No. 6010.* Hearings before the Surface Transportation Subcommittee, Senate Committee on Commerce in S. 2560 and S. 2764, 87th Cong. 2d sess. Washington, D.C.: GPO, Feb., Apr., 1962.

––––––. *Intercity Ton-miles 1939–1959. Statement No. 6103.* Washington, D.C.: GPO, Apr., 1969.

Kennedy, Edward M. "Opening Statement." *Oversight of Freight Rate Competition in the Motor Carrier Industry,* Hearings. U.S. Senate, Committee on the Judiciary, Subcommittee on Antitrust and Monopoly, 95th Congress, 1st and 2d sess., Washington, D.C.: GPO, 1978.

McElhiney, Paul T. *Motor Carrier Common Carrier Freight Survey*. Washington, D.C.: U.S. Department of Transportation, 1975.

Miklius, Walter. *Economic Performance of Motor Carriers Operating under the Agricultural Exemption*. Marketing Research Report No. 838. Washington, D.C.: USDA, 1969.

Motor Carrier Act of 1980. Hearing before the Subcommittee on Surface Transportation of the Committee on Commerce, Science, and Transportation, U.S. Senate, 97th Cong., 2d sess., Dec. 14, 1982. Washington, D.C.: GPO, 1982.

Oversight-Motor Carrier Act of 1980. Hearings before the Subcommittee on Surface Transportation of the Committee on Public Works and Transportation, House of Representatives, 97th Cong., 2d sess., June 23, Nov. 30, Dec. 1, 1982. Washington, D.C.: GPO, 1982.

Regulation of Interstate Motor Carriers. Hearing before a Subcommittee on Interstate and Foreign Commerce, House of Representatives, 74th Cong., 1st sess., Feb. 19–Mar. 5, 1935. Washington, D.C.: GPO, 1935.

Regulation of Transport Agencies: A Report of the Federal Coordinator of Transportation. Senate Document No. 152, 73d Cong., 2d sess. Washington, D.C.: GPO, 1934.

Roberts, Merrill J. "Transport Costs, Pricing, and Regulation." In *Transportation Economics: A Conference of the Universities*. New York: National Bureau of Economic Research, 1965, 3–40.

Shenefield, John H. "Prepared Statement." U.S. Senate, Committee on the Judiciary, Subcommittee on Antitrust and Monopoly, 95th Congress, 1st and 2d sess. *Oversight of Freight Rate Competition in the Motor Carrier Industry*. Hearings. Washington, D.C.: GPO, 1978.

Snitzler, J. R., and R. J. Byrne. *Interstate Trucking of Fresh and Frozen Poultry under Agricultural Exemption*. Marketing Research Report No. 224, Washington, D.C.: USDA, 1958.

_____. *Interstate Trucking of Frozen Fruits and Vegetables under Agricultural Exemption*. Marketing Research Report No. 316. Washington, D.C.: USDA, 1959.

Sutton, R. M., R. S. Potter, and D. W. Weitz. *Private Carriage Motivation and Impact of Rural Location*. Prepared for U.S. Department of Transportation. New York: Drake Sheehan/Stewart Dougall, Mar. 28, 1985.

Trucking Deregulation: Is It Happening? Hearing before the Joint Economic Committee, Congress of the United States, 97th Cong., 1st sess., Nov. 17, 1981. Washington, D.C.: GPO, 1982.

U.S. Bureau of the Census. *1972 Census of Transportation: Truck Inventory and Use Survey*. Washington, D.C.: GPO, 1974.

U.S. Department of Agriculture. *For-Hire Carriers Hauling Exempt Agricultural Commodities*. Marketing Research Report No. 585. Washington, D.C.: USDA, Jan., 1963.

U.S. Department of Agriculture. *The Role of Truck Brokers in the Movement of Exempt Agricultural Commodities*. Marketing Research Report No. 525. Washington, D.C.: USDA, Feb., 1962.

U.S. Department of Labor. *Indexes of Output Per Man Hour: Selected Industries, 1939 and 1947–65*. Washington, D.C.: GPO, 1966.

U.S. Department of Labor, Bureau of Labor Statistics. *Technological Trends in Major American Industries*. Washington, D.C.: GPO, 1966.

U.S. Senate. *Control of Illegal Interstate Motor Carrier Transportation.* Hearings before the Surface Transportation Subcommittee, Senate Committee on Commerce. In S. 2560 and S. 2764, 87th Cong., 2d sess. Washington, D.C.: GPO, Feb. and Apr., 1962.

U.S. Senate. *National Transportation Policy.* 87th Cong., 1st sess. Washington, D.C.: GPO, 1961.

U.S. Senate. *Trucking Mergers and Concentration.* Hearings before the Senate Select Committee on Small Business, 85th Cong., 1st sess. Washington, D.C.: GPO, July, 1957.

Wright, Bruce H. *For-Hire Trucking of Exempt Farm Products.* Marketing Research Report No. 649. Washington, D.C.: USDA, 1964.

ICC CASES

Aluminum Extrusions from Miami to Chicago, 32 I.C.C. 188 (1965).

Animal Feed – Kansas City, Mo., to Chicago, 325 I.C.C. 147 (1965).

Applications to Substitute Single-Line for Joint-Line Operations, Ex Parte No. MC-109.

Armored Motor Service, Inc., Conservation Proceeding, 77 M.C.C. 433 (1958).

Associated Transport, Inc. – Control and Consolidation – Arrow Carrier Corp., et al., 38 M.C.C. 137 (1942).

Atchison, Topeka and Santa Fe Railway Company v. *Morris,* 329 I.C.C. 326 (1967).

Bass Transportation Co., Inc., Extension – St. Louis, Mo., 125 M.C.C. 233 (1976).

C & D Oil Company Contract Carrier Application, 1 M.C.C. 329 (1936).

Carbon Black, Southwest to Ind., Ohio and Mo., 325 I.C.C. 138 (1965).

Central Territory Motor Carrier Rates, 8 M.C.C. 233 (1938).

Central Transport, Inc. – Purchase (Portion) – Piedmont Petroleum Products, Inc., 127 M.C.C. 284 (1978).

Change of Policy Consideration of Rates in Operating Rights Application Proceedings, 359 I.C.C. 613 (1979).

Charles F. Geraci Contract Carrier Application, 7 M.C.C. 369 (1938).

Clipper Express Co., Petition for a Declaratory Order: Exempt Agricultural Commodities, 361 I.C.C. 301 (1979).

Coffee, Roasted, from Omaha, Ne., to Twin Cities, 22 M.C.C. 529 (1940).

Composition Roofing, Stroud, Ok., to St. Louis, Mo., 329 I.C.C. 612 (1967).

Connell Transport Co. Extension – New York, N.Y., 91 M.C.C. 113 (1962).

Contractors Cargo Company – Extension of Operations, 96 M.C.C. 306 (1964).

Coordination of Motor Transportation, 182 I.C.C. 263 (1932).

Direct Routes for Regular Route Movements, Ex Parte No. MC-136 (not printed), decided Aug. 8, 1980.

Dry Goods, Piece Goods, Dependent on Value, 53 M.C.C. 157 (1951).

Dual Operations, Ex Parte No. 55 (Sub. No. 27) 43 Fed. Reg. 14664 (1978).

E. A. Gallagher & Sons v. *Cleveland General Transport Co., Inc.,* 98 M.C.C. 356 (1965).

Elimination of Gateway Restrictions and Circuitous Route Limitations, Ex Parte No. MC-142, 132 M.C.C. 174 (1980).

Ex-Water Traffic, Ex Parte No. MC-105, 44 Fed. Reg. 3723 (1979).

Foodstuffs from Jacksonville to Georgia and Alabama, 62 M.C.C. 689 (1954).

General Increase – Middle Atlantic and New England Territories, 319 I.C.C. 168 (1963).

General Increase, Middle Atlantic and New England Territories, 332 I.C.C. 820 (1969).

General Increase — Southern Motor Carriers Rate Conference I. and S. Doc. No. M-29772 43 Fed. Reg. 15550 (1978).

General Increases — Eastern Central Territory, 316 I.C.C. 467 (1962).

Grant of Operating Authority to an Applicant Who Intends to Use It Primarily as an Incident to the Carriage of Its Own Goods and Its Own Non-transportation Business, Ex Parte No. MC-118, 43 Fed. Reg. 55051 (1978).

Greenfield Transport Company, Inc., Extension-General Commodities, United States, 132 M.C.C. 485 (1981).

Gypsum, Paper, from Kansas City, Mo., to Chicago, 304 I.C.C. 125 (1958).

H. B. Church Truck Service Company Common Carrier Application, 27 M.C.C. 191 (1940).

Implementation of Public Law 90-433 — Agricultural Cooperative Transportation Exemption, 108 M.C.C. 799 (1969).

Increased Common Carrier Rates in the East, 42 M.C.C. 633 (1943).

Increased Common Carrier Truck Rates in New England, 43 M.C.C. 13 (1943).

Increased LTL, AQ, and TL Rates, to, from, and between New England Territory, 335 I.C.C. 185 (1969).

Increased Motor Carrier Rates in New England, 1949, 49 M.C.C. 477 (1949).

Increased Rates and Charges, Central and Southern Territories, 335 I.C.C. 676 (1969).

Increased Rates and Charges, from, to, and between Middlewest Territory, 335 I.C.C. 142 (1969).

Increased Rates and Minimum Charges within, from, and to the South, 335 I.C.C. 77 (1969).

Increases, Middle Atlantic and New England 1948, 49 M.C.C. 357 (1949).

Increases, Transcontinental-Intermountain Coast, 304 I.C.C. 15 (1958).

Independent Movers — Rates on Household Goods, I. & S. No. M-2640, 46 M.C.C. 878 (1946), *Commerce Clearing House,* Federal Carrier Cases — ICC, vol. 2, CCH No. 31, 218, pp. 516–7.

Intercorporate Hauling: Proposed Policy Statement, Ex Parte No. MC-122, 44 Fed. Reg. 42838 (1979).

Intermediate Point Restriction, Ex Parte No. MC-132 (not printed), decided Aug. 8, 1980.

Interpretation — Intercorporate Hauling, Ex Parte No. 122 (Sub-No. 3), 132 M.C.C. 736 (1981).

James La Casse Extension — Dairy Products, 79 M.C.C. 222 (1959).

John Klann Moving & Trucking Company Contract Carrier Application, 29 M.C.C. 409 (1941).

J. V. McNicholas Transfer Co. — Control — Tom's Express, Inc., 127 M.C.C. 309 (1978).

Keystone Transportation Company Contract Carrier Application, 19 M.C.C. 475 (1939).

La-Bar's Inc., Extension-Mountaintop Insulation (Wilkes-Barre, Pa.); Sub-No. 14, 132 M.C.C. 263 (1980); CCH, 1980-82 Carrier Cases, Section 36,941, p. 47,742.

Lawrence G. Willman Contract Carrier Application, 77 M.C.C. 535 (1958).

L. C. Jones Trucking Company, Extension — Utah, 69 M.C.C. 273 (1956).

Lease of Equipment to Private Carriers, Ex Parte No. MC-122, Sub-No. 2, 132 M.C.C. 756 (1982).

Lenoir Chair Co. Contract Carrier Application, 51 M.C.C. 65 (1949).

Liberty Trucking Co., Extension — General Commodities, 130 M.C.C. 243 (1978).

Liberty Trucking Co., Extension — General Commodities, 131 M.C.C. 573 (1979).

Lukens Steel Co., Contract Carrier Application, 42 M.C.C. 672 (1943).

McCormick's Express, Inc., Common Carrier Application, 12 M.C.C. 632 (1938).
Middle Atlantic States Motor Carrier Rates, 4 M.C.C. 68 (1937).
Midwestern Motor Carrier Rates, 27 M.C.C. 297 (1941).
Milk from Iola to Kansas City, 304 I.C.C. 13 (1958).
Motor Bus and Truck Operation, 140 I.C.C. 685 (1928).
Motor Transportation of Property Incidental to Transportation by Aircraft, 131 M.C.C. 87 (1978).
Motor Ways Tariff Bureau v. *Steel Transportation Co., Inc.,* 62 M.C.C. 413 (1954).
New England Motor Carrier Rates, 8 M.C.C. 287 (1938).
New York Central Railroad Company Extension, Congers, N.Y.-Jersey City, N.J., 61 M.C.C. 457 (1953).
Notification of Rate Proposals Following Prior Independent Action, Ex Parte No. 297, Sub-No. 2, 358 I.C.C. 487 (1978).
N. S. Craig Contract Carrier Application, 31 M.C.C. 705 (1941).
Oil Carriers Company Extension—Colorado, 79 M.C.C. 169 (1959).
Onions and Potatoes from North Dakota to Twin Cities, 26 M.C.C. 153 (1940).
Pan-American Bus Lines Operation, 1 M.C.C. 190 (1936).
Paper Articles—Twin Cities—Chicago and Milwaukee, 12 M.C.C. 453 (1939).
P. E. Gallot Jr.—Purchase—Max Emil Holst, 45 M.C.C. 1 (1946).
Petition for Enlargement of the Amount of Operational Circuity Reduction Permitted under Certain Provisions of the Property Motor Carrier Superhighway and Deviation Rules, 121 M.C.C. 685 (1975).
Policy Statement Regarding the "Rule of Eight" in Contract Carrier Application, Ex Parte No. MC-119, 43 Fed. Reg. 38756 (1978).
Pre-Fab Transit Company Extension-Nationwide, General Commodities, 132 M.C.C. 409 (1981).
Protest Standards in Motor Carrier Application Proceedings, Ex Parte No. MC-55, Sub-No. 26, 43 Fed. Reg. 17008 (1978).
Rail General Exemption Authority—Fresh Fruits and Vegetables, Ex Parte No. 346, 361 I.C.C. (1979).
Railroad-Freight Forwarder Contract Rates, Ex Parte No. 364.
Ralph A. Veon, Inc., Contract Carrier Application, 92 M.C.C. 248 (1963).
Rate Bureau Investigation, Ex Parte No. 297, 349 I.C.C. 811 (1975).
Rate Bureau Investigation, Ex Parte No. 297, 351 I.C.C. 437 (1976).
Rate Increases and Charges, Southwestern States, 335 I.C.C. 361 (1969).
Rates over Carpet City, 4 M.C.C. 589 (1938).
Refrigeration Material from Memphis, Tenn., to Dayton, Ohio, 4 M.C.C. 187 (1938).
Regulations Governing the Transportation in Interstate or Foreign Commerce of Hazardous Materials by Motor Vehicle over Direct Routes, 111 M.C.C. 575 (1970).
Released Rate Rules—National Motor Freight Classification, 316 I.C.C. 499 (1962).
Removal of Restrictions from Authorities of Motor Carriers of Property, Ex Parte No. 12, Sub-No. 1, 132 M.C.C. 372 (1980).
Rules Governing Applications for Operating Authority, Ex Parte No. 55, Sub-No. 43, 364 I.C.C. 508 (1980).
Rules to Govern the Assembling and Presenting of Cost Evidence, 337 I.C.C. 298 (1970).
Southwest Equipment Rental, Inc.—Purchase (Portion)—Interstate Contract Carrier Corp., 127 M.C.C. 223 (1978).
Special Limited Authority: Proposed Procedures, Ex Parte No. MC-131, 45 Fed. Reg. 2871 (1980).

Special Procedures Governing Applications for Motor Carrier Authority Complementary to Movements of Exempt Agricultural Commodities, Ex Parte No. MC-127, 45 Fed. Reg. 61648 (1980).

Special Tariff Authority, Decision No. 79-3070-M, decided July 31, 1979.

Substituted Service—Charges and Practices of For-Hire Carriers and Freight Forwarders (Fishyback Service), Ex Parte No. 230 I.C.C. 301 (1964).

Substituted Service (Fishyback Service)—Water For Motor Service (Fishyback Service)—Alaskan Trade, 361 I.C.C. 359 (1979).

Sunkist Growers, Inc., Petition for Declaratory Order—"Member Transportation," 121 M.C.C. 448 (1975).

Superior Trucking Co. Extension—Agricultural Machinery, 126 M.C.C. 292 (1977).

Telishak Trucking, Inc., Extension—Precast Concrete Slabs and Beams, 92 M.C.C. 553 (1963).

Toto Purchasing & Supply Company, Inc. Common Carrier Application, 128 M.C.C. 873 (1978).

Transportation Activities of Midwest Transfer Co. of Illinois, et al., 49 M.C.C. 383 (1949).

Trunk Line Territory Motor Carrier Rates, 24 M.C.C. 501 (1940).

T. T. Brooks Trucking Co., Inc., Conversion Application, 81 M.C.C. 561 (1959).

Umthun Trucking Co. Extension—Phosphatic Feed Supplements, 91 M.C.C. 697 (1962).

Union Bus Lines, Inc.—Purchase—Joe Amberson, 5 M.C.C. 201 (1937).

Walter C. Benson Company, Inc., Extension New York, New Jersey, and Pennsylvania, 61 M.C.C. 128 (1952).

Woitishek Contract Carrier Application, 42 M.C.C. 193 (1943).

Zephan Odell Clark Common Carrier Application, 1 M.C.C. 445 (1937).

COURT CASES

American Bus Association v. *United States,* 627 F. 2d 525 (1980).

American Trucking Association v. *Atchison, Topeka and Santa Fe,* 387 U.S. 397 (1967).

American Trucking Associations, Inc. v. *United States* 627 F. 2d 1313 (1980).

Appleyard's Motor Transportation Co. v. *United States,* 592 F. 2d 8 (1st Cir. 1979).

Association of American Railroads v. *United States,* 603 F. 2d 953 (1979).

Atchison, Topeka and Santa Fe Railway Company v. *Morris,* 329 I.C.C. 326 (1967), 334.

Brooks Transportation Company v. *United States,* 93 F. Supp. 517 (1950); 340 U.S. 925 (1951).

Buck v. *Kuykendall,* 267 U.S. 307 (1925).

Cooley v. *Board of Port Wardens,* 53 U.S. (12 How.) 299 (1851).

D.C. Transit System, Inc. v. *Washington Metropolitan Area Transit Commission,* 350 F. 2d 753 (1965).

Dixie Highway Express, Inc. v. *United States,* 268 F. Supp. 239 (1967).

E. A. Gallagher & Sons, et al. v. *Cleveland General Transport,* 98 M.C.C. 356 (1965).

East Texas Lines v. *Frozen Food Express,* 351 U.S. 49 (1956).

East Texas Motor Freight and Regular Common Carrier Conference of American Trucking Associations v. *Interstate Commerce Commission and United States,* No. 79-1121 (1981).

Frost and Frost Trucking Co. v. *Railroad Commission of California,* 271 U.S. 583 (1926).

Georgia v. *Pennsylvania Railroad Company,* 324 U.S. 439 (1945).

I.C.C. v. *Dunn,* 166 F. 2d 116 (1948).

I.C.C. v. *J-T Transport Co.,* 368 U.S. 81 (1961).
I.C.C. v. *Milk Producers Marketing Co.,* 405 F. 2d 639 (1969).
I.C.C. v. *Parker,* 326 U.S. 60 (1945).
I.C.C. v. *Service Trucking Co.,* 91 F. Supp. 533 (1950), 186 F. 2d 400 (1951).
McLean Trucking Co. v. *U.S.* 321 U.S. 67 (1944).
May Trucking Co. v. *Interstate Commerce Commission* 593 F. 2d 1349 (D.C. Cir. 1979).
Mercury Motor Express, Inc. v. *United States* 648 F. 2d 315 (1981).
Michigan Public Utilities Commission v. *Duke,* 266 U.S. 570 (1925).
Morgan Drive-Away, Inc. v. *United States,* 268 F. Supp. 886 (1967).
Motor Ways Tariff Bureau v. *Steel Transportation Co., Inc.,* 62 M.C.C. 413 (1954).
Nashua Motor Express, Inc. v. *United States,* 230 F. Supp. 646 (1964).
Northwest Agricultural Cooperative Association, Inc. v. *I.C.C.* 350 F. 2d 252 (1965).
Petroleum Carrier Corporation v. *United States,* 258 F. Supp. 611 (1966).
The Regular Common Carrier Conference v. *United States,* 627 F. 2d 525 (D.C. Cir. 1980).
Schaffer Transportation Co. v. *United States,* 355 U.S. 83 (1957).
Schechter Poultry Corp. v. *U.S.,* 295 U.S. 495 (1935).
Schenley Distillers Corp. v. *United States,* 61 F. Supp. 981 (1945); 326 U.S. 432 (1946).
Smith v. *Caihoon,* 283 U.S. 553 (1931).
Stephenson v. *Binford,* 287 U.S. 251 (1932).
United States v. *Contract Steel Carriers, Inc.,* 350 U.S. 409 (1956).
United States v. *Drum,* 368 U.S., 370 (1962).
United States v. *Joint Traffic Association,* 171 U.S. 505 (1898).
United States v. *Trans-Missouri Freight Association,* 166 U.S. 290 (1897).
Wabash, St. Louis and Pacific Railway Co. v. *Illinois,* 118 U.S. 557 (1886).
Younger Brothers, Inc. v. *United States,* 289 Supp. 545 (1968).

Miscellaneous

Cowen, Janna L. "The Operating Ratio and Alternative Earnings Control Standards for Regulated Highway Freight Carriers." Lincoln: Ph.D. diss., University of Nebraska-Lincoln, 1979.

Dobesh, Larry. "Earnings Control Standards for Regulated Motor Carriers." Pullman: Ph.D. diss., Washington State University, 1973.

Falcon, Elmo. "Impact of Motor Carrier Deregulation on a Small Rural Community: A Case Study." M.S. thesis, University of Nebraska-Lincoln, 1981.

Hannahs, Stephen, and Joseph Tune. "1977 Financial Analysis of the Motor Carrier Industry." Union Oil Company, Union 76 Division, n.d.

Szto, S. "Federal and State Regulation of Motor Carrier Rates and Services." Philadelphia: Ph.D. diss., University of Pennsylvania, 1934.

Trinc's Blue Book of the Trucking Industry. Washington, D.C.: Trinc Transportation Consultants, various years.

Yearbook of Railroad Facts. Washington: Association of American Railroads, various years.

Index